TALLAHASSEE
LIBRARY
COMMUNITY COLLEGE

Gods, Ghosts, and Ancestors

Taiwanese view of the author offering incense in a temple. (Source: 台灣畫刊 [Taiwan Pictorial], rural edition, 10 June 1967.)

台灣鄉下信仰

# Gods, Ghosts, and Ancestors

## The Folk Religion of a Taiwanese Village

David K. Jordan

University of California Press
Berkeley, Los Angeles, and London

University of California Press
Berkeley and Los Angeles, California
University of California Press, Ltd.
London, England

ISBN: 0-520-01962-8
Library of Congress Catalog Card Number: 70-149945
Printed in the United States of America
Designed by Eileen Lavelle

# Contents

# Preface

This study is based on field materials collected during my residence in a Hokkien-speaking [1] village in southwestern Taiwan between autumn 1966 and summer 1968. It is appropriate to begin by describing my situation in Taiwan and some of the particular problems I had in the course of my researches. My language preparation for this work was two quarters of intensive Mandarin accomplished in summer programs at Stanford University. This preparation was very substantially less than would have been beneficial. Two quarters of summer-school Mandarin (a total of about five months) does not equip one adequately for productive work with written materials among Hokkien-speaking people. No small amount of field time—probably somewhere between a third and a half—was therefore spent directly or indirectly on language, and precautions taken against misunderstanding had to be much more elaborate than might have been necessary. Far too many interviews during all but the last month or two of my residence had to be conducted in Mandarin or with a Hokkien-Mandarin translation.[2]

The situation in the village itself was extremely good. I had the initial confidence and enthusiasm of an influential village elder and his well educated, Mandarin-speaking son, who made it his business to introduce me to numerous friends both in the village itself and in the surrounding area. People seemed pleased with my interest in Taiwanese culture from the very beginning, and wondered only that Americans had not come to study their fascinating village many years ago. I had also the interest and enthusiastic assis-

1. Taiwanese are native speakers of Hokkien. Since 1945, compulsory universal education in Mandarin has made that language very widespread among people under thirty or so. Among other things, this means that one can do fieldwork with Mandarin. But it also means that the ability of many informants to converse in Mandarin subverts the anthropologist's study of Hokkien. And one can of course do better fieldwork in Hokkien. I suspect that this is an important problem in most bilingual fieldwork situations.
2. Interviews conducted in Hokkien were not simultaneously interpreted, but either conducted by an assistant and later written out from his notes and from memory, or else tape recorded and later written out. I was able to understand just enough to follow the general trend and be certain that most points were covered. This proved to be preferable to the acute unnaturalness of simultaneous or intermittent translation. English was of course not used at any point for any purpose other than my own diary.

tance of the local police and township officials, which made access to census and other records comparatively easy. Nearly universal courtesy, interest, and cooperation of local people makes Taiwan a truly pleasurable place to do research.

The first three months or so in the village were spent poring over Taiwanese textbooks. These are inevitably in romanization, and Taiwanese equally inevitably are unable to read romanization. Accordingly, there was little possibility of a teacher able to work with me with these textbooks. I am convinced that this was much the wrong way to proceed. Nevertheless, it had a number of advantages, even if I would not do it again. One was that it established me as relatively harmless (in case there were village people who were initially more suspicious of my motives than I thought).[3] Another was that my incubation over textbooks suggested very strongly that I was what I had announced myself to be—a student—and the status of student is very highly respected in China. And third, it meant that I was "at home" to a large number of young, Mandarin-speaking visitors, and through them I was rapidly learning a good deal, probably more than I realized.

At the end of this three months I engaged a research assistant from a nearby town and with him began serious census taking and interviewing. By midsummer I was ready to hire another man, as well as a temporary girl to interview village people on subjects more intimately related to the role of women and the raising of children, and the summer of 1967 was a kind of perpetual seminar on Taiwanese culture among the four of us, each with his tasks to do. Both of the men continued in my employ virtually until I left Taiwan in late July 1968.

The principal target of my research was religion, and in pursuit of material we traveled more than ten thousand miles by motorcycle nearly all of it within Tainan city and Tainan county. However, I wanted to collect as many other data and other kinds of data as possible. Because I had not intended to work with religious material before I went to Taiwan, I did not have explicit hypotheses to test. Obtaining and comprehending religious information was in any case difficult enough that I am not sure I could have fitted the available data to any prefabricated hypotheses anyway.

3. So far as I know, the only suspicion entertained about me among Taiwanese I met was that I might secretly be a Christian missionary hoping to win converts in the village.

The result of my disorganization and wide-ranging objectives has been that I have notes on many things, but that many of them are superficial, and on few topics are they extensive.

As the reader will readily discover for himself, there are places where the argument becomes a bit chancy as the data grow thin. I am very aware of this problem, and I have tried to parade it rather than hide it, because I think it is best for anthropologists to be both honest and explicit about such matters, generally a good deal more honest and more explicit than is comfortable.

The present essay is an attempt to expose and explore certain regularities that have emerged from some of these data both while I was in Taiwan and as I have considered them after my return. It is a first approximation of a systematization of certain logical principles that seem to lie beneath a number of kinds of Taiwanese religious expression. Two competent and companionable research assistants helped me in my research work in Taiwan: Mr. Chern Jau-yann 陳昭彥 and Mr. Lii Maw-shyang 李茂祥. In addition, Miss Hwang Shiow-menq 黄秀孟 (the present Mrs. Wang Gong-tyan 王宮田) conducted interviews among the village women during the summer of 1967 and assisted also in the collection of proverbs and other material. To these loyal fellow workers I wish to express my heartfelt thanks.

Much assistance and stimulation were offered me while I was in Taiwan by Professor Chen Chi-lu 陳奇祿 of National Taiwan University and by Dr. Ling Shun-sheng 淩純聲, Dr. Li Yih-yuan 李亦園, Dr. Liu Chi-wan 劉枝萬, Mr. Wang Sung-hsing 王崧興, and Madame Inez de Beauclair, all of the Institute of Ethnology of Academia Sinica. Much day-to-day advice, reinforcement, and companionship were offered by other friends living in Tainan city, particularly Mr. Chen Shao-ting 陳少庭, Rev. and Mrs. Peyton Craighill, Dr. and Mrs. William L. Parish, and Dr. and Mrs. Kristofer Schipper. To all of these distinguished friends I am most grateful.

Much of the material presented here was incorporated into a Ph.D. dissertation (Jordan 1969) submitted to the Department of Anthropology of the University of Chicago. For assistance in preparing that dissertation and in generally organizing my thoughts about what I had seen, particular thanks must be expressed to Professor Melford E. Spiro, my research adviser while I was in Taiwan, and to Professor Nur Yalman, who gave generously of his time, helping me to make the long and painful move from fieldnotes to insights after my return. Professor Victor Turner and Dr. Kenneth Starr discussed my material at some length with me in Chicago, and I have benefited from criticisms offered by both. To all four teachers I wish to express thanks. Where I have followed their advice my work has been better for it. Where I have not followed it, it has never failed to stimulate much thought and the reconsideration of many problems.

Professor Spiro and Dr. Thomas W. Johnson have read earlier drafts of the present work, and I have benefited from discussing it with them.

Thanks are also due to Mr. Raymond Ford of the University of California Press for rendering successive drafts progressively more readable and for seeing the work through the printing, to Mr. Charles Y. C. Liu 劉耀紀, who wrote the characters appearing through the book, and to Dr. John W. Haeger, who did the calligraphy for the cover.

By far my largest debt is to the people of the village I shall call Bao-an, who accepted me in their midst and generously gave me their time, their knowledge, their trust, and their interest that I might pursue what must have seemed at times most obscure and curious ends. It is the life of Bao-an that this work describes, and what there is of real interest here is what the people of Bao-an were generous enough to show me. In a very real sense this is their work, more than mine, and I am most grateful for the part I have played in it.

It is not possible to acknowledge individually the help of village people. The catalog would be far too long for a brief introduction. If I were to single out one or two village friends who were most valuable in providing for my needs and educating me in the ways of the Taiwanese countryside, I should unhesitatingly select my gracious landlord, Mr. Guo Chaur-shinq 郭朝性 and his family, especially his son, Mr. Guo Deng-chau 郭登超. Their assistance to me in Taiwan was indispensable, and I am most grateful.

This research, as well as the bulk of my training in graduate school, was supported by National Institute of Mental Health grants 5-F1-MH-24,257 and 1-R04-MH-13526-01. A small grant from the Academic Senate of the University of California, San Diego, financed the preparation of the pictures and diagrams. This public support is gratefully acknowledged.

# A Note on Romanization and Other Conventions

## CHINESE PLACE NAMES

Chinese place names in this book which appear in the gazeteer section of the *China Yearbook* for 1969–1970 follow the spellings used in that book.[1] Names of dynasties follow the dynastic table in the same work (pp. 792–797). These spellings do not accurately represent the sound of the Chinese words involved. Their continued use is justified only by their being conventional English representations of the Chinese words. I have regarded these as English words.

## ROMANIZED CHINESE

Chinese words have been unavoidable in the text. Whenever possible I have used an English gloss in the discussion, followed by the Chinese term at the first occurrence of the gloss and occasionally thereafter as it seemed necessary to clarity. In other cases only the Chinese word would do, and I have used it in a romanized form.

Romanized words used in the text are divided into those in Mandarin and those in Hokkien.[2] The former are romanized according to the National system of romanization (*Gwoyeu Romatzyh* 國語羅馬字), which is the official system of romanization of the Republic of China. Hokkien words are written in the Standard

1. *China Yearbook* 1969–1970: 816–838.

2. Hokkien refers to the group of Chinese dialects of southern Fukien generally called Miinnan 閩南 in Chinese. Alternative English designations are Fukienese, Amoy, and Taiwanese. Hokkien dialects are spoken not only in Fukien, but also in Taiwan and in numerous Asiatic overseas Chinese communities. For a discussion of Mandarin and Hokkien in Taiwan, *see* Jordan 1969a.

romanization, familiar to all students of Hokkien.[3] A small number of Cantonese words have been used, and these are clearly marked as such. The romanization is that used in the dictionary of Chyau Yann-nong (1965). Chinese characters are provided in the text at the first occurrence of each romanized term other than bibliographic references. A table at the back lists all Chinese words used in the text, plus place and dynasty names, and provides Mandarin and Hokkien pronunciations and Chinese characters.

I have preferred Mandarin to Hokkien romanizations because Mandarin is the more widely used "dialect" outside Taiwan, and Hokkien terms would be less immediately recognizable to many readers. It should be understood, however, that my knowledge of Mandarin is very heavily influenced by the Mandarin usages peculiar to Taiwan, and despite care and attention to the differences it is not impossible that in some cases Mandarin terms are rather calques on the Hokkien than *bona fide* northern Chinese usages. When the Mandarin deviates conspicuously from the Hokkien, I have tried to explain the difference or use the Hokkien.

All Mandarin words and phrases begin with a capital letter, whereas Hokkien words or phrases never do, even in titles, or when beginning a sentence. I write Mandarin *Jiatyng* and *Sai,* but Hokkien *ka-têng* and *sai.* All romanizations (as distinct from English spellings) are italicized, with the exception of proper names.

#### BIBLIOGRAPHIC CITATIONS

In citations from the literature, Chinese authors writing in Western languages or translated into Western languages have been treated as Western authors and are cited in the spellings used in the works in question.[4] Names of authors writing in Chinese are romanized in Mandarin. For works in Chinese, both the surname and the given name of the author appear in citations. Because in Chinese possible surnames are limited in number, this device eliminates classification together of many different authors sharing the same surname.

Many of these conventions are innovative. Some of them may

3. I have described both systems and compared them with other romanization systems in another work (Jordan 1971a).
4. One work in romanized Hokkien is considered a Western-language book for these purposes.

seem trivial, but each is directed to the solution of a problem I have had to face when reading works by other writers, and I sincerely believe that each of them makes the work of the reader easier, the message of the author clearer, and the text of the book more accurate than most other procedures that could be adopted.

# Introduction

This book is a case study of Chinese religion. It is about religion as it is lived in one village, here called Bao-an 保安, at one point in time: the present. The pseudonym *Bao-an* means "safeguarding harmony"; religion in Bao-an is directed to that end. The nature of the harmony, the dangers that threaten it, and particularly the means by which it is preserved will be our theme.

In preparing the book, I have had three objectives. Most obviously, but least importantly, the book is a description of a southern Taiwanese village. As such it is one of a small number of accounts in western languages of particular Chinese villages and is a contribution to the available data on rural Chinese life and its variation across space. Anyone who has tried to study regional variation in China on the basis of ethnographic accounts realizes how tantalizing it is to discover differences between ethnographies and not know whether they are due to regional differences or to differences in the experiences and interests of the ethnographers. The more ethnographies we have for a region, the clearer the picture becomes. The concentration of work in Taiwan and Hong Kong in recent years is at last beginning to provide a certain depth of coverage in these areas that allows us to see how they are different and how similar. One goal of this book is to contribute to this collection of data.

That objective is subordinate, however, to a second, for I am also attempting to provide a new perspective on rural Chinese society by focusing on the tight relation between religious beliefs and practices on the one hand and social structure, particularly family and village structure, on the other. When one approaches Chinese folk religion from this point of view (essentially from the point of view of social anthropology), what attracts one's attention is not so much the customs of the great tradition, such as cleaning the tombs at the "clear and bright" festival or giving money to the children at New Year, but rather practices that are directly relevant to the functioning of society at the local level—the constant re-ranking of local gods, for example, or the distribution of local ghosts. My second objective, then, is to provide a view of south-western Taiwanese religion as an integral part of a living society, rather than merely as a catalog of customs.

In working with these materials, it has become evident that Bao-an religion is concerned with human relationships with three kinds of supernatural beings: gods, ancestors, and ghosts. It is difficult to say which of these is most important—they are all essential to the scheme—but surely the gods with their temples and oracles are the most prominent to the casual visitor to the area, and the ghosts the most striking to the analyst seeking explanations and interconnections in the events that make up the history and the daily routine of Bao-an life. Not surprisingly, therefore, I have devoted less attention to ancestors, somewhat more to gods (and their oracles), and most of all to ghosts. If such a procedure seems jarring—it is, after all, nearly the exact opposite of what most of our stereotypes of Chinese religion lead us to expect—it is well to remember that studies of Chinese folk religion are few, that such studies written from the standpoint of social and cultural anthropology are fewer, and that anthropological case studies of specifically Taiwanese religion are virtually nonexistent. We must expect surprises. I rather suspect—though it is only a guess—that work guided by a range of interests and mode of analysis similar to mine in the study of Bao-an would yield equally unexpected results from almost any area of China, results that would contrast with our presuppositions and probably also with my data from southern Taiwan. The "jarring" quality is a function—and perhaps an advantage—of remaining true to a local tradition even when it runs contrary to the great tradition, and of seeking to understand a *local* religious manifestation in its relation to *local* problems.

A third objective is made possible by the second; that is, to examine the dynamic of the relation between society and religion in Taiwan. I shall seek to discover the way in which the relation between the social life and the religious beliefs of rural people adapts itself to the shifts and changes of day-to-day life and to subtler changes wrought by the passing of longer periods. The picture that emerges is one of much greater flexibility than we usually imagine in connection with Chinese religion.

My conclusions occur passim in the text, because many of them are unintelligible without the data from which they are derived, and because many of the data are confusing without immediate interpretation. Even the data alone are rather intricately related to one another at times. It is hardly possible to present all the facts simultaneously, and so it is useful to begin by summarizing the picture about to emerge before moving ahead with the detailed material.

The first chapter sets the scene. It describes the agricultural village of Bao-an on the southwestern Taiwanese plain. The fact that Taiwan was settled as a frontier area in the seventeenth century makes its history somewhat different from that of other provinces of southeastern China, and we shall consider the effects of its frontier position on the development of lineages and ancestor worship, two institutions of Chinese life that so often seem to Westerners the essence of all that is Chinese. I shall argue that frontier conditions were inappropriate for the elaboration of either of these traits, and shall show how a different social group, defined by residence and surname and unified by religious allegiances, became the basis for much social activity throughout most of the history of Bao-an and the neighboring villages.

How do these "unifying religious allegiances" work? The allegiances, we shall see, involve patron gods, who enter into alliance with a village, and who are believed to protect it against certain kinds of dangers. The manipulation of these gods, I shall maintain, allows the playing out of a variety of relations between and among villages, as well as the governing of various activities within the village.

But how do people "manipulate the gods"? The process by which such manipulation is accomplished is divination, particularly divination through spirit mediums. We shall consider the role of the rural medium in some detail, for it is he who must keep religion and social action in a productive interplay with each other. The village, of course, is not the only group of importance. The name of China is almost synonymous with the notion of family. We shall find that the same alliance that obtains between gods and villages can also obtain between gods and families. We shall see how families and groups of families parallel the village in the way they enter into relations of reciprocity with the supernatural, informed by the same understandings and enacted through the same symbols as occur at the village level. The dangers that threaten families, however, are somewhat different from those that threaten villages. I shall argue that there is an ideal image of the family, to which village people try to make their families conform, an image summed up in Chinese by the twin notions of "roundness" (structural completeness) and "harmony" (the smooth functioning of things). When violations of harmony occur—in other words, when people get sick, when financial ruin threatens, or when family relations deteriorate—divine revelation often blames ghosts. And ghosts, it develops, are often shades of family members involved in irregularities in the structure of the family: violations of roundness. We are thus provided with the beginnings of a theory of ghosts, a theory relating belief in ghosts, ways of coping with family disaster, and Chinese ideals of family structure. A theory of ghosts is something new in books about China, and we shall examine the ghosts of Bao-an rather carefully.

From frontier settlers to village and surname alliances, from alliances to patron gods, from patron gods protecting villages to patron gods protecting families, from protection of families to dangers that threaten them, we shall arrive in the end at a fuller understanding of the relations among a variety of kinds of rural Taiwanese supernaturals, and at a model of Taiwanese religious explanation and ways of coping with the world. This model differs from the usual functional models of anthropologists because it is logically independent of changes in social structure, capable of continued functioning in the face of the evolution of social relationships in Bao-an. Far from being rigid and unresponsive (as we are accustomed to think of traditional religion as being), Taiwanese folk belief is fluid and adaptable, capable of providing explanations for and means of dealing with a wide range of human problems in conditions of changing values and practices.

# Gods, Ghosts, and Ancestors

# Chapter 1
## *Bao-an: A Taiwanese Village*

This work centers about a village in southwestern Taiwan, a province of the Republic of China. I shall call the village Bao-an 保安.[1] Bao-an is located not far from the town of Hsikang,[2] a township 鄉 capital just north of the legal limits of Tainan city, the former capital city of the island and the area of earliest Chinese settlement in Taiwan.[3] Bao-an is located beside the Tsengwen Chi, a river that runs a meandering course from the eastern mountains to the sea. Because the Taiwanese mountains are high, and the plain narrow, Taiwanese rivers flow high and fast when there is rain, quickly draining the mountain sources. But when there is no rain, they dry up, sometimes entirely, until the next rain in the mountains. The Tsengwen Chi is no exception, and it has made for itself a wide wadi it seldom actually fills, but in which it unpredictably flows first at one side, then at the other, sometimes covering most of the area, sometimes only a tiny stream. In 1932 the river was confined to this bed by two dikes, about a kilometer apart and running from a point some distance west of Hsikang to the sea, which were constructed by the Japanese administration (1895–1945). In 1967, on President Chiang's birthday, work was

1. This name was picked as a pseudonym by one of my village friends from a collection of names selected to sound similar to names of villages in this area, to be easily pronounceable in English, and to be representable by the same spelling in more than one system of romanization. The name means "safeguarding harmony" and is taken from a name used for the village temple in many Taiwanese villages: "temple for safeguarding harmony" (*Bao-an Gong* 保安宮).
2. For the geographically precise, Hsikang is located at 23°7′35″ north, 120°11′36″ east.
3. For historical background on Taiwan, *see* Alvarez 1930, Davidson 1903, Goddard 1963 and 1966, Imbault-Huart 1893. Recently released histories of the island in Chinese include Ferng Tzuoh-min 1966 and Anonymous 1964. For a brief summary treatment, *see* Hsieh 1964: 123–194, or C. L. Chen 1967.

begun for a dam in the mountains far upstream from Hsikang. The new dam, to be completed in 1973, is expected to reduce flood expectancy from once every twelve years to once a century and to provide substantial amounts of electricity and irrigation water from what will become Taiwan's largest lake.

Bao-an is an agricultural village, and the people of Bao-an raise most of the crops common to the area, including three harvests of paddy rice per year, and dry rice, sweet potatoes, and sugarcane. These, plus watermelons (both those produced for their pulp and those grown for their seed) are the principal cash crops. Jute, sesame, sorghum, maize, taro, cotton, or other crops are also planted in smaller amounts. Numerous fruits are grown, though only bananas are sold outside the village.

In addition to their other land, the people of Bao-an farm the fertile land within the wadi of the Tsengwen Chi. This soil is so well endowed by the annual flooding that oxcarts of it can be dug out of the lowest part when the water is low and carted to other areas for sale. But it is always farmed with the understanding that floods will wash out the crops in some years, and this element of chance makes it unprofitable for any but fast-growing crops. The portions of the wadi most often flooded by the river are used for watermelon, while beans, sweet potatoes, sesame, and other crops are grown in the remainder. Rice and sugar, the major cash crops, are confined entirely to safer land beyond the flood dikes.

According to the June 1966 township census records, the population of Bao-an was 1,669. In the early months of 1967, when I did census work there, they were organized into 227 households. Every resident of Taiwan constitutes or is a member of a household 户 with a known address. Each household has a head 户長, and census records specify the relationship (by kinship or otherwise) of each individual member of the household to the head. For most purposes the household corresponds with the family 家, but not always. Particularly in urban areas, extraneous people (such as distant relatives, boarders, servants, or apprentices) may be members of the household but not of the family. In Bao-an the correspondence between household and family is in general very close (with some exceptions that will be considered later on), and to avoid tedious repetition of the word *family* I have tended to use the two words interchangeably except in a few passages in which

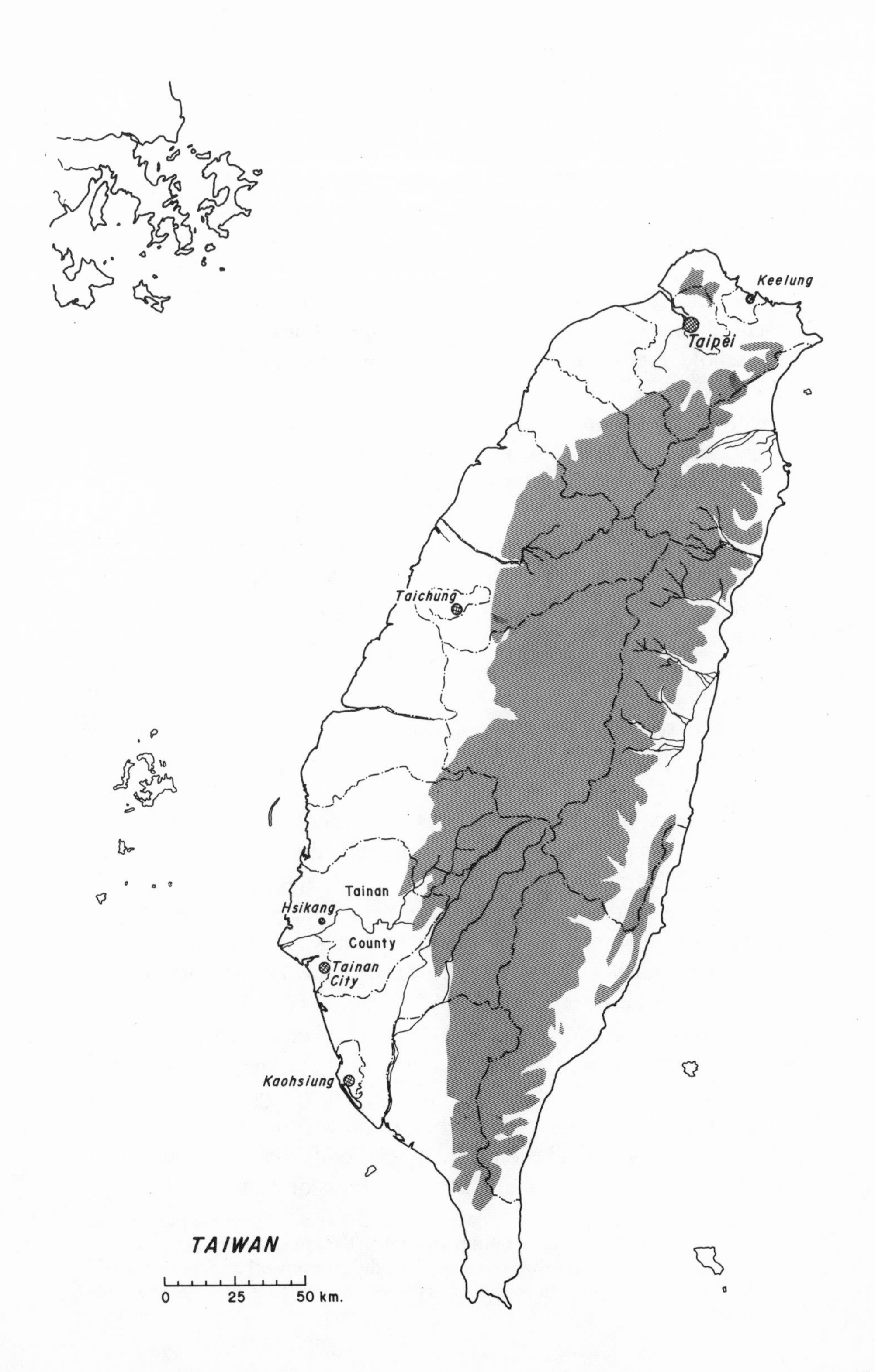
Keelung
Taipei
Taichung
Tainan
Hsikang
County
Tainan
City
Kaohsiung
TAIWAN
0
25
50 km.

the distinction is clearly indicated by inserting the Chinese words. One other point should be noted: as in most Taiwanese villages, a certain proportion of registered "resident" family members in fact do their residing in other parts of the island, often for educational or military reasons, but not infrequently also in order to earn money in urban industries, especially in Kaohsiung. The government makes noble efforts to encourage people to change their household registration in such cases, but the campaign is not entirely effective. Accordingly, most village household statistics are slightly higher than the actual resident population, and correspondingly urban records, I suspect, are slightly lower. This inflated figure is entirely in accord with the Chinese notion of a family (if not, strictly speaking, of a household), for family division occurs ritually, and not by moving away, and the nonresident residents are considered to be people of Bao-an as much as anyone else. Moving away has nothing to do with it. Furthermore, they frequently make trips back to the village, especially at holidays, and one is constantly coming up against village people whom one has not seen before. I initially made attempts to differentiate "real" residents from "part-time" residents, but ended by accepting the native categories.

Bao-an is a "pure" village, entirely Taiwanese ethnically, with no admixture of Hakka, aboriginal, or mainland immigrant populations.[4] It is pure in another way as well: there is but one, rather apologetic, Christian family, and no declared agnostics or atheists. Although a small number of village men hold jobs in Hsikang or Tainan and commute by bicycle or motorcycle, the vast majority of the residents of the village are farmers with tracts of land situated within about a three-kilometer radius of the village. There were some eight to twelve shops in 1968. The number varies according to the season: in summer many people open small watermelon stands or sell their produce in the village. One of these establishments belongs to an herbalist and another to a maker and mender of bicycles. The remainder sell foodstuffs, and when they become prosperous enough, lay in a stock of stationery, writing

4. The trivial exception is two women from mixed Taiwanese-aboriginal villages in the foothill areas of northeastern Tainan county. Both women are native speakers of Hokkien, and if they differ from other village women at all it is perhaps only in a slightly greater forcefulness in handling their household affairs.

brushes, ink, candles, spirit money,[5] cigarettes, pencils, matches, pickles, firecrackers, candies, soy sauce, twine, straw hats, soap, paper fans, wine, copybooks, household medicines, and other small items of daily need and comfort. With the exception of the young bicyclesmith, all the shopowners also maintain fields.

The village is fairly pure in one more respect: about three-quarters of the inhabitants share the surname Guo 郭, although they belong to at least five stocks of Guo, as we shall see in more detail below. Because of the high concentration of Guo in this village, and a neighboring sister village, both are under the special patronage of King Guo, a god whose principal Taiwanese temple is located in Tainan city, from which a joss[6] tours and visits both villages once in three years, to which a good deal of money was contributed by individuals and villages a few years ago for its construction, and to which village people have recourse in spiritual need when local gods are unable or unwilling to assist them.

Bao-an is a tightly nucleated cluster of buildings. Many of these are houses of the inhabitants, of course. They tend to face south (for reasons of aesthetics as much as of geomancy) but are placed at just slightly different angles from each other (for reasons of geomancy alone). In the remote past these were simply built wherever there was land geomantically well endowed in the village. In Japanese times a grid of roads was laid out, and today houses are lined up, after a fashion, along these roads, though many buildings also continue to be laid out in the same disorderly, old-fashioned way in the interstices between the roads.

If the human dwellings are built hard by one another, the spacing is rendered yet tighter by the presence of countless pigsties,

5. Spirit money is sheets of paper bearing a thin tinfoil square and overprinted with designs showing gods and bearing expressions of earthly joy. It is burned to provide money to gods or to the dead. This paper is also used by spirit mediums to write charms, and in the handling of religious objects too hot to touch (such as the pan in which such paper is burned) and for sundry other purposes. Other terms for spirit money include *joss-papers, paper money,* and *mockmoney*. None of these terms has much to recommend it. For a summary of information on spirit money, *see* Hwang Der-shyr 1967: 58.

6. According to the *Oxford English Dictionary,* the word *joss* first appears in English in 1711, borrowed from Chinese Pidgin English and apparently a corruption of Portuguese *deos,* "god." The term denotes a carved image of a Chinese god, used as an object of worship.

brick latrines, and enormous spherical wattle-and-daub grain bins in a shape that reminds Western visitors of outsized birdhouses.

Before the construction of the dikes defining the limits of the river wadi, Bao-an was situated in the area that is now enclosed between them. Because of periodic flooding, some people built houses on the present Bao-an site. When the dikes were built, Bao-an and one other village in the flood zone area were dissolved. Most of the Bao-an population moved to the present site. Land holdings, however, were distributed over a wide area, interpenetrating the holdings of other villages, the usual Taiwanese pattern.[7] Some of this land was on the opposite side of the Tsengwen Chi, and some families even had most of their land in that area. In time a few families established a new settlement across the river so that they could be closer to this land.

Today there are 135 houses in Bao-an proper, and another 20 across the Tsengwen Chi in the daughter settlement, also considered part of Bao-an. This makes a total of 155 houses for 227 households, or an average of 1.47 households to the house. This figure seems low for Taiwan.[8] Perhaps the lower ratio of households to houses in Bao-an can be attributed originally to a spate of housebuilding connected with the move of some families out of the primary village in the wadi land to the present Bao-an site before the dikes were built. In recent years the effect may have been amplified by (1) increased prosperity, hence greater funds for housebuilding, (2) the inclusion of adjacent parcels of land within the ritually defined limits of the village, rendering them accessible for building, (3) restricted building land immediately adjacent to some existing buildings into which they might easily be expanded to hold more residents, and (4) recent migration across the river and the construction there of 20 new buildings. In Bao-an even the largest compound contains only 26 people, whereas I have visited compounds in other villages with twice that many inhabitants or more.

In addition to shops, houses, and pigsties, the village has one

7. Cf. Gallin 1966: chapter 4, especially the map on page 100.

8. Gallin (1966: 29) reports a population for Hsin Hsing in 1958 of 656 people in 115 households (an average of 5.7 as against 7.3 inhabitants per household in Bao-an), and his map on page 27 shows 39 houses, which would make 2.9 households per compound (assuming he has mapped all the buildings).

The village temple provides a site for village meetings as well as a focus for religious activities.

other building: a small temple, or *kong-chhò·* 公厝.[9] This was dedicated during the Dawguang 道光 period of the last dynasty (1821–1850), but the present structure was built in the early 1930s. The temple has served at various times as a village office, as a meeting hall, and as a primary school or kindergarten. When the public health service calls to give inoculations, it is done at the temple. When the manufacturer of puffed-rice confections comes to town, he sets up on the porch of the temple. But its primary function, and today very nearly its only function, is religious. The temple is the site of semimonthly worship by all the village families, as we shall see below. It is also the site of extraor-

9. The term *kong-chhò·* means "community hall" in Hokkien. The usual characters used to write the expression are 公厝. The second of these in Mandarin is *Tsuoh,* a temporary shelter in which a coffin may be stored pending its burial. Whether the words are etymologically related, or whether the Hokkien word *chhò·* has simply borrowed an homonymous character, is not clear to me, but in either case it is important to recognize that the word has somewhat different and potentially confusing meanings in the two languages. Recently the trend in Taiwan has been to build a community center in addition to a temple, the usual term for this being "education and recreation centre"育樂中心. During the period I lived in Bao-an, the village acquired such a building. This is not inevitable, however, and in many villages even very new temples still provide facilities for a kindergarten and a village office, the latter usually equipped with a public address system that can be heard throughout the village.

dinary worship at New Year and on other festival days, such as the birthdays of important gods. The temple owns two of the many josses in the village, or, more exactly, the village owns them in the name of the temple. I do not know the history of these two josses, except that they are considered to be very old. They represent the Queen of Heaven 媽祖 or 天上聖母 and Marshal Shieh 謝府元帥, both popular deities in Taiwan. Like most josses, they are decorated with gold plaques worn about their necks, the presents of grateful worshippers. Unfortunately, cases are known of thieves visiting some villages and stealing such readily accessible gold. For this reason a publicly owned joss is not kept in the temple, but is circulated from house to house, remaining at one house until another family wishes to consult the god represented by the image, then remaining with the second family until a third uses it.[10] The temple altar bears only one statue: an old one in poor condition representing the goddess Guan-in 觀音. Most people do not consider it very powerful, and some consider it to have lost its efficacy completely. It bears no gold, and the temple in this way contains little of intrinsic interest to potential thieves.[11] A volunteer temple keeper burns incense in the building mornings and evenings, but the actual administration of temple affairs is in the hands of a committee based upon the "portions" into which the village is divided for political purposes, as we shall see in a moment. At New Year, divination blocks are dropped before the temple in connection with the name of each household head, and the number of successive positive throws made in the name of each is recorded. Within the set of names for each portion, run-off throws are made until two names have more points than any others, and these two households are the portion's representatives 股首 to the temple committee for that year. At each semimonthly sacrifice before the temple, one of these families (selected by rotation) provides the sacrifices for the altar itself and sees to the organiza-

10. As we shall see below, many privately owned josses also circulate widely in the village. The usual motive in borrowing a joss is that one wishes to consult the god on some subject in a séance or by other means of divination.

11. In some villages better doors on newer temple buildings can be securely locked at night, or in some cases iron bars are installed before the naos. At larger temples, such as that at Hsikang, good locks at night and constant attendance in daylight hours obviate the need for bars or absent gods, although a substantial wooden picket fence guards the naos nevertheless.

tion of the rites. In addition to the fourteen families thus selected, a censer master 爐主 is chosen, also by divination blocks and points, who has general authority over the temple, including such matters as setting up benches if there is to be a meeting, and tending to the provision of offerings of fruit and flowers on the altar.

For more efficacious consultation with the gods, village people often visit the temple of the Queen of Heaven in Hsikang.[12] The Hsikang temple is much larger and serves many more worshippers. It is more elaborately fitted than the temple in Bao-an, and provides more elaborate means of divination.

Politically, Bao-an regards itself as a unitary entity, almost entirely free of factions. It participates vigorously and enthusiastically in the election of officials at all levels of government, from the provincial down to the purely local. At the township level one can distinguish two important factions, associated with the surnames Guo and Hwang 黃, but incorporating people of all surnames in each faction. Although these seem to derive directly from factions that competed with some bloodthirstiness during Ching times, today they coexist inconspicuously, almost harmoniously, and share the government of Hsikang in an equilibrium that shifts slightly with each election. During the period I was in Bao-an, the Guo faction, with which Bao-an associates itself, was clearly dominant in the township government.

Bao-an is governed internally by a town-meeting system. Until 1968, when the new education and recreation center was completed, these meetings took place in the village temple, and the officers who preside over the meeting still bear titles related to the temple.[13] The offices, corresponding approximately to president, vice-president, secretary, and treasurer, are: chairman of the temple board 廟宇董事長; temple director of miscellaneous affairs 廟宇雜事管理; temple secretary 廟宇書記; and temple treasurer 廟宇會記. These officials are elected, but only the chairman of the temple board is officially rec-

12. The temple is officially called the "hall for celebrating peace" 慶安宮. I shall refer to it as the Hsikang temple. A description of this fascinating edifice has been published by Chern Ching-gaw and Shieh Shyr-cherng 1963: 281ff.

13. The government of everyday temple affairs is in the hands of the censer master and the temple committee, as we have seen. The use of the word *temple* in the present context is more or less equivalent to *village* in connotation.

ognized by higher governmental levels, and not in his capacity as chairman of the temple board, but as mayor, for the mayor is, *ex officio,* the chairman of the temple board.

The mayor is the chief administrative officer of the village. He is assisted in administrative tasks by a committee of headmen chosen from the portions 股 .[14] For administrative purposes, Bao-an is divided into seven traditional portions. In each portion one household head is regarded as headman (*thâu-kē-á* 頭家仔), and the council of seven headmen, together with the elected mayor, provide the administrative apparatus of the village.[15]

Mayors were the only legally elected officials during Japanese times, and seem ordinarily to have served fairly long terms (ten years and up). Two of these elderly and honorable gentlemen are still active in village affairs today. Ex-mayor A is doctrinaire and outspoken, famous for his sharp tongue and his churlish temper. He is noted also for his great knowledge of religious matters and for his fine skill as a storyteller and local historian. Ex-mayor B is more even tempered and easy going, and maintains his political influence in the village through his willing role as a just peacemaker in disputes and through the active and vigilant political intervention in village affairs by his two sons, both men of skill, ambition, and some education, with jobs outside the village but strong local loyalty and interest. These two men often differ with each other on public issues, and B is continuously the victim of A's vilifications even when they are in agreement. Bao-an is not a faction-ridden village by any means, but there are occasional disagreements about public matters, and it is normal for these two elderly men to be important figures on opposite sides of such issues. Each of these men has the backing of his friends as well as of his immediate kinsmen. Both are named Guo, and they are distantly related to each other. Accordingly, their influence is not extended

14. The "portions" are traditional village divisions. Three of them are named after Taiwanese villages from which Guo moved to Bao-an, and two of these contain only Guo families. The other four are named after sections of Bao-an (e.g., North Road Portion), and of these one contains only Guo families (not surprising considering the number of Guo families).

15. On paper, there are fifteen *Lin* 鄰 districts in Bao-an, each with a *Lin* head, but the *Lin* system, introduced by the national government after the retrocession from Japan, seems less natural than the seven headmen, and the *Lin* heads are seldom called together.

following surname loyalties or even following kinship loyalties to more than a limited degree, but rather on the basis of individual personalities, and to a certain extent of individual issues. The finesse with which these men are able to make themselves spokesmen for different ranges of village opinion, combined with the fact that they are kinsmen, seems to provide a way of channeling village disagreements into a single common decision with few hard feelings.

The present mayor, C, also named Guo, is unrelated to either of the older men, and tends to a course designed to maintain friendship with both sides. He is a man of great prestige, and his decisions are respected, whether they are about the village and its development or about the settling of private disputes submitted to him for arbitration. When I asked about the most important men in the village, one young woman recited a rhyme that the local children used to sing about it:

| D gâu tōa-sia$^n$; | D (an elderly and well respected Bao-an man) can really shout; |
|---|---|
| C gâu ko·-chia$^n$; | C can really talk people into things; |
| B kiâ chhia bān-bān; | B rides his bicycle very slowly; |
| A kàn-kiāu ū chhut miâ$^n$. | A has made a name for himself scolding. |

Bao-an has other officials who are primarily concerned with government and economic cooperation at higher levels. Five men from Bao-an sit on the representative council of the Hsikang Agricultural Association 農會; two Bao-an men are representatives to the Sugar Committee 蔗糖原料委員會; three citizens of Bao-an represent three districts in the Irrigation Association serving Chiayi and Tainan counties 嘉南農田水利會小組長.[16] The principal Bao-an official with an outside post, however, is the representative of this village in the township assembly 鄉民代表會. This last is an office of great prestige in the village, and an object of keen competition (often in the form of behind-the-scenes maneuvering) at election time. The township assemblyman and the mayor were commonly represented to me when I first arrived as

16. These districts are not drawn to coincide with village boundaries, and accordingly one of the representatives represents a territory largely outside of Boa-an. The other two represent territories roughly corresponding to the parts of Bao-an on each bank of the Tsengwen Chi.

the most important officials in Bao-an, and are often mentioned together in the same breath as the true governors of the village.

## SURNAMES AND LINEAGES

After this quick overview of Bao-an, let us return to a loose end that was (by contrivance) left dangling somewhere between the apologetic Christians and the tightly nucleated buildings; that is, the large number of Guo in the village who are not all related to one another. The point is worth following in some detail, for it is directly related to one of the major differences between southeastern continental China and southern Taiwan: the difference between a lineage-dominated society and one based on other principles and other solidarities.[17]

The majority of the modern Taiwanese are descendants of immigrants from Fukien. But although Fukien is a province particularly remarkable for its baroque lineage organization, Taiwan shows little evidence of this tradition. The Chinese word that has been translated "clan" or "(corporate) lineage" is *Tzwu/chók* 族. I originally arranged that my census forms should include a space in which the *Tzwu* affiliation of each household might be recorded. Unfortunately race or ethnicity is often expressed with the same word, and it is this latter meaning that occurred first to the minds of the village people. When I would ask what *Tzwu* a man belonged to, he would reply that he was Chinese 漢, that everyone in Bao-an was Chinese, and that it seemed to him a benighted item to include in a questionnaire. The reason was simple: in Boa-an there are no corporate lineages. My question, instead of being sophisticated and within-the-culture—and I had been very proud of it for just these reasons—was irrelevant and prejudiced the case.

Fragments of the complex of things associated with lineage on the Chinese mainland apparently have existed in Taiwan in the past, and one still comes upon maddeningly suggestive hints of them. Although today no descent groups own common land or other com-

17. It is not clear to me how much of what I am about to say applies also to northern Taiwan, which was settled somewhat later and under somewhat different circumstances. Although it is convenient to speak of Taiwan and the Taiwanese, what I have in mind is principally southern Taiwan and the southern Taiwanese, particularly the area near Tainan where Bao-an is situated and where earliest settlement took place.

Only one household in Bao-an has a statue of an ancestor: a Ching official.

munal wealth, nevertheless one group of related families is still somewhat embittered by the alleged embezzlement of funds deriving from a small plot of collectively owned land in the 1930s. But only one group.

Another group of families in Bao-an has a written genealogy, a small copybook containing names of male descendants and some collaterals beginning with a ninth generation ancestor who immigrated from Fukien and ending with the present nineteenth generation.[18] The document is kept as a matter of curiosity primarily, and not used in any obvious way. For example, to the best of my knowledge, these families do not worship ancestors more remote than those worshipped by other people because of their knowledge of them through the written genealogy, nor do they attempt to maintain a wider network of kinship ties. Another group of families was recorded on a genealogy kept in another village (and again a bit out of date), but none of the Bao-an families had a copy, and once again the document was not considered particularly important. Gallin's comment on lineage organization in Hsin Hsing (1966: 136) could equally well apply to Bao-an: lineages are of "relatively small size and minimum formalization" in Taiwan, probably in all areas.

There is a fairly straightforward reason why extensive and well-organized corporate lineage groups should be less imposing in Taiwan than in Fukien, and it relates to the nature of early settlement patterns on the island. Taiwan, throughout the history of Chinese settlement, has been almost exclusively a haven for refugees. The bulk of early Chinese settlers seem to have come during the seventeenth century. During the thirty-seven years of the Dutch administration (1624–1661) subsidies were offered to settlers growing rice and sugar on government-owned land, and Chinese settlement was actively encouraged to provide cheap labor (Liao 1949: 13). The seventeenth century was, of course, the period of the decline of the Ming dynasty, and in the course of things the southeastern coastal area fell into the hands of a certain Koxinga, a pirate loyal to the Ming dynasty, whose programs included expelling the Dutch from Taiwan and the Manchus from the main-

18. Previously it was not kept that well up to date. In a frenzy of enthusiasm one day, one of my field assistants added the last two or three generations.

land.[19] In the former he was successful, in the latter frustrated. In any case, in the course of his crusades he recruited a large army along the mainland coasts, most of whom ended up in Taiwan. Chen Ta writes (1923):

> Many of his soldiers who were discharged from the army made homes in Formosa. According to whether they came from Kwangtung or Fukien, they were known as Hakkas or Hoklos. . . . Numerically the Hoklos predominated, for in 1661 Koxinga recruited about 30,000 soldiers and marines from the coast villages in Fukien, and three years later his son again recruited between 6,000 and 7,000 from southern Fukien. A great majority of these were unmarried and afterwards settled in Formosa (pp. 42–43).
>
> Up to 1760 emigrants' sweethearts, wives, and relatives who had been left behind in their own villages were allowed to join them in Taiwan. But when the coast was made dangerous by the frequent raids of the pirates, the Chinese Government prohibited further emigration of emigrants' relatives . . . (p. 42).

In addition to the army of Koxinga and their relatives, numerous other refugees from the Ming collapse found their way to Taiwan (Liao 1949: 13), just as numerous refugees from communist China have done in our own day.

When the settlers were not political refugees, they were economic ones, either forced from Fukien by famine and poverty, or attracted to Taiwan by promises of unlimited land at the frontier, or both. Writes Chen:

> Fukien is a mountainous Province whose scanty production of rice and other food articles is not sufficient to feed its local population. Consequently the inhabitants of the coast villages were under a strong economic pressure to emigrate (p. 39).
>
> During the fifteenth century about 25,000 Chinese settled in and around Anping [situated on the coast at Tainan city] and were engaged in agriculture and industry. Fishermen visited the southwestern shore of the island and had temporary homes in the coast villages. . . . These were pioneer days in Formosa (p. 40).

19. The name Koxinga is a corruption of the Hokkien *kok-sèng-iâ* 國姓爺, "lord of a national surname," an appelation referring to the privilege extended to him by the last Ming emperor of assuming the surname of the royal house. His own name was Jenq Cherng-gong/te$^{n}$-sêng-kong 鄭成功, and this is the usual name used for him in Taiwan today.

According to De Mailla, who visited the area in 1715, the only force that prevented truly massive migration to Taiwan at that time was the extortionate price demanded for passports and other "necessary" papers by the mandarins controlling migration across the straits.[20] Nevertheless, in commenting on this passage of Father De Mailla's account, Davidson (1903: 69) speaks of "many hundred thousand emigrants" from Fukien, Kwangtung, and the city of Chinkiang who apparently succeeded in getting through this gamut of payments.

However encumbered by official policy or abuse, immigration into Taiwan apparently continued throughout Ching times until it was prohibited under Japanese law. Chen reports arrivals and departures of steamship passengers at the ports of Tamsui and Kaohsiung, the two international ports in Ching times (Chen 1923: 44). In most years arrivals exceeded departures, and between 1873 and 1895, 9,833 persons arrived in Tamsui and 4,479 at Kaohsiung in excess of the number leaving during the same period.[21] Because the bulk of immigrants might have been expected to arrive by junk at these or at domestic ports, the actual number of immigrants during this period must surely have been higher. Immigration to the island was actually encouraged at various times. Davidson (1903: 210) speaks of an immigration bureau organized in the 1870s to bring "coolies from the overcrowded districts of Swatow and vicinity" to Taiwan, where they were "given grants of land in the sparsely settled districts between Takow [modern Kaohsiung] and the extreme south of the island," presumably both to relieve population pressure on the China coast and to populate Taiwan.

It has been suggested that these settlers were lower class to begin with. They would have come from nuclear or minimally extended families for the most part (or would have come to Taiwan in nuclear family groups), with little direct experience in the leadership of truly successful or elaborate lineage organization, with little direct knowledge of the management of lineage ancestor cults and no money to operate such things even had they had the necessary

20. Father De Mailla's account, originally in Portuguese, was published in English in the Shanghai *Celestial Empire* and reprinted in Campbell 1903: 504–518.

21. The number is actually slightly higher, because figures are incomplete for 1885 and 1891 and thus excluded from these totals. The total arrivals at Tamsui were 151,982 as against 142,149 departures. The equivalent figures for Kaohsiung were 15,873 as against 11,394.

knowledge. Indeed, they would for the most part have lacked immediately known illustrious ancestors who had served in high offices such as always formed the particularly attractive objects of worship in the cults of the wealthy. More importantly, it would often have been the case that an immigrant would have arrived in Taiwan with few relatives on the island with whom cooperation along lineage lines would have been useful or even possible. Furthermore, many intended to return to Fukien later and would have seen no point in the establishment of full lineage trappings in their semicolonial environment.

But another form of social organization emerged from the wealth of available Chinese social traditions, one that was much better adapted to the frontier conditions. By a polite fiction, Chinese assume that all men of the same surname are relatives, even though no link can be traced.[22] Accordingly a man with my surname, wherever he be from, bears a relationship to me that is in some way special, and different from the relationship which I have with people of other surnames.[23] Furthermore, the total set of Chinese surnames is not large, and no more than ten surnames account for more than half of the population.[24] Thus identity of surname can be made a basis of political support and economic cooperation. It is like a letter of introduction or having a friend in common. In the great reshuffling of different elements of the Fukienese population as they drifted to Taiwan, surname

22. A Taiwanese proverb puts it with all the conciseness of the Napoleonic Code: "A common surname means a common ancestor" (*kāng sè$^{n}$ to-sī* kāng chó· 共姓就是共祖).

23. For this reason Taiwanese surname groups are effectively exogamous, and marriage within the surname group is considered degrading and unfortunate, and possibly dangerous to the children. A girl marries within her surname group only because she is so undesirable that she is a "person with no place to find a husband" (*bô-tàng-kè-á* 無地嫁仔).

24. Liaw Hann-chern (1960) found a total of 737 surnames in a sample of 828,804 Taiwanese households, of which the ten most common surnames accounted for 429,249 households, or nearly 52 percent of the total, and 479 surnames—more than half—were represented by ten or fewer households. The Taiwanese proverb is not far from the truth when it says, "Chern, Lin, Lii, Guo, and Tsay are half the people in the world" (tân, lîm, lí, koeh, chhòa: thian hā chiàm chít pòa$^{n}$ 陳林李郭蔡天下占一半). For the ten most common surnames, the actual ordering in Taiwan, following Liaw's sample, is Chern, Lin, Hwang, Jang, Lii, Wang, Wu, Tsay, Liou, Yang 陳林黃張李王吳蔡劉楊. In Tainan county, where Bao-an is situated, the ordering is Chern, Lin, Hwang, Lii, Wang, Wu, Yang, Jang, Tsay, Guo 陳林黃李王吳楊張蔡郭.

identity together with place of origin could easily have provided the quickest and most efficient way to form important kinds of alliances.[25]

The use of surnames to form social groupings seems to be characteristic of Chinese colonial expansion into other areas as well as Taiwan.[26] One short guide to San Francisco's Chinatown contains the following interesting passage:

> More important [than special-purpose organizations] are the family associations—the Chans, Wongs, the Four Families and a score more—made up of people who bear the same name. Presided over by a council, each family organization looks after the welfare of its members, and its influence extends across the continent. At their last San Francisco convention, for example, the Wongs attracted 10,000 other Wongs from all corners of the United States (Walls 1960: 37).

One result of the importance of Taiwanese surname groupings, at least in the Hsikang region where Bao-an is situated, is that vil-

25. The importance of surname groups in Taiwan, at least in recent times, is revealed by a Japanese government survey published in 1919 (summarized by S. H. Chen 1956: 10). The survey included religious organizations, but since most organizations have some religious symbolism involved in them, Chen points out that "In fact these were associations in response to various social needs." Of 6,159 associations surveyed, 160 (under 4 percent) were "associations to help the education of kinsmen" and none other were directly related to kinship. On the other hand 1,685 (27 percent) were associations organized by people of the same trade; 1,851 (30 per cent) were associations "organized by people living in the same village or town"; and 1,077 (17 percent) were associations organized by people of the same surname. No doubt the trade organizations are urban phenomena. However the local and surname organizations, nearly half of the total, are presumably general and by their very existence and formality reveal the importance of these principles in organizing Taiwanese society.

26. Cf. Freedman 1966: 162 ff., in which he discusses the colonization of south China during the Tang and Sung and the overseas expansion from these areas. Although Freedman tends to make the argument in terms of "lineages," he concedes that "the large-scale organization of overseas Chinese on the basis of agnatic kinship has typically taken the form of clan association and not the lineage" (p. 165). A clan association is a form "in which men of a common surname are grouped together for limited purposes" for Freedman. The probable circumstance is put even more clearly by Pasternak (1969), who also suggests a number of other ways in which associations might be created to meet the exigencies of the frontier situation and maintains (probably realistically) that real lineages are next to impossible to form in the face of massive organizational need and fairly random migration.

lages in many cases include several different groups of related families, with most of the groups bearing the same surname, but unable to trace relationships of kinship between them. Of 227 households in Bao-an in 1967, 164 (72.3 percent) of them bore the surname Guo. These are considered to be divided into five groups according to the town in Taiwan to which their ancestors migrated from Fukien, and from which they emigrated to Bao-an.[27] There are in addition some Guo households who are unsure of their identification with one of these origin groups, and others who, though associating themselves with one of the origin groups, cannot trace a genealogical connection within it.

In addition to this core of same-surname households, families with other surnames also join a village. Table 1 shows the proportions of minority surname households in Bao-an in 1967. Both Hwang and Shyu settlements seem to date from at least the mid-nineteenth century, and the Jang group is probably almost as old. Like the Guo group it consists of a group of related households plus others not known to be related to them. Single families of various surnames, on the other hand, appear to be of fairly recent introduction. Thus the single Chern household was the result of a matrilocal marriage in 1926 that brought the father of the present household head into the village. During 1967 a neolocal Fang 方 household moved to Bao-an in order to set up a bicycle shop in an area that seemed commercially ready.

It is far from clear whether groups of surname mates founded the villages or whether a village having, more or less by accident, a preponderance of one surname attracted other settlers who happened to share that surname.[28] It seems certain, in any case, that

27. There are no traditions about the founding of Bao-an. One man, now in his sixties, claims that when his grandfather's great-grandfather (that is, the plus-five generation) first came to Bao-an, it was already a functioning village. Allowing twenty years to the generation, this would place his ancestor's immigration sometime before one hundred and twenty years ago, or before 1847. Allowing twenty-five years to the generation, it would place his ancestor's immigration sometime before one hundred and sixty years ago, or before 1807.

28. Chen (1956: 3 ff.) opts for the former model, and suggests that the typical surname village begins "pure" and later expands through the encrustation of matrilateral kinsmen, craftsmen, and itinerant merchants. Whichever pattern applies, the phenomenon seems common. Chen cites a Japanese government survey of a Lin 林 village called "Lin-ts'o-Hau" near "Peikan, Tainan" in which the proportion of Lin in the village is 76.6 percent, startlingly close to the percentage of Guo in Bao-an.

TABLE 1
BAO-AN SURNAME DISTRIBUTION

| | *Surname* | *Number of Households* | *Percentage of All Households* |
|---|---|---|---|
| 郭 | Guo / koeh | 164 | 72.3 |
| 張 | Jang / tiu$^{n}$ | 14 | 6.2 |
| 黃 | Hwang / n̂g | 11 | 4.9 |
| 徐 | Shyu / chhî | 11 | 4.9 |
| 林 | Lin / lîm | 7 | 3.1 |
| 王 | Wang / ông | 4 | 1.8 |
| 侯 | Hour / hâu$^{n}$ | 3 | 1.3 |
| 賴 | Lay / lōa | 3 | 1.3 |
| 李 | Lii / lí | 2 | .9 |
| 謝 | Shieh / chiā | 2 | .9 |
| 陳 | Chern / tân | 1 | .4 |
| 丁 | Ding / teng | 1 | .4 |
| 鄭 | Jenq / te$^{n}$ | 1 | .4 |
| 江 | Jiang / kang | 1 | .4 |
| 消 | Shiau / siau | 1 | .4 |
| 葉 | Yeh / ia̍p | 1 | .4 |
| | Total | 227 | 100.0% |

from earliest times Bao-an was a mixed village, dominated however by the Guo surname group. However the villages were originally founded, the identification of surname with village rapidly became crucially important in local wars.

## THE SURNAME WARS

It is possible to get some hint of how the system of surname villages worked in the climate of Taiwan during the Ching by reviewing what is known of the history of intervillage conflicts at that time.

Historians of Taiwan speak of battles, even wars, raging between different factions during the late Ching period.[29] One has

29. *See* Davidson 1903: 63–122, Goddard 1966: 92–110, Imbault-Huart 1893: 103–122. Imbault-Huart writes: "The first objective of the Chinese government after gaining possession of the island was to set up administrative machinery capable both of moving and of holding in check the turbulent population" (p. 105). [Le premier objet du gouvernement chinois,

the impression from the Western sources that at least for the island as a whole the major contingents in these struggles were place-of-origin groups from different parts of Fukien, identified partly by dialect (for the Hokkien language is a multidialectical one). At the local level, however, the relevant unit of antagonism seems to have been the surname group. In the Hsikang region some villages, because the predominant surname was Guo, constituted a Guo faction, including members of these villages whose surnames were not Guo. Other villages, where the predominant surname was Hwang, constituted a Hwang faction, opposed to the Guo villages, and including members of the Hwang villages whose surnames were not Hwang.

Two villages in the immediate vicinity were made up predominantly of Guo: Bao-an and Wulin.[30] At least seven villages were composed largely of persons bearing the surname Hwang. For reasons that are no longer remembered (though they are thought to relate to land tenure [31]), the Hwang and Guo found themselves increasingly antagonistic to one another until, sometime between 1855 and 1870, open war broke out between the two groups. So few were the Guo in comparison with the Hwang that they are said to have dressed their women as men so that from a distance their forces would look more formidable than they were and thus they might avoid attack.

Little is remembered of these "great wars" of the Ching period. Those who participated, even as children, are now long dead, as are most of their children, and the tales that are still told are

---

après sa prise de possession de l'île, fut d'y établir des rouages administratifs capables de mettre en mouvement et de tenir en bride cette population turbulente.] An anonymous traveller to Taiwan at the beginning of the eighteenth century is quoted by Davidson: "Though they are industrious, yet the emigrants have deservedly a reputation for insubordination and lawlessness. They associate much in clans [probably referring to surname groups], and clannish attachments and feuds are cherished among them; but they are very fond of intercourse with foreigners. Many of them are unmarried or have left their families in China, to whom they hope to return after amassing a little property" (p. 69). On the treatment of foreigners during this period, *see* Pletcher 1949.

30. Wulin 梧林 means "Forest of *Sterculia platanifolia.*" The name is somehow more felicitous in Chinese.

31. A somewhat whimsical Taiwanese proverb enjoins the young that "your land comes first, your wife and children second" (*tē-it chhân-hn̂g, tē-jī bó·-kiáⁿ* 第一田園第二妻囝).

scattered, contradictory, and blurred with the passing of time. Even most of the antagonisms are forgotten, though such standing intervillage antipathies as seem to appear today are often along the same lines that were apparently battle lines a century ago, and the local (township-level) political factions are still those of the Guo and the Hwang, however much they may become complicated by individual issues and particular personalities.

The incident that began this war was trivial enough: an ox, belonging to a Guo family, wandered into a Hwang field and was slaughtered by the owner of the field. For thirteen years thereafter battles raged. The Hwang seldom made direct forays into Bao-an or Wulin, but preferred to ambush individuals on the roads, and accordingly people named Guo could not safely travel to sell their produce or to obtain provisions from the outside. (Indeed, as we shall see, there were problems even for people who were not named Guo if they were allied with the Guo.) On roads now often paved and busy with motorcycle traffic, lone travellers on foot were ambushed and occasionally killed. In fields where today one finds only sugar cane and rice paddies, the "soldiers" of the opposing sides met in formal battle and fought with wooden and bamboo swords, clubs, and tridents, and occasionally with rather primitive firearms.

The battles seem to have been inspired partly by the desire that one's own dead should be fewer in number than the enemy dead. Reports vary on the number of people killed in total, the highest estimate being eighty-two (forty-one on either side), but most agree on the figure of thirteen Hwang against twelve Guo when at length government authorities forced the war to a close and decided upon reparations to be paid for the imbalance in the dead. (The Guo faction avoided the reparations by disinterring a recently buried corpse, decapitating it, and presenting its head to the mandarin as a thirteenth victim on the Guo side. The Hwang apparently did not realize the victim was not theirs and did not protest.)[32]

The Guo did not win the war. It was at best a draw. Even a

32. To the best of my knowledge the numbers eighty-two, forty-one, thirteen, and twenty-six have no importance in Chinese numerology. *See* Granet 1934: 127–248. What is significant is not the figures themselves, but the effort to keep the number of casualties exactly equal.

draw is impressive, however, considering the situation in which Bao-an and Wulin found themselves when hostilities originally broke out. Insofar as it is possible today to reconstruct the events of the period, the local Guo seem to have done as well as they did because they engaged in various kinds of alliances with other groups.

One major source of assistance seems to have been other people named Guo (not known to be relatives) who lived in Tainan city. The Guo of Tainan were worshippers of King Guo, a patron god of places in which Guo are particularly numerous. One heavily mythologized account speaks of a visiting god being implored by a goddess worshipped in Bao-an to assist her in protecting the village. The visiting god suggested that King Guo, divine protector of the Guo surname, was the appropriate deity to apply to, and the goddess accordingly obtained the cooperation of King Guo, who directed his followers in Tainan to assist Bao-an and Wulin. The cooperation with the Guo in Tainan city seems to have been based heavily upon surname solidarity, and it is assumed by most informants today that the Guo of Tainan contributed their bit in these early struggles *because, and only because,* they shared a surname. However suspicious we may be of this as a total explanation, it is clearly an important part from the Taiwanese point of view. The assistance, by the way, was rendered by the Guo of one district of Tainan only, and apparently not by any city-wide surname organization.

The aid given by the Guo of Tainan was not directly military, but rather consisted of providing such goods as the people of Bao-an were unable to bring into the village through normal trading channels because of Hwang blockades and ambushes on the roads. The supplies from Tainan were floated on bamboo rafts along the coast and up the Tsengwen Chi to Bao-an. To avoid ambush from Hwang-allied riverside villages downstream, much of this work was done at night and apparently was successful.

A second source of assistance came from alliances with other surname groups in the area. One of these was named Chern 陳 and lived in a small village some three or four kilometers to the north of Bao-an. The Chern lent manpower and in at least one celebrated incident provided an armed escort for rafts being brought up the river from Tainan. The basis for the alliance with the

Chern is not certain. Local tradition says simply that the patron god of the Chern in that village, Marshal Shieh, commanded them to assist the Guo of Wulin and Bao-an. Before such a command would have been credible, sentiment must have been running heavily in favor of helping the Guo already.

Village tradition maintains that Marshal Shieh himself joined the Chern in assisting Bao-an, and it is not difficult to imagine a delegation of Chern, perhaps armed, proceeding with the Marshal's palanquin to Bao-an where, through his spirit medium, the god revealed the god of the Hwang to be nothing but a transformed dog demon, formidably powerful in the human world but an inferior being in the supernatural sphere, and revealed a charm for the defeat of the Hwang.

> Now a large number of those who bore the name of Hwang lived at XYZ village, and when they were making war a certain god called the Red Duke [紅公祖] was helping them. The Red Duke was a transformation of a black dog devil [黑狗精], so their strength was very great. At that time we were very pathetic here. So Marshal Shieh . . . came and helped us. . . . Of course he knew what kind of god the Hwang's god was, so he told the people of this village to make a dog tub [33] and carry a [black] flag [of the kind used in exorcism]. When we went to war we were to recite a charm: He who meets the black will fall [見黑就倒]. From the time we began doing this, we won every battle with the Hwang, that is we defeated the Hwang.
>
> . . . I understand that after they had produced the dog tub, they won every battle. Whenever they spoke this sentence, the Hwang people would fall down.

Although we do not know the basis of the Chern-Guo alliance, the important point is that it was somehow contracted, and that the unit that seems to have been involved was defined on the basis of surname and locality.[34] Informants maintain that other such alli-

33. I have been unable to identify the item in question. The Chinese term 狗桶 means simply "dog tub" but may apply in a metaphorical sense to some other item.

34. To the best of my knowledge research is still wanting concerning "traditional" alignments between surname groups in Taiwan. At the present time there are hints of such alliances at least in restricted areas, but it would be of interest if, say, all Chern were (now or in the past) conceived to bear a friendly relation with all Guo, while all Hwang were assumed to be hostile to all Guo.

ances were also contracted with surname groups in various villages, to a degree that enabled their faction to hold its own against the Hwang villages, but there is disagreement about which villages were involved, partly due to changes in village names at various times.

A third source of assistance was immigration of additional Guo families into Wulin and Bao-an from villages where they were harassed by Hwang. Some villages seem to have been able to maintain neutrality, and minority Guo populations in them were comparatively safe. In other cases, their safety was more chancy, and at least one family still recalls that they moved to Bao-an because their house in another, unallied village was burned to the ground by the Hwang.

A fourth source of assistance came through ties of village solidarity which compelled non-Guo of the Guo villages to assist in various ways. The war was between surname groups, and particularly between surname groups further delineated by village affiliations. At the same time, village dwellers of other surnames apparently could not remain entirely neutral, but had obligations to the dominant faction. In some cases, village loyalties even took precedence over surname loyalties (not surprising if the alternative is having one's house burned to the ground). Provisions were obtained for Bao-an, for example, by village people bearing other surnames, and, in particular, families named Shyu and Hwang (!) are remembered for this service to the Guo of Bao-an. These non-Guo participants were clearly resented by the enemy and apparently were interfered with from time to time, but they enjoyed nevertheless the status of nonantagonists in the struggles. A keen appreciation of this point is displayed by the informant who spoke of a Shyu provisioner who ran afoul of the Hwang while on a mission: "I have heard that one time one of our Shyu runners was caught by the Hwang and his ear was cut off. This was to symbolize that he was not named Guo, and the Hwang couldn't kill him."

The point of all this is that the relevant units in the Hwang-Guo conflict were surname groups, which were in various ways further defined by village association. The basic units seem to have been same-surname subsets of particular villages, which then contaminated, as it were, sharers either of the surname or of the village with secondary responsibilities in the conflict. The Guo ultimately emerged undefeated because of their successful manipulation of surname and village loyalties. This manipulation entailed enlisting the aid not only of people of their same village and of their same surname, but also of *at least* one other group defined by other surname and village boundaries, namely, the Chern. It is significant that no specific mention is made by any informants about reliance on kinship links in the formation of these alliances. The units are always the Guo of such and such a place or the Hwang of this village or that; and the authority for participation of outsiders is cited as that of a god who patronizes a group delineated by surname and locale.

I am *not* saying that the loosely structured units that emerge are not lineage units. That depends upon how one defines lineage, and I understand that Taiwanese surname-village units are similar in some ways to lineage units in other parts of the world. But I *am* arguing that they are not *Tzwu* 族 (Chinese lineage) units. They are not *Tzwu* units because they do not recruit their membership as a *Tzwu* recruits its membership, because they do not have common holdings of land or other wealth as a *Tzwu* does, and because they are not called *Tzwu*, but are referred to merely by the surname involved (the Guo of Bao-an, the Lin of Tainan, the Chern, the Wang).[35] They represent an alternative form of social organization, similar in certain ways to *Tzwu* organization, but distinct from it: a natural outgrowth of Chinese ideas about social organization that is also well adapted—and I would prefer to say preadapted—to a colonial area such as Taiwan.

35. Traditional *Tzwu* units are sometimes referred to in the same way. The point here is that this is the *only* way in which informants refer to these southern Taiwanese social units.

# Chapter 2
## *The Religion of the Taiwanese*

Having developed a picture, however sketchy, of the history and organization of Bao-an village, we now turn to religion. In the present chapter we shall consider some aspects of Taiwanese folk religion in general. In the chapters that follow we shall explore religious phenomena of Bao-an in particular and consider their relation to other facets of village life.

### BUDDHISTS AND TAOISTS

One question that is often asked about religion in Taiwan is whether the people are Taoists or Buddhists, and perhaps it will prove easiest to begin consideration of Taiwanese religion by answering this reasonable question. There is something called Taoism, with certain tradition and religious specialists and books associated with it; and it is Chinese. There is also something called Buddhism, with certain traditions, religious specialists and books. It is different from Taoism, but in most ways it is equally Chinese. There is in addition to these two traditions, with their specialists and their books, a corpus of beliefs and practices, the folk religion, which has variously been described as Confucian [1] (which it is not), as animistic,[2] and as popular.[3] All three of these strains, Taoism, Buddhism, and folk religion, have contributed heavily to Chinese religious life, and their interpenetration is so extensive as to prevent a thoroughgoing sorting of the elements one might associate with each in its "primal" state. It is important that we note how closely these three strains are mixed. At the same time, however, there are certain traits that still carry a specifically Taoist or Buddhist tinge, and, most important, there are separate Taoist and Buddhist clergies whom village people call upon to perform certain rituals. Both the pantheons and the personnel of the Taoist

1. Groot 1910. 2. Reichelt 1951. 3. Maspero 1923.

and Buddhist faiths must be clearly distinguished from each other and from folk religion if we are to understand the dynamics of religion in Taiwan today.[4]

Buddhism has a hierarchy of supernatural beings which is, as I understand it, clearly and explicitly worked out, if not by a universal Buddhist church, at least by individual schools. Taoism also has a hierarchy of supernatural beings which is, as I understand it, worked out in some detail. These supernatural beings include some gods worshipped only by the Taoist priests, for they are founders of various schools of Taoist philosophy, alchemy, and magic. Both clergies engage in worship of the beings in their respective hierarchies, but only certain members of either hierarchy are worshipped by the people at large.

In the Buddhist religion, popular worship is confined almost entirely to three figures: Guan-in, the Amida Buddha, and the Śākyamuni Buddha, in that order of popularity. The arhats are represented in many temples by tiny statues on the wall of a room devoted to Guan-in, where they are more items of pious and conventional decoration than objects of worship.

In the case of the Taoist figures, the intergrading with popular religion is more complete. The primary difference is that the

4. Contemporary Chinese writers unanimously distinguish Buddhism and Taoism from other beliefs, which are variously treated. For Jiang Jia-jiin (1957, 1959) the classification of religions in Taiwan is Taoism, Buddhism, Christianity, and "popular beliefs" 民間信仰, the last category including nature worship, divination, and a variety of other things. For Lii Tian-chuen (1956) the categories are Taoism, Buddhism, Christianity, and "common beliefs" 通俗信仰, but unlike Jiang Jia-jiin's "popular beliefs" this last category includes cults of three popular gods, two of whom Jiang Jia-jiin (1959) specifically classes as Taoist. For Her Lian-kwei and Wey Huey-lin (1966) the category of popular beliefs is itself composed of Taoism, Buddhism, Lay Buddhism, and individual cults of various historical figures (e.g., Guangong 關公, Jenq Cherng-gong 鄭成功) plus the cults of patron gods, plus many other subdivisions each given equal rank with the rest. A separate category of wizardry 巫覡 includes all practitioners other than orthodox Buddhist and Taoist clerics, and this is considered separate from the category of popular beliefs. Approximately the same format is followed in Her Lian-kwei's contribution to the Taiwan provincial gazeteer (Her Lian-kwei 1955).

What is more significant than the particular classifications of these authors is their agreement that whatever Buddhism and Taoism may be, they are not the whole story, and that some additional categories are necessary to include the parts of Taiwanese folk belief that they are unwilling to subsume under one or the other of these major traditions.

masses ignore (and are ignorant of) the deified magicians, and the priests pay little attention to most of the popular gods, although either side would acknowledge the importance of all these beings as gods 神. The pantheons are intellectually continuous.

The Taiwanese Buddhist clergy dwell in monasteries, and the Buddhist monastery-temples are therefore clearly understood to be Buddhist, despite various practices not historically a part of Buddhism (such as the use of divination blocks and *chhiam*-papers).[5] Taoist priests, on the other hand, practice in public temples, which they neither own nor control, or in the houses of their clients. Taoist priesthood is entirely a private practice, like that of an American lawyer or physician.[6] There is no such thing as a Taoist temple, over and against a folk temple, in the way that there are distinctive Buddhist temples, for the "Taoist" temples (that is the places where Taoist rites are performed) *are* the folk temples.[7] These temples, because they are public, folk temples, often contain Buddhist images as well as non-Buddhist ones,[8] but Buddhist temples do not ordinarily contain non-Buddhist images.

5. The one religion introduced during the Japanese period and still surviving in Taiwan is *Tenrikyō* 天理教. The first postwar Japanese *Tenrikyō* missionary arrived in Taiwan during my stay there and was dismayed, as I was, to discover that since the war the Taiwanese *Tenrikyō* adherents had introduced divination blocks into the temple. In one *Tenrikyō* home I even found a carved joss representing "the *Tenrikyō* god" rather than the mirror used as a semi-mystical symbol of *Tenri-ō-no-mikoto* 天理王命 in Japan.

6. This situation does not seem to be typical for China as a whole. In many parts of the country there have been Taoist institutions very similar to the Buddhist monasteries, as well as a variety of types of Buddhist religious organizations. In Taiwan, however, the Taoist clerics are a dwindling handful of men who are not associated in formal organizations.

7. The term *Taoist* is often used in Taiwan to cover everything that is not Buddhist, Christian, or Moslem, and I have often slipped into this usage myself. The usage is convenient and harmless, as long as we remember what it means.

8. It is widely held that during the Japanese years, the government resolved to destroy all Chinese temples. Buddhist figures were placed in them, and it was pointed out that they were now Buddhist temples, and hence Japanese. The Japanese were apparently convinced, it is said, for they did not burn the temples. Even the most recent temples, however, are still built with niches or even halls for Guan-in, often surrounded by the arhats, so it is difficult to accept this historical incident as the explanation for the presence of Buddhist figures today. Basically, certain Buddhist figures are objects of popular and not merely Buddhist worship, and as such they are (naturally enough) placed in popular temples.

The Buddhist faith is considered foreign in some way, and Chinese delight in explaining that it is ultimately Indian. Buddhist clerics dress in grey or white or brown robes of distinctive cut, and are celebate and vegetarian, whereas Taoist priests are indistinguishable from the remainder of the population, have families, and eat what they please except during particular rites.

All of this sounds rather complicated. In practice it is very simple. There is a set of village beliefs and practices related to the supernatural. There are, in addition, two traditions represented by clergy. Both clergies are outside the village, and are related to village religion only in being outside specialists called in to perform needed rituals, particularly funerals and temple festivals, but also exorcism and other rites. These occasions are not frequent, and the liturgies and rites the priests perform are not understood by anyone who is not a priest. In the Taoist case the liturgy is typically secret; in the Buddhist case it is heavily sanskritized and requires an extensive special education before it is intelligible.

In the present chapter we shall be concerned with the religion of village people, not of clergymen. To the extent that village people have ideas about the clergy, or about what the clergy do when they are called to the village to perform ceremonies, we do not exclude the clergy from our consideration. But to the extent that the clergy have their own version of religious doctrine or practice, which is different from the version popular in Bao-an, they are not our present concern. There is a practical reason for this limitation: I have not studied and do not understand the religious ideas of any group of clergy. I agree that such study is important and interesting, and that it is necessary to an understanding of the religious system of China as a whole, just as the religion of the imperial court is important, interesting, and necessary to an understanding of the whole system. I have not included the study of the clergy because it would have taken many, many more years in Taiwan than I spent there, and because it would take many more years in a good library working with materials in languages I do not now read.

If I need a theoretical rationalization, however, it is this: this essay is about folk religion. One of the problems in discussing folk religion is deciding who are the folk. Is it reasonable to consider that folk religion includes elements in fact unknown to most of the participants in the system? If one answers categorically that it is not, then one is reduced to making use only of such knowledge as is common to everybody or nearly everybody. Such a decision means excluding a great many data that might be of great significance for the integration of the system at levels higher than those at which the most ignorant people in it may bother to integrate it. On the other hand, if one answers that it is reasonable to include elements that are arcane to the participants, then one finds oneself moving to the other extreme, and trying to include a world of details that are unknown to all but a very few participants (indeed to all participants if the details are the concern of outside specialists). When this happens, it seems to me it is difficult to draw conclusions bearing on the dynamics of social and cultural life, for I do not see how people can be directly influenced by ideas they do not in fact have.

What one ends up doing in practice, of course, is learning everything one can from everyone who is willing to talk about it, and relating it to everything one can think of to relate it to. But as a general theoretical bias, in drawing social and cultural conclusions about ritual activities, I am more inclined to the proletarian view than to the elitest one. For this reason I would be inclined to exclude from a study of village religion most of the testimony of religious elites from outside the village, even if I had it. But of course I do not, and that is why I call this stand I have taken a rationalization.

## GODS AND GHOSTS

A man's body lives by virtue of its animation by two or more souls; this is clear beyond question to a Taiwanese farmer. Scholars may dispute, as they have for centuries, about how many souls there are: two, four, or myriad thousands. For simple folk the details are irrelevant. Everybody knows there are at least two. One soul is the *Poh/phek* 魄. It is the lower soul, associated with the earth, with femaleness, with darkness, and in general with all things *In* 陰.[9] This soul is necessary to life, but is unimportant in the greater scheme of things. It tends to linger in coffins or

9. For a discussion of *In* and *Yang*, usually spelled *yin* and *yang* in English, *see* Fung 1948: 129–142, Granet 1934: 101–126, or van Praag 1966: 76–100.

around graves, and eventually to burn itself out and expire.[10] A man has another kind of soul too—an ethereal soul, of brightness and maleness and celestial realms, in other words of *Yang* 陽. This soul is called by scholars a *Hwen/hûn* 魂 or a *Ling/lêng* 靈, and in ordinary parlance a *Linghwen/lêng-hûn* 靈魂.

This *Linghwen* is of immortal stuff. There are various points of view as to how this immortal being spends its time after death. One view (by origin a Buddhist one) would send the *Linghwen* to hell 地獄, where it suffers hideously for its shortcomings in the world of the living. The descriptions of these torments are elaborate and various.[11] In certain contexts any Taiwanese is prepared to explain the importance and the inevitability of hell, and some maintain that Taiwanese who convert to Christianity do so because they have done evil deeds and wish to escape punishment by adopting a religion that provides no place in its cosmology for hell.[12] When the soul at length arrives at the final court of hell, penitent after its deservedly hideous purgatorial experiences, it is (somewhat unpedagogically) fed a drink inducing forgetfulness[13] and is reincarnated into an earthly form appropriate to the degree of virtue that informed it in its previous existence.

A second view, held simultaneously with the first, considers the *Linghwen* to continue life in the world of the shades 陰間, a ghostly sphere, invisible to mortals, yet interpenetrating the world of the living in time and space. Their existence can be comfortable if they are well provided by their descendants with food offerings,

10. But for a discussion of confusion as to the presence of various categories of soul in the grave, *see* Groot 1892–1910: vol. 4, pp. 5 f., 64 f.

11. For a fairly complete recent account taken from texts of various periods, *see* Eberhard 1967: chap. 2. Another readily available description in the context of traditional drama is provided by Laufer 1923: 4–28. For one of the Taiwanese variants see Nĝ 1955: 70–72 in the Hokkien edition; 99–103 in the English edition.

12. I have yet to meet a non-Christian Taiwanese who is aware that hell figures also in Christian thinking.

13. This drink is served by the Venerable Goddess Grandmother Menq 孟婆尊神, whom Werner (1932: 312) describes as the Buddhist Proserpine. DuBoise (1886: 314) writes that when scholars arrived in hell, able by Buddhist chants to avoid punishment, they were transferred to Grandmother Menq's department and given this liquid. In their next incarnation they died after birth or as infants and were thus delivered anew to the first courts of hell, now defenseless. The usual Taiwanese view is less inclined to pursue the workings of hell to so logical a conclusion.

clothing, housing, and above all with money. Small suits of clothing, papers folded to represent silver and gold ingots, or printed to imitate paper money, and paper houses of enormous complexity are all to be had in any Taiwanese town to be burned and thus communicated to the shades of the deceased. Indeed the artistry of these paper houses, equipped as they are with furnishings, gardens, and a staff of servants, easily surpasses the level of many a folk art that has received more attention as art. But the lot of such a shade is not always so pleasant. It sometimes happens that the dead has no descendants to provide him with offerings as the years go by. Slowly he is reduced to dire poverty and becomes a most pitiable creature. In desperation, and often in rage, he attacks human beings to gain direct fulfilment of his needs or at least to win attention to his plight. And in attacking human beings he changes categories, for a *Linghwen* (soul) who becomes vicious is a ghost, or *Goei* 鬼.[14] One village story I recorded tells of the visitation of such an unfortunate supernatural.

In a neighboring village a man died and was buried with all the appropriate ritual. A few months later his daughter was working in a field where her father had formerly worked, and he appeared to her, smoking, and wearing very tattered clothes. She was frightened and ran home, and explained about the bad clothes her poor father had to wear in the world of the shades, and that the living ought to provide him with better.

Another tale illustrates the malice to which the ghost may be forced.

Near Tainan there is a building with a section where no one dares sleep. One night a brave man and four companions went to the forbidden

14. Some writers associate the *Hwen* soul with gods (*Shern*) and the *Poh* soul with ghosts (*Goei*), which is admittedly a tidier scheme. Thompson (1969: 10f.) writes: "Now the material or *yin* component of the soul (called *p'o*) was that which would turn into a *kuei* if not placated by suitable burial and sacrifices. . . . This power of the *hun* soul derived from its nature as *shen*, which not only was a generic term for kindly spirits, but was used in reference to all deities." All I can say is that no one in Bao-an ever explained the scheme to me this way, and many people explained it to me the way I have described it. I suspect that the root of the problem is the change in the meaning of the difficult term *Goei* over time (or between "dialects"), but I am not sinologist enough to be able to trace this in detail.

place. As usual a ghost appeared, an old woman begging. They attacked her with bamboo clubs and she vanished. Subsequently they all fell ill. Four repented and went to ask her forgiveness. They recovered. The fifth is ill to this day.

In a general way, these pathetic and desperate *Goei* can be referred to by a common euphemism: the Good Brethren 好兄弟, known in the English literature by the less polite but more descriptive Chinese term: Hungry Ghosts 餓鬼.[15] The Good Brethren are dangerous because they are desperate, and to avoid incurring their jealousy or wrath one sacrifices to them at the gate of the house on the occasion of any important sacrifice to other supernaturals.[16] In Bao-an there is no question that the Good Brethren are the single most common category of supernatural worshipped simply because they exact sacrifices whenever sacrifices are to be offered for any reason.

In this view, then, there are two fates for a *Linghwen:* either it has descendants who provide it with offerings piously or it is ground down in poverty. The *Linghwen* with descendants who see to its welfare is also an ancestor 祖 先. Technically, some informants insist, a *Goei* and a *Linghwen* (and hence also an ancestor) are the same thing. The difference is that the term *Linghwen* communicates nothing save that the individual is dead, while the term *Goei* has rather ugly connotations that he may be danger-

15. In Bao-an the usual term is "lonely spirit" 孤 魂, although the term "hungry ghosts" is also used. Apparently in earlier times the ghosts were hungry not because they were not tended, but because they were being punished for avariciousness in life. They are accordingly sometimes portrayed with enormous bellies and mouths, but a gullet too small to pass food or water, causing eternal hunger and thirst. This latter interpretation, however, does not seem common in Bao-an.

Chinese hungry ghosts derive originally from Hindu *preta*. Soothill and Hodous (1937: 341), in an article under 鬼 in their dictionary of Chinese Buddhist terms, discuss various subdivisions of hungry ghosts. Although the hungry ghosts have long since lost much explicit connection with Buddhism or its doctrines, Soothill and Hodous do list various Chinese transliterations of the Sanskrit word *preta* that are clearly intended as sound transcriptions: *Biiliiduo/pi-lé-to* 俾 禮 多 (p. 320); *Bihlihduo/pit-lī-to* 畢 利 多 (p. 361); *Bihlii(duo)/phek-lē(-to)* 薜 荔 (多) (p. 462). This last writing, however, is apparently used only in the more Chinese sense of a *preta* seen as an ancestral spirit, become a hungry ghost living among men, and potentially harmful.

16. Although the term "Good Brethren" is itself a euphemism, the practice of worshipping them at the gate provides the source for a secondary euphemism, for the act is often called "worshipping the gate" 拜 門 口.

This table of food offerings is prepared for the use of wandering ghosts, lest they interfere with offerings to gods and ancestors.

ous or that he is not properly taken care of by descendants. The word tends to be avoided save as a term of abuse.[17]

But *Goei* are also set in opposition to another category: gods or *Shern* 神.[18] The conceptualization relevant in making this distinction is that the condition of a *Linghwen* after death is dependent—and if we are to be consistent with our earlier description, we can only insist that this means *partly* dependent—upon the merit it has accumulated in its terrestrial life. If you are good you become a god; if you are bad you become a ghost, say many village people, as though that were the whole story.

> When we men are good, we have a good report; and when we are bad, we have a bad report. The idea is always the same. Gods are those who

17. As an abusive term it has extensions among the living. A naughty or uncooperative child, for example, is a "little ghost" 小鬼. The English expression "little devil" seems similar in many contexts. A man fond of liquor is an "alcohol ghost" 酒鬼, a term used in playful scolding (covering some of the contexts in which American "wino" might be used).
18. Classically the opposition is another manifestation of *In* and *Yang*. Cf. Groot 1892–1910: vol. 4, pp. 407 ff.

A man and his grandchildren burn paper money and offer food and wine to the Good Brethren, or wandering ghosts.

> have done good deeds as men, those who love virtue and study the ways of the buddhas and after death join the buddhas [ 佛 ]. Those who devote themselves to the salvation of others become gods [*Shern*] at death.
>
> . . . The notion is that men of a good nature become gods; men of virtue become gods, and those without it become ghosts. A ghost who did very bad things before death may decide to practice virtue after dying; he can in that case become a god. A man may be very poor yet desire to be rich, and he can become rich. The situations are the same.

In this conceptualization there is a continuity between *Goei* and *Shern*, and some informants, when pressed to distinguish between the two, declare that there is no real difference save in their being bad or good. Still, a *Shern* is conceived to occupy an enviable position as an official in a celestial hierarchy, a salaried sinecure in an ancient and honorable tradition, dispensing decisions with the force of law. A *Goei,* on the other hand, is deprived of such honor, and spends his days in misery and dark doings.

To review: When a person dies, he becomes a *Linghwen*. Or, if you prefer, his *Linghwen* lives after him. He goes to hell, where he is punished for his earthly transgressions and is then reincarnated to try again. At the same time another theory tells him that what is crucial is whether or not he has descendants. If he does, and if they worship him and provide him with sacrifices, he lives a fairly content life as an ancestor in a shadowy afterworld that is not known in detail. If he has no descendants (or if the unfilial wretches fail to provide for him), he lives in the same shadowy afterworld as a miserable and starving *Goei*. If he was in life a man of exceptional virtue, he may be appointed to a position in the celestial bureaucracy and be a *Shern*, although the chances for this are, frankly, slim, given the number of virtuous competitors and the small number of positions that seem to be available. As a *Shern* he presumably has a coterie of worshippers who provide for him, and his position is substantially better than it was when he was merely an ancestor, not to mention a *Goei*.

This scheme or, more exactly, these two schemes are not without their contradictions. This same *Linghwen* that is suffering in hell pending reincarnation is obliged to reside in ancestral tablets at least part of the time, and this same ancestor that is worshipped in the tablets may simultaneously have duties in a celestial hierarchy. Village people do not seem to make any attempt to put the eschatology together more compactly. No one I asked about the matter could give a pat answer as to how an ancestor could go on being an ancestor once he had been reincarnated, for example. Yet it is clear that the two conceptualizations do coexist and occasionally come into revealing conflict with each other. At one funeral in Bao-an, for example, various ancestors were invited to reside in small paper effigies in order to observe the funeral games and other festivities, but great difficulty was experienced in getting one of the *Linghwen* to the effigy because the ancestor was in hell and had to get special permission to leave. This required several extra verses of the priestly chant before divination blocks revealed that the spirit had at last arrived. Historically such problems result from syncretism, particularly of Taoist and Buddhist elements with folk beliefs. But the Chinese are not a people given to apologetics, and authoritarianism in religion has traditionally concentrated on outlawing sects considered politically dangerous or subversive of the state rather than on doctrinal issues.[19] Accordingly there is little concern for tight logic in the folk system.

*Goei*, *Shern*, *Linghwen*, ancestor: these more or less exhaust the terms we shall need to consider the supernatural in Bao-an. At the risk of generating a loose end, however, I ought to concede that there are other words relating to the supernatural. These categories of beings are spoken of in traditional tales especially, and are not quite the same as the supernaturals we have been dealing with, but are not altogether different either. Several religious traditions, immensely imaginative writers of fiction and fantasy, and a wide variety of popular theater, all perpetuated by a literary tradition surpassed in antiquity by none other on this planet, have maintained in popular understanding and belief a wealth of other beings. To draw a loose parallel, we might say they are similar in many ways to the traditions of "little people" or "good fairies" in Europe, although the Chinese beings are more sacred. How, we ask, do immortals 仙 [20] or buddhas 佛, as well as sundry evil fairies 妖精 or 妖怪, devils 魔神 and false or evil gods 邪神 fit into the scheme?

When I questioned several informants and demanded of them that they make a nice tidy chart showing how these various kinds of beings relate to one another, the results were inconclusive. One informant simply listed buddhas, immortals, gods, and men in that order, as a kind of hierarchy of importance. Another provided a list of beings into which man can be transformed: as a living being a man can become an immortal or a buddha. Immortals, he explained, live in the mountains and are Taoist. Buddhas live in "the east" and are Buddhist. That is about the only difference. At death a man can become a god, gods dwelling also in the mountains, or he can become a ghost. Ghosts too may die, and both ghosts and men are therefore mortal, in contradistinction to gods, immortals, and buddhas, who are immortal.[21] A

19. Cf. Groot 1903.
20. To avoid confounding the following discussion with too many Chinese words, I have used a single gloss for each term, selecting the most common or self-evident glosses, not necessarily the most accurate, and making them isomorphic with the Chinese terms. I have not necessarily followed the same convention in other parts of this work, however.
21. Therefore it is to one's advantage to be good in life so as to become a god at death and attain immortality. It is something like receiving tenure.

third informant agreed that it is a living man who becomes a buddha or an immortal, and a dead man who becomes a god or a ghost. Buddhas are different from immortals, however, in that they lack an individual soul and therefore have no freedom, whereas immortals have these attributes. No immortal would want to become a buddha, she explained. Then she added that immortals struck her as rather "cute," possibly thinking of the famous eight immortals who appear so often as a rather lighthearted artistic and literary motif. Gods live in heaven for the most part, although it is impossible to be sure about some. The Five Kings surely dwell in heaven, but the Queen of Heaven she could not be certain about. Ghosts are most pathetic, for they are homeless, and they are always subject to extinction if killed by supernaturals of superior categories.

The fourth informant had the most complicated and ultimately the most interesting scheme of all. It centered in man: as a living being, man can become an immortal, although there is at the moment only one immortal in the world, a certain Liou Boruen 劉伯温.[22] Not all immortals were originally men, however. It is possible also for animals to become immortals. When they die, men become either gods or ghosts. Ghosts are of several kinds. Fallen gods become ghosts, but are designated "false gods." Animals can also become ghosts, although not gods, and are designated "evil fairies," a category also including anthropomorphized inanimate objects (which are properly called *Iaujing* 妖精, according to this view, although *Iauguay* 妖怪 and *Iaujing* tend to be confused with each other). Buddhas live in the Western Heaven; immortals dwell in the mountains; but gods live in their temples, where they can tend to human affairs.

Interesting as these results may be, they do not betray a clear, shared, detailed conceptualization of any single scheme, even among willing and verbal informants. This is not surprising, for the unity "supernatural being" is imposed, and it makes as little sense to suppose that all will be easily arranged into a single scheme as to suppose that a European is prepared to arrange

22. He is listed in most Chinese biographical dictionaries by his given name, Liou Ji 劉基. The historical Liou Ji (1311–1375) was a statesman of the early Ming. To him is attributed the *Hot Biscuit Song* 燒餅歌, interpreted prophetically in a way similar to the Western *Nostradamus*.

Oberon and Father Christmas on the same chart with Saint Hilary and the Angel Gabriel. I propose for present purposes to leave Oberon and Father Christmas off the chart. For Taiwan, we do not need Oberon very often, and we will learn more without him, at least for a time. In this book we may productively confine ourselves to the *Linghwen* in its three important manifestations in Bao-an: as a god, an ancestor, and a ghost.

The gods are conceived as occupying positions in a celestial government very similar, at least in broad outlines, to human governments. The traditional view, and the one most often expressed by Chinese, is that the hierarchy is a sort of mirror of the Chinese governmental structure of imperial days (even to civil service examinations). Today, some Taiwanese explain it, and perhaps conceptualize it, as resembling the Republican government, ruled over by a president, vice-president, various underlings and directors, and divided into divers ministries and commissions.

The same theme is repeated in symbolism within the temples themselves. The usual Chinese temple is in the form of a yamen, with the statue of the god of the temple situated where the official would sit. Many temples are provided on either side with racks where tall poles are placed, each of which terminates in a highly stylized emblem, usually carved in wood. Individually, these emblems are not readily interpretable by anyone I have talked to; but collectively they are understood to represent the offices of a kingly court—the subordinate officials who, in the nature of things, would normally be part of the court attached to the yamen (with little attention to what level yamen we are talking about). In processions they are carried by young boys before the palanquin of the temple god to "represent" the presence of his subordinates. These staffs are not found in all temples, for they are expensive. Nor are they in any way a necessary part of even the largest temple. But they are a way of making the temple more beautiful 好看. It is interesting and significant that the way chosen to make the temple beautiful also emphasizes the official nature of its object of worship.

Prominent as the bureaucratic theme is, the hierarchism is seldom very neat if one looks closely. The only figure whose position is universally agreed on is the Jade Emperor 玉皇上帝, who is at the top. Below him is a group of gods who are higher than other gods, but whom one tries in vain to rank. Some Taiwanese place Guangong 關公 just below the Jade Emperor himself (and indeed it is even whispered about that Guangong has recently succeeded to the office of Jade Emperor). In Hsikang the Twelve Plague Gods are immediately below the Jade Emperor. Some informants insert most of the Buddhist pantheon at this point, including and especially Guan-in. Others include the gods who preside over the dead.

Hazy as all this is, in any given region there is a general sense that such and such a god is "high" (Mandarin 高, Hokkien 大), and that because of this he may have advantages that make it easier for him than for some lower god to accomplish certain things a petitioner wants to have him do. Many conditions can effect the degree to which a community focuses on a particular deity and regards him as important: the presence of a shrine, particularly a large and important one, naturally brings the importance of its enshrined objects of worship to the attention of people in the area. It is difficult to live in southwestern Taiwan without being aware of the Five Kings enshrined in huge temples at Nankuenshen 南鯤鯓 and Matou,[23] for example, even though they may not be otherwise relevant in a given community. Another important consideration influencing the position of a deity in the eyes of a community is the presence or absence of a particularly efficacious religious effigy carved in his likeness. The efficaciousness of a joss in turn depends upon other factors: the willingness of its owner to lend it for séances is important, because a joss builds its reputation through its successful use in divination. A third and very important factor in the status a god is perceived to have in a community is the presence or absence of a spirit medium whom he may possess and through whom he may advise the community with an intimacy impossible through other means of divination.

We shall consider such matters as josses and spirit mediums below. The point here is that at least among the farming people the hierarchy of gods is not the same from place to place or from time to time, even though it is believed to be more or less permanently fixed in heaven.

23. For a discussion of the shrine at Nankuenshen, *see* Chern Ching-gaw and Shieh Shyr-cherng 1963: 309–313. On the shrine at Matou see the same work, pp. 223–229; also a special edition of the journal *Faahae* [法海] vol. 4, no. 1 (5 May 1959).

# Chapter 3
## *Divine Guardians of the Village*

With an introduction to the supernatural behind us, let us turn back to Bao-an village. We saw earlier that two organizing principles were important: surname and village, and the point was illustrated by a description of warfare in the Hsikang region. In the present section we shall see how the intersection of these two principles of social organization is ritually symbolized in Bao-an in the person of King Guo,[1] a patron deity. After this we shall examine the village defined as a sacred domain, which must be protected, and the nature of the enemy that must, with King Guo's help, be kept out.

### SUPERNATURAL PROTECTORS OF BAO-AN

The individuality of a village is inseparable from the particular configuration of gods who guide its policy, and its conflicts with other villages necessarily entail conflicts between the divinities that each side is able to muster. Accordingly, alliances between men and gods are a common idiom in which historical events are recounted. In some villages, including Bao-an, a single god is elevated to a position of supreme authority as the recognized protector of the village, and in Bao-an this god, King Guo, is the prime symbolization of the unity of surname units and village units.

Of the gods who are most frequently spoken of in Bao-an, King Guo is the "highest" and "most powerful." [2] King Guo is both a patron of those who bear this surname and a generalized god whose assistance is available to others. In the Hsikang area he is the

1. 郭姓王 or 郭聖王, more formally known as 廣澤尊王. Although the identity of surname is probably not entirely a matter of chance, most patron gods do not bear the same surname as their worshipping villages. Certainly in no sense is King Guo thought of as ancestral.
2. For a recounting of several traditions about the earthly life of King Guo, *see* Liaw Yuh-wen 1967: 78–83, and Jenq Sheng-chang 1967: 49–52.

patron of villages in which the Guo surname is predominant or which were allied with the Guo faction against the Hwang in the wars of a century ago, as they are in the political factions of today. In particular he is of great importance in Bao-an and Wulin.[3]

It should be noted that, despite the surname, King Guo is *not* considered to be ancestral to anyone living today. His wife was a celestial maiden deliberately "planted" on earth to marry him, and their offspring were a series of semiautochthonous stones that mysteriously appeared in the floor of the home temple. These are understood to symbolize "sons" to whom virtually all worship of King Guo is actually directed. And the sons have no offspring, being nonhistorical (or non-"historical") beings confined to their ethereal manifestations. The word used to designate a son of King Guo means "guardian" plus a birth-order number.[4] Functionally this serves nicely to allow the god to be worshipped simultaneously in many places, or to permit different mediums to contradict each other, since it is always a different "guardian" in question. The same device is *not* used to multiply other, even more popular gods, however.

It is important to emphasize that King Guo today is the patron not only of the Guo as a surname group, but of the *villages* of the Guo faction, including such of their inhabitants as are *not* named Guo. His tie to these villages is due to their Guo inhabitants, but

3. Her Lián-kwei and Wey Huey-lin (1966: 136 f.) present a simplified scheme of "protective gods of immigrant groups" 移民守護神 such that Taiwanese of Tsinkiang 晉江 or 泉州 stock worship King Guo and the Great Emperor Who Protects Life 保生大帝, alias Wu Jen Ren 吳真人, and Taiwanese of Lunghsi 龍溪 or 漳州 stock worship King Chern 陳聖王. Minorities with origins outside Fukien have also appropriate and separate deities. However, the Guo of Bao-an (as of southern Taiwan generally) consider themselves to have come from Lunghsi and speak the Lunghsi rather than the Tsinkiang dialect of Taiwanese Hokkien; nevertheless they are under the patronage of King Guo. The Her-Wey scheme may generalize accurately for the island as a whole—I do not know—but it apparently predicts little at the level of the individual village.

4. The Chinese is Taybao 太保, a term formerly used to designate the Guardian 太保 to the heir apparent 太子, and in this original usage also written 太子太保. Its use to designate the "sons" of King Guo has never been clear to me. Can it be the invention of a Fukienese medium of long past? I have rendered it "guardian" to avoid introducing a Chinese term, but I suspect that the implication of high court office is more relevant here than the notion of trusteeship.

his commitment is to them as total villages. In social terms, his cult represents the acceptance of affiliation with a Guo dominated faction by the non-Guo of the village; he is the prime symbol of the integration of village solidarity and surname solidarity even though village and surname personnel do not entirely overlap.

His dual aspect as protector of the Guo surname and of the villages of the Guo faction is well illustrated by his local name. King Guo is locally called *koeh-sèng-ông*. This may either be written 郭聖王, meaning "Sacred King Guo," or it may be written 郭姓王, meaning "King of the Guo Surname."[5] No doubt people are to be found who will insist that one form is right and the other wrong. Both writings do occur, however, and it seems clear that both meanings of *sèng* are thought to apply.[6]

The center for King Guo's worship in Taiwan today is the Shiluo Diann 西羅殿 of Tainan city, which it is claimed was founded in 1714 by direct transfer of its incense fire from the home temple in Fukien.[7]

The Shiluo Diann is too far away to be easily accessible for daily visits and divination. If it is true that a prophet is without honor in his own house (and I have always been told that this is the case), then no arrangement could be better calculated to preserve the prestige of King Guo and the sanctity of his oracles. Problems not satisfactorily solved within Bao-an, or which arise

5. The pronunciations are identical in Hokkien only, not in Mandarin. When mentioning the god to me in Mandarin, informants would use now one title, now the other.

6. It is inviting to speculate that the writing with 姓, "surname," is earlier than that with 聖, "sacred," and that the change follows a gradual change in his role from more strictly surname-related concerns toward greater generalization, perhaps at the time of the Guo-Hwang conflicts, perhaps after the pacification of the region. Unfortunately, evidence is lacking on earlier usage. Neither form is frequently written, since for most purposes where writing is employed a yet more formal title is used: The Venerable King of the Broad Marshes 廣澤尊王. At the risk of going yet further out on a limb I would suggest that this formal title is seldom used in speech in southwestern Taiwan because (unlike *koeh-sèng-ông*) it makes no statement at all about the special relation of this god to Guo concerns.

7. Transfer of a pot of smoldering incense is the key act by which a daughter temple is founded from a mother temple. The daughter temple is said to "separate" 分 from the parent temple. When parent temples are politically available, regular pilgrimages, usually yearly, are made to the parent temple for "renewal" of the fire. The home temple of King Guo is located at Phoenix Mountain Monastery in Fukien province 福建省南安縣泉州府鳳山寺.

A palanquin bearing gods is carried into Bao-an by people from a neighboring village.

between Guo villages, can be brought to the god's attention in a situation that marks the problem off as something out of the ordinary, and provides it with a "special" solution of greater sanctity and authority than is usually possible. Today it is rare for the village as a whole to refer problems to (the medium of) King Guo in Tainan, but it is not at all rare for individuals to do so when they are not satisfied with decisions handed down by local gods through their spirit-mediums or by other means of divination.

But King Guo is not *merely* a benevolent outsider who puts in his oar only at local invitation. He is also the protector of the village, and accordingly from time to time he makes a visit. Bao-an, like other villages in the Hsikang region, participates in a triennial festival. The festival is called a *Wangjiaw* 王 醮 and is performed in honor of visiting divine inspectors of extraordinarily high rank.[8] The rites involve, among other things, a procession in which local gods move through the villages of the area for

8. These inspectors are derived from "plague gods," and the temple rites are, strictly speaking, those appropriate for plague gods. The details are not relevant to the present discussion. The interested reader should refer to Liou Jy-wann 1963 for a discussion of plague gods, and to the same author's more recent monographs (1967 and forthcoming) for a discussion of various types of *Jiaw,* including the Hsikang rites.

three days to provide themselves with a chance (1) to inspect their territory, (2) to drive out misfortune and correct injustice, and (3) to pay their respects on behalf of their village constituencies to the visiting inspectors. The core elements of this procession are palanquins containing the gods of the participating villages. Normally, each village is represented by at least one palanquin filled with small josses belonging to individual families or owned collectively.

In addition to the palanquins containing many small josses there are larger ones containing much larger images often belonging to large temples rather than to individual villages. These are patron gods of whole villages or clusters of villages, including, of course, King Guo. They are normally placed near the end of the procession. Because local custom maintains that the last place is the place of greatest honor, there is a certain amount of behind-the-scenes maneuvering for a place as near to the rear as possible. The order of march is decided by the officials of the Hsikang temple [9] and depends partly upon temporary ranking given to local gods as "officials" in the festival for that year. Thus in 1964 it was decided that "The Tour of Inspection Representing Heaven has by Imperial Decree gloriously appointed the Venerable King of the Broad Marshes [King Guo] as Vice-Commander, the Grand Tutor *Yang of A* Village as Great General of the Rearguard, Marshal Shieh of *B* Village as Vanguard, and Wugongshern [蜈蚣神] of *C* Village as Sage of the Hundred Steps." [10]

The permanent positions of these gods in the celestial hierarchy are, in theory, relevant; but the temporary assignment of each to an ad hoc role during the festival allows other considerations to take precedence.[11] The decision is supposedly made by divination, but

9. Larger temples, such as that at Hsikang, are not administered in the same way that we described earlier for the temple in Bao-an. They are managed instead by a temple committee, which elects its own new members and typically includes the most wealthy and powerful men of the area. The system of prestigious posts in towns like Hsikang seems to play off the temple committees, the agricultural associations, and the more strictly political offices against one another. The subject is worth further study.

10. From a brochure issued by the *Chinq An Gong* 慶安宮 Hsikang Temple. I am grateful to the *Chinq An Gong* for lending their only remaining copy for photoduplication. Village names have been replaced by single roman letters.

11. This means, among other things, that the question of "permanent"

because the way one asks a question can influence the outcome of divination, the temple officials, like imperial advisers, may always be suspected of influencing the gods.

What is important is that the order of march should be in accord with political reality, and the position of King Guo *behind* the protector of another village is a symbolic expression of the precedence of Guo influence over that represented in the other village. When priorities are unclear, the way is open for decisions to be made by the astute manipulation of these palanquins, but when they are clear, or when there is open and clearly defined dispute, the authorization of the "wrong" order of march can provoke serious disagreements. Thus in 1967 a conflict developed between Bao-an, Wulin, and other Guo villages on the one hand and a traditional "enemy" affiliated with the (today subordinate) Hwang faction. The latter claimed that the order of march should be decided anew each time, whereas the Guo villages maintained that the question had been decided finally a time or two before, with King Guo (naturally enough) in the most prestigious position. The Guo view prevailed, and the opposing village withdrew from the festival entirely rather than endure the mortification of being consigned to subordination to King Guo. According to letters from village people after I left the area, in the 1970 festival the opposing Hwang village prevailed upon temple authorities (among whom Hwang influence was apparently strong) to arrange divine consent to change the ordering. In 1970 Wulin and Bao-an therefore withdrew after extensive negotiations both with the temple authorities and among themselves.

The point of all this is that one of the ways in which a divine village protector protects is in sharing his rank and glory with that of his protégé villages. Seen the other way about, a divine protector provides a concrete symbol that can be invested with the rank and glory of the protégé village and can be manipulated in relation to similar symbols from other villages. This allows the village people to play out in a cooperative religious rite conflicts

precedence in the hierarchy is never actually solved. Because there does not seem to be a clear notion of precedence covering the locally worshipped village gods, an attempt to organize a procession in which such precedence was important would be foredoomed to failure. In some sense, assigning temporary roles can be seen as a dodge to avoid the issue. The temple has authority only to assign temporary roles.

and questions of priority deriving originally from conflicts and questions of priority in other areas.

But there is another aspect to the presence of King Guo in Bao-an. Within and among the Guo villages themselves, of course, the visit of King Guo represents more than just a chance to get one up on a neighboring faction. The statue used in the festival is the fourth "guardian" we spoke of earlier. It is kept in Bao-an or Wulin (chosen by lot) for about four and a half months after the festival (or until after the seventeenth day of the eighth moon, which is the official birthday of the particular guardian used), and during this time he occupies a place of honor seated on his palanquin placed squarely in the door of the village temple. The statue is considered to be especially beautiful as well as efficacious, and the universal reaction to it, in Bao-an at least, is one of great admiration and reverence. In 1967 King Guo was in Bao-an on the birthday of another local god worshipped primarily by the Jang within the village. King Guo's palanquin was placed in the courtyard where the ceremonies were held, as a guest of honor, and was as much an object of worship as the statue of the god whose birth was being celebrated.

King Guo also arrives in the Hsikang area about a week before the festival begins. His presence provides an opportunity for numerous visits between Guo villages, in which he is serially entertained. Besides the palanquins of gods, most villages submit troupes of performers to the festival procession, and these performers normally rehearse for two or three months before the festival begins. King Guo's visit to each Guo village is accompanied by the festival troupes from the previous village, who perform in their host village and are treated to noodles or other refreshment for their trouble.

These troupes of performers are without overt religious significance for the most part, many taking their inspiration from classical novels or other bits of Chinese folklore. However, a very large number of them are distinctively military in character and consist of men dressed as soldiers and carrying weaponry of the same kind used in the Hwang-Guo war of the late Ching. Their performance consists of an athletic ballet, magnificently rehearsed and enthusiastically performed, in the pugnacious tradition of Chinese shadow boxing. Such an escort is entirely appropriate for a god, and in-

Two papier-mâché water buffalo struggle in a performance prepared for the triennial Hsikang festival. Many procession acts have no religious content.

deed is common in processions throughout Taiwan, for the "soldiers" represent a god's "army" just as an emperor or general would proceed with his military forces. In Hsikang the soldiers also recall to local minds the days when each village actually had soldiers for combat purposes. Bao-an has heightened the imagery, for her soldiers are inevitably young boys from ten to fifteen years old or so because, it is said, "after the Hwang killed our adults, we had only children to dance in the festival."

In this way, King Guo's visit provides occasion for the formal expression of good relations (and communal military exploits!) between these traditional allies: the social equivalent of phatic communication in language if you like. It also provides them with a focus about which to organize actual cooperative interaction (mutual entertaining), so that each visit is both a reminder of traditional cooperation and an instance of it.

To what extent can Bao-an represent other Taiwanese villages? Probably not at all. So far as I am aware, Bao-an is not particularly

Village youths rehearse to be soldiers in a festival procession. The martial aspects of processions provide a dramatization of earlier wars and lasting conflicts.

typical of the villages in its area. Villages today are seldom so completely dominated by a single surname; few villages share a patron god knowingly with other villages in a common and semi-communal cult; very seldom, to the best of my knowledge, do patron gods correspond in surname with the groups they patronize. But typicality is perhaps beside the point. Bao-an seems to represent the kind of structure that is in some way "natural" to the area rather than that which is most common. Even if Bao-an and the Guo represent an extreme instance, fostered by a particularly benignant happenchance, still this is what these principles *can* produce. And that in many ways is more revealing than what is merely statistically usual.

Bao-an village is not merely a collection of people. It is a physical place, with legal boundaries and with ritual ones. Four enormous trees located near the four corners of the village represent forts 營 manned by supernatural soldiers, and a fifth fort is located immediately opposite the temple at another tree. There is nothing about these trees in normal times that distinguishes them from other trees in the eyes of human visitors. But they are the first line of defence against undesirable supernatural forces.

The soldiers who man the forts and patrol the streets and byways of the village are deputies sent by King Guo to protect the harmony of the village. Sacrifices of food are made twice monthly by way of provisioning these soldiers. The rites go by the name of *Shaangbing/siú*ⁿ*-peng* 賞兵, which we may translate as "appreciating the soldiers" for the time being.[12]

Rites to the soldiers are not particularly complicated. Some time in the midafternoon of the first and fifteenth of each lunar month the family of one of the headmen, among whom the duty of leading these rites rotates, appears before the temple to place a temporary altar on its porch and lay offerings on it. Sometimes a group of village boys playing near the temple will be recruited to carry a drum about the village to announce the beginning of the rites. Sometimes an announcement will be made over the public address system. Sometimes, both. Meanwhile, the "head" family (that is, the family in charge of the rites for this time) has lit some sticks of incense, bowed before the temple altar, bowed out the door,[13] and placed the incense sticks in the various dishes of food. Shortly, more families join, bringing baskets of food (their dinner, usually), which are set out in symmetrical lines of baskets running out from the door of the temple and across the square. The baskets are normally brought by women and children, or sometimes by children alone, who set the baskets down, light the sticks of incense, bow, and install the burning incense in the food. With this finished, they are at liberty to run and play or stand in groups talking, tak-

12. Diamond (1966: 267) uses the same term to describe sacrifices to divine soldiers held once a year on occasion of the patron god's birthday. Apparently Bao-an formerly held its *Shaangbing* rites once a year also. It is said that about thirty years back King Guo (in his manifestation as the second guardian) possessed a medium and announced that for unspecified reasons he had overextended himself protecting the villages of the vicinity and had been forced to borrow five million troops from the Five Kings of Tuucherng 土城, a village to the south. Nonannual sacrifices were apparently held to welcome and send off the guest soldiers, and to welcome back King Guo's soldiers. The rites have been semimonthly since. "I want my soldiers to eat well," King Guo instructed.

13. Bowing first to the altar, then toward the door is common also in household rites. It is so usual that it is more or less automatic, and many people are at a loss to explain what it means; some suggest that it is a gesture to the Good Brethren lest they be insulted and goaded to mischief.

ing care only that the incense sticks are supplemented with new ones before they burn out.

After most of the worshippers have about burned up their third stick of incense, the head family throws divination blocks to determine whether the soldiers have had their fill yet. If not, more time is allowed, and the blocks are thrown again. At length the blocks indicate that the military is happily stuffed, and the rites draw to a close. The children are summoned before the temple to kneel and move their hands before them in a gesture of worship (usually a most unheartfelt one, for they are all eager to be home, and it is in fact a moment of great hilarity). Then a bonfire is made of the paper spirit-money brought by each family in addition to its food offerings. Usually some of the children have been employed ahead of time carefully making a tower of the packs of money. As the fire dies down a pitcher of water is fetched and a circle of water is made about the fire three times. With this act the rites have ended. The remains of incense sticks are unceremoniously snatched from the baskets of food and dumped on the remains of the bonfire, then the baskets are carted home again. The square is effectively empty within about ninety seconds after the last circle of water is poured, and the baskets are well on their way home to be eaten.

The rite of appreciating the soldiers fulfils an agreement with King Guo. Bao-an provisions the soldiers of King Guo, and King Guo protects the village. It makes little difference who brings a family's offerings to the temple, for what is important is that the offerings be made. The soldiers want merely to be fed; they are not fussy about who in the family serves them. And it does not seem to matter whether all the families are present. The rites begin when the censer-master's family burns the first sticks of incense. It would be a poor showing, somewhat lacking in etiquette perhaps, if very few families ever came to feed the soldiers. But the terms of the rite have been met even if but one family sacrifices. No one seems upset if, on a cold and rainy evening, only thirty families huddle on the porch of the temple with their damp sacrifices. But the normal attendance is much greater; usually three-fourths or more of the families bring baskets of food to fulfil the obligations of the village.

There are important gods in the village other than King Guo, as we shall see presently. Accordingly, not everyone speaks of the soldiers as the subordinates of King Guo, but simply as soldiers provided by "the gods" for the protection of Bao-an. This more general interpretation seems to be reinforced by and at the same time helps to justify certain of the details of the rite. No statues are used to represent the soldiers, but such of the village josses as are not confined to their home altars by overzealous curators are placed on the temple altar on the days of sacrifice. No one is immediately able to explain their presence in rites dedicated to the soldiers, but it makes sense in its way if we look again at the term I translated as "appreciating the soldiers" (*Shaangbing*). *Shaang* has another meaning besides appreciate: to reward or bestow, as a superior rewards an inferior. The presence of the josses on the altar seems quite appropriate if they are overseers of their soldiers, on whom food is being "bestowed" in the rite.

### SUPERNATURAL ENEMIES OF BAO-AN

What is the enemy that requires such an extensive military establishment to protect the village? For the most part it is the ghosts of the dead. Not all the dead. Not the dead who are ancestors and are properly worshipped and looked after. Not the dead who lived to a ripe old age in their time among the living and died peacefully in their beds. Rather the less "proper" dead; the hungry ghosts, and the ghosts of those who died by suicide or by murder, of those who were executed or died by drowning in the river or in irrigation canals.[14] These ghosts are generally concentrated "to the north" of Bao-an, and there are tales of odd things happening in the fields and along the roads to the north. When "things begin to go wrong" in the village, when there are unusual disasters, when many people are sick or there are agricultural reverses, or when means of divination do not seem to be producing workable decisions, one explanation is that despite the divine defences the ghosts have somehow got in.

14. Chinese seem to have a special fear of death by drowning. One of the twenty-four dangers to the lives of young children 關 which traditional almanacs attempt to predict is drowning. When ancestral spirits are called to participate in a funeral, those who have died by drowning require separate summoning. The ghosts of people who died in this way are said to linger at the place of death in order to pull other victims into the same pool of water and drown them. Drowning may be more frequent also among Chinese, since few of them know how to swim, and we may suppose that the continuation of special attitudes about death in water may promote panic when faced with water emergencies.

Should there be reason to suspect that this has happened, or that Bao-an is in imminent danger of being invaded by ghosts, the forts may be strengthened by means of an exorcism consisting of purification by fire of the temple and the five forts. One such exorcism was performed during the time I lived in Bao-an.[15]

This exorcism was performed by a hired priest and was presided over by the gods themselves, either through their mediums or through divination chairs. The priest called in for such an event is called an *âng-thâu-á* 紅頭仔.[16] Taiwanese *ạng-thâu-á* are basically exorcists, who are invited and paid to purify villages, houses and families of forces causing illness and misfortune. They also perform a limited number of other rites, including "opening the eyes" of newly acquired josses. The nearest *âng-thâu-á* who can be called to Bao-an lives in a village to the east of Hsikang, and to the best of my knowledge he is the only "red head" in the immediate area.

The *âng-thâu-á* arrived in Bao-an in the early afternoon and

15. Unfortunately for clear exposition, this was the occasion of much more than merely village exorcism, although that is the only aspect of it directly relevant here. A new spirit medium had been possessed, and the exorcism was preliminary to his initiation and was designed to ensure that he was possessed by a benign and not an evil presence. The initiation itself, which need not concern us here, consisted of purifying the body of the medium and instructing him in the use of his mortification instruments. All of this had to take place on an appropriate, felicitous day, and the day chosen was the birthday of the Queen of Heaven, the twenty-third day of the third moon. So far as I know, none of the activity here described relates to the Queen of Heaven. In the previous year, 1967, no village-wide observance of her birthday was celebrated, which tends to confirm this.

16. Literally, a "red head" priest, in opposition to a "black head" priest or *Heitour Dawshyh* 黑頭道士, more often simply *Dawshyh*. Whereas the *âng-thâu-á* is primarily an exorcist and uses only a small corpus of liturgy, the *Dawshyh* performs in other capacities as well, although in Taiwan there appears to be more overlap in the two liturgies than is common in other parts of the country (*see* Schipper 1966: 81n). In the vicinity of Bao-an, *âng-thâu-á* are more common than *Dawshyh* and charge less for their services; accordingly they are the most usual outside religious practitioners called upon to perform occasional rites in the village. *Dawshyh* were called to the area during my stay only to officiate at funerals and in connection with the triennial festival at Hsikang. On schools of Taoist priesthood for China as a whole, *see* Welch 1957: 83–163 and Fuh Chyn-jia 1937: 207–230; for Taiwan, *see* Lii Tian-chuen 1956: 20–46 and Jiang Jia-jiin 1957: 124 f. and 1959: 12–15.

recited chants for about an hour before the temple[17] while village people performed rites of "appreciating the soldiers."[18] When he finished his chant, the *âng-thâu-á* prepared five sturdy bamboo stakes, with magic charms written on yellow paper securely bound to the tops of them, to be driven into the ground at each of the five forts to supplement the power of the soldiers. When the stakes were ready, the *âng-thâu-á* busied himself with the preparation of purification oil. In a large cooking basin of the kind that is usual in China he placed a thick wick tightly wound into approximately the shape and size of a bamboo shoot. This he soaked with rice liquor to render it more inflammable. Then he added about an equal quantity of peanut oil to the rice liquor now flooding the bottom of the pan. The basin was then heated over a small charcoal stove and the wick was lit, while the *âng-thâu-á* performed his chant, dancing in a circle about the pan. When the oil was hot, the charcoal stove was placed in an inverted bamboo stool to which wires were attached so that the stool, the stove, and the pan of oil might be slung from a pole carried by two bearers.

The rite about to be performed by the *âng-thâu-á* was a kind of purification called "passing through oil"過油. The oil used in the rite is usually designated by the same term.

17. Chanted Hokkien is incomprehensible to native speakers as well as to me. The priests themselves make every effort, moreover, to mutter their chants less articulately if they know people are listening to what is being chanted, for the content is often secret and may be communicated only to the initiated. Nor does the priests' schedule during these rites allow of extensive interviewing on the spot, and interviewing at a later date has generally been unsatisfactory due to the disinclination of most clerics to say very much about what has transpired and the difficulty of being sure what part of a series of chants one is talking about. For all these reasons I do not have material on these chants. For purposes of the present analysis, such material is not essential—the people of Bao-an have no more idea what is being chanted than I do—but for a full understanding of the event and its relation to other parts of the greater Chinese religious tradition one naturally needs the view of the officiating *âng-thâu-á*, including the texts he chants.

18. "Appreciating the soldiers" was accomplished in the midafternoon. Not long after the participants had returned home, however, they were called back over the public address system to perform the rite again, in exactly the same way. For some reason my notes are hazy on the point, but I *believe* that the first time the sacrifices were directed to the soldiers, and the second time to the Good Brethren, that is to wandering and potentially malicious hungry ghosts. This, as we shall see, is the format of the "same" rites performed at the family level.

As the *âng-thâu-á* prepared the oil, a succession of village youths held the two divination chairs and waited for the gods to descend into them. As the chairs began to shake slightly, they turned them over to more experienced, older men. About the same time the gods descended into the divination chairs, a medium, who had appeared somewhat earlier for the sacrifices to the soldiers, went into trance. With the gods in attendance and the oil hot, all was ready to purge the village of its ghosts. This was done by successively firing—I can think of no more appropriate word—the oil. The *âng-thâu-á* spat a fine spray of rice liquor onto the hot oil, causing a momentary column of flame and smoke to rise several feet in height, through which incense pots and other objects in the temple were passed to purify them. When the temple building and its sacra had been purified in successive columns of flame and black peanut-oil smoke, the apparatus followed the medium and the divination chair to each of the five forts successively, where the oil was fired, a charm stake was posted, a banner with charms written on it was nailed to the tree, and firecrackers were set off.

By these comparatively simple acts the positions of the soldiers in the forts were strengthened, and the invading evil forces were frightened away. Also by these relatively simple acts the action of the gods, including King Guo, as protectors of the village was dramatized. For the gods, in their mediums and their divination chairs, are present at such rites, and are visibly and dramatically fulfilling their end of the agreement, honoring the same contract by which the soldiers are cared for with semimonthly sacrifices.

When unnatural deaths occur in the village, rites must be conducted to drive out the untoward forces they leave behind. In July 1967 King Guo was still in the village after the Hsikang triennial festival. Another festival was to take place in Chiayi to the north, and a group of Bao-an men travelled to Chiayi with the palanquin of King Guo to march in the procession. No sooner had King Guo left than a child drowned in the fishpond in the center of Bao-an, causing no small consternation to all who lived in the village. It seemed strange to me that he should have drowned, for people said that he could swim a little, and the pond is shallow and often used for bathing. One man told me: "He was pulled in by a ghost. Someone died there before, and when someone dies, his ghost often wants to pull a second one after him . . . A lot of people have died there. I don't know how many." Another speculated that the ghosts to the north had somehow managed to get into the village.

The dead child left behind a malign ghost, which, it was feared, would do untold harm if permitted to remain in the village. Properly it would have been called a "water ghost" 水鬼, but so dangerous was it that this term could not be spoken. (After my repeated inquiry one man wrote the word for me, but would not speak it.) Instead it was referred to merely as a "bad thing" (*pháiⁿ-mih* 歹物). Such beings appear to have caused alarm on the Fukienese coast at the end of the last century as well as in modern Taiwan. Groot (1892–1910: 5.525) writes of them: "The common opinion in that part of China is that those . . . 'water-spectres' mostly are souls of the drowned. Having spent their time in their wet abode in the bondage of the watergods, they may be redeemed from this servitude by substitution, and therefore they lie in ambush for victims to draw into the water and make them take their place. Thus they are a constant lurking danger for people on the waterside, fishers, boatmen, and washer-women."

People in Bao-an were less explicit about the workings of a "bad thing" in the village, but it was clear it ought to be removed. The death took place on July 22 (the fifteenth day of the sixth moon). The twenty-seventh (that is the twentieth by the lunar calendar) was chosen as a calendrically appropriate day for the exorcism.

A little past noon two altar tables were placed on the porch of the temple, and the instruments of divination were placed by them so that the gods might provide instructions on how to perform the exorcism. These instruments I have called "divination chairs." The Taiwanese word is *kiō-á* 轎仔, or "little palanquin." They will be described in some detail below. At the moment it is enough to know that the object involved is a small chair, with arms and a back, that measures about thirty centimeters from the top of the back to the bottom of the legs. It is held by two bearers, who are said to "support" 扶 the chair. The *kiō-á* is used to provide a seat for the divine presence, and the descent of a god into it results in a bouncing motion of the chair, and sometimes in violent lateral movements as well. In divination the chair traces characters upon a tabletop with one of the protruding arms. Variations on this chair also occur; there is, for example, a larger model slung on poles in the manner of a sedan chair and wielded by four bearers rather than two. The differences seem to be more regional than functional.

The first god to appear was His Highness Chyr池府二千歲, whom we shall meet again (p. 106), because he is the patron of the Jang families in the village and a frequent visitor in séances. He advised that people should desist from speaking "bad words" to one another; that is, scolding or arguing. The death had disrupted the "harmony" of the village, and the village people were being instructed not to make matters worse by adding interpersonal disharmony, but to create as harmonious an atmosphere as possible.[19] His second word of advice was that people should keep their children away from the fishpond and watch them. He himself had business to tend to other than watching village children every minute. All of this was interpreted from the characters traced upon one of the altar tables by the divination chair. The second chair was now possessed by King Guo. He reiterated the same advice offered by His Highness Chyr, and then proceeded with instructions for the exorcism of the water ghost (or rather of the "bad thing"!). The two gods, represented by the divination chairs, would go in person to the pond and drive the "bad thing" from it. The bystanders must be very careful that it not lodge in their bodies, and to this end women and children were not to approach the pond, and those men who chose to do this work were to carry with them one sheet apiece of spirit money on which His Highness Chyr would write a protecting charm. His Highness now caused the arm of his divination chair to be dipped in ink, and with the ink he made a blot on each of twenty sheets of spirit money laid out on the altar before the chair. The men stuffed these into their pockets and left in a great hurry for the fishpond, following the two wildly swinging divination chairs, which fairly dragged their wielders along the road.

Upon arrival at the pond the chairs ran madly about the perimeter of the pond, then hurled themselves and their bearers into the water where they circled the pond several times more swinging up

19. We shall see later in connection with the family that the notion of inharmony 不平安 includes sickness, financial reverses, death, and numerous other disasters, as well as interpersonal relations. Attention to interpersonal relations during the exorcism of an inharmonious water ghost is not therefore so odd as it may at first seem.

and down into and out of the water to drive out the bad thing. At the same time the onlookers shouted high-pitched shouts, hurled burning firecrackers over the pond, and threw handfuls of sesame seeds into the water.[20] The shouting, the rain of sesame seeds, and the continual and ubiquitous explosions of firecrackers were all calculated to terrify the ghost, and added to this were the chairs of the gods ploughing through the water, hot on the trail of the startled ducks. When the gods climbed out at one bank, they would leap in wildly elsewhere and beat the water with renewed vigor. Had I been the water ghost, I should surely have fled.

The body of the drowned child had been encased in an unpainted wooden box, and in the afternoon of the day on which the exorcism was held it was carried out of the village to the cemetery and buried.

20. The objective of this last, I was told, was that the bad thing would try to count the seeds, but as there were so many he would surely lose count. In a fit of frustration and pique he would run away and never return. It struck me as unlikely, but that is the only explanation I was able to elicit. Sesame was in season. As I understand it, any small seeds would do.

# Chapter 4
## *Divination*

At several times in the discussion so far, mention has been made of decisions made through divination, although little has been said about the sort of divination involved. The instruments for communicating with the gods are many, and selection among them depends upon a number of factors, including the nature of the question to be put, the intricacy required in the response, the amount of money one is able to spend, the personnel involved in the manipulation and interpretation of the instruments and one's relations with these people, the usual mode of communication used by the supernatural one wishes to consult, and various other factors, not excluding a healthy element of pure fashion and caprice. But for the trivial exceptions of mountebanks or of occasional instances of ghosts and demons being thought to interfere, all revelations are equally true and valid. When they are in contradiction it is customary to accept the most recent one as valid at the expense of earlier ones, or, should one be suspicious of it for some reason, to continue inquiries until responses are clearly applicable and reasonable.[1]

Bao-an has people able to read traditional almanacs correctly, and makes use of the services of professors of geomancy both from the Hsikang area and from more distant places. People in Bao-an also consult wandering fortunetellers and soothsayers, often blind, who visit the village or who can often be found in the bazaar of any larger town. Our concern at present, however, is with divina-

1. I have tried pursuing the question of just how it happens that a reliable mode of divination can later be contradicted. Accepting the second revelation as correct, is it not astounding that the first revelation, proceeding from a source of known reliability, should be wrong? With a keen sense of the limits of the system and of questions that should not be too closely examined, informants will agree only that it is very strange, perhaps past understanding.

tion as it involves communication with divine agencies. The major devices for this sort of divination are described below.

### THE POE

By far the most common act of divination accomplished in Taiwan makes use of *poe* 筶, known in English as "moonboards," or "divination blocks." [2] A pair of divination blocks is two pieces of wood or, preferably, of bamboo root, each cut into the shape of a crescent moon, rounded on one surface and flat on the other. The two are mirror images of one another, and if the flat sides are placed against each other, the pair looks as though it were a single block of wood.

In divination these objects are held out upon the two palms, raised about to the level of the forehead of the kneeling worshipper, and allowed to drop on the floor.[3] There are two positions in which each block can land: rounded side up or rounded side down. Therefore there are three combinations of positions: both blocks might land flat side downward, both might land rounded side downward, or each might land differently. This last combination is taken to indicate agreement by the deity with the proposition as stated, briefly a yes response. Both of the other combinations indicate failure of the deity to agree, although the degree of disagreement is open to dispute. There is never an irrevocable no in this. Most people report that when the two blocks land rounded side downward and rock giddily on the floor before coming to rest, the god is amused at the statement put to him, and this position is called "laughing *poe*" (*chhiò-poe* 笑 筶). But when the flat sides come to rest on the floor, so that the blocks fall and come immedi-

2. The northern Chinese term is *Jiaw* 珓 or 筊, occasionally pronounced in the third tone: *Jiao*. This would be pronounced *kàu* in Hokkien, but is not in colloquial use in this area. In Taiwan the usual Mandarin term is *Bei*, conventionally written with the character for the homonymous word "cup" 杯 or 桮 or 盃. This writing is apparently a very ancient one. The Tang poet Harn Yuh 韓愈 (A.D. 768–824) used both words in the following lines: 手持杯珓導我擲，云此最吉餘難同. "He handed me divinity cups [*Bei-jiaw*], he showed me how to use them / And told me that my fortune was the best of all." (Translated by Witter Bynner 1929: 22.) I am grateful to Professor Lao Kan 勞榦 for bringing this verse to my attention. For descriptions of the use of *poe* in other parts of China, *see* Doolittle 1865: 2.107 ff., Doré 1917: 353–355.

3. An occupational danger of investigating Taiwanese temples is the likelihood of being hit by ricocheting *poe*.

ately to an abrupt standstill, then anger is indicated. This position is called "negative *poe*" (*im-poe* 陰筶). The positive fall is called "sacred *poe*" (*siūⁿ-poe* 聖筶). These interpretations of negative replies are seldom taken very seriously, however, and what is important is to determine what form of a statement the god will confirm as a correct statement of his point of view, rather than to develop an emphatic yes or no to a given question.[4] The question is typically presented in a murmured silent prayer and the blocks dropped. If they indicate an affirmative, they are dropped again. A validly affirmative reply requires three positive falls running, and the occurrence of either negative reply requires the reconstruction of the question and another attempt, or requires that one give up. The chances of a block landing on one or the other of its sides appear to be about the same, though in fact they probably differ from block to block depending upon the exact height from which the block is dropped (since it is dropped rounded side downward), the evenness of the floor or other surface upon which they are thrown, and the condition of the blocks themselves, since those made of bamboo roots—the majority—become pitted in time as base sections of former subsidiary roots drop out of their sockets leaving holes. Even if the chances of landing with one side or the other skyward were the same, the probability of having three throws of "unlikes" should be but one in eight, so it may be seen that considerable effort is spent before the exact form of the answer is settled upon.

These blocks are used in ordinary consultations with household and temple josses, as well as with ancestors. Questions that might be put in this way are limited, but as the method is cheap, it is the one most often used for a start on eliciting divine information, even should other methods later be resorted to. Another important use of *poe* is in conferring with gods as to whether rituals are being conducted to their satisfaction, and a very common question put is whether the offerings have been in place long enough for the god to have eaten his fill.

Because of the purely mechanical nature of *poe*, there are sta-

4. Somewhat to the consternation of the foreign student, Chinese lacks convenient terms for *yes* or *no*. The conversational devices used instead are the repetition of a verb of the question (with or without a negative prefix) and the use of the word *right* or the word *is* (with or without a negative prefix). The *poe* are therefore performing within a context more similar to ordinary conversation than might at first glance be thought.

tistical regularities over time, even though their behavior might be quite erratic in response to any single question. Questions, accordingly, must be composed with due appreciation of the probabilities of a positive response. Whereas in theory the *poe,* because they are controlled by the gods, are manipulated by supernatural forces to reinforce correct answers and therefore could be requested to perform in defiance of the law of averages, in fact the statistical nature of the device is apparently fully appreciated, and on one occasion was even articulated, during one of the semimonthly worship sessions before the temple. The *poe* were being thrown by one of the two former mayors of the village whom we met earlier. This man, for reasons clear to no one but himself, was expecting a miraculous descent of a god to choose a new spirit medium on this particular evening. When it did not happen, he contrived to put questions to the *poe* that would stand a good chance of prolonging the proceedings to provide a better opportunity for the anticipated divine descent. As the evening wore on, many people bcame more and more uneasy about the unusual length of the sacrifices, an uneasiness made the more intense by their growing hunger. At length, about ten o'clock, the second former mayor ordered his sacrifices brought home, in great disgust, and with no small show. "He is asking questions in such a way," he declared, "that he can't possibly get an affirmative answer." A quarter of an hour or so later the *poe* declared that the gods had eaten their fill.

The incident is of interest because it suggests that there is a clear realization that *poe* are statistical devices. Existing simultaneously with the belief that they are a vehicle of communication controlled absolutely by divine agencies, there is a healthy realization of the limits imposed by the nature of the device, and an understanding that *poe* require human cooperation to function correctly. The lack of apologetics in Taiwanese religion is unfortunate, for it makes the point difficult to follow up, but it would be of great interest to know to what extent man can be governed by absolute pragmatism in the manipulation of religious symbols invested by himself with great sanctity.

For more elaborate questions, people of Bao-an may go to a larger temple, where they can make use of *chhiam* 籤 verses. These are small slips of paper, usually displayed on a board at one side of a temple, bearing numbers from one to sixty or from one to one hundred. On the altar is a vase of bamboo slips correspondingly numbered. Such a slip is drawn from the vase and *poe* are used to confirm that the correspondingly numbered slip of paper will indeed contain the answer to the question at hand. When this has been established, the slip of paper is itself consulted. It contains a verse of four lines. Such verses are often difficult to interpret, and in many temples an explanation is added below the verse, applying its message to particular questions the worshipper might have asked. In larger temples an old man is usually to be found who can provide additional instruction on the interpretation of these verses. Although most small villages in southwestern Taiwan seem to provide their temples with sets of *chhiam* papers, Bao-an does not, and it is necessary to go to Hsikang to divine in this way.[5]

### THE KIŌ-Á

For more serious consultations with the divine, the people of Bao-an have recourse to a *kiō-á* 轎仔, which I described briefly in the previous chapter, and which I have glossed "divination chair" for want of a better term.[6] This object, we recall, is a small wooden chair, usually about twenty centimeters on a side and about twenty-five or thirty centimeters high at the back. Around the sides of the chair are set small pickets of wood that are free to move up and down in their sockets, causing a clicking sound when the chair is bounced or jostled. Divination by means of a *kiō-á* is accomplished by two men [7] holding it by its legs in an up-

5. Many temples, Hsikang's among them, are now installing coin-operated *chhiam* dispensers that obviate the need for positive *poe* and simply present one with a printed verse (in a spherical plastic capsule) upon receipt of a coin. I have never seen such a machine actually used, and so far as I know it is not taken very seriously, but perhaps I did not inquire so diligently as I might because the whole thought of a coin-operated *chhiam* machine offends my Western sensibilities. It appears that such machines *are* taken seriously in Japan (Thomas W. Johnson, personal communication).

6. The Hokkien word *kiō-á* is cognate with Mandarin *Jiawtz* 轎子. A *Jiawtz,* however, may also be the palanquin in which a joss is carried (called a *kiō* 轎 in Hokkien). In Hokkien a *kiō-á* is only the object here described, not a palanquin (although various specialized types of *kiō-á* may have carrying poles and vaguely resemble palanquins).

7. Women do not perform this task in Bao-an or in any séances that I have seen elsewhere. Other lines of evidence suggest to me that this is probably not because they are prohibited from doing so, but rather because in some sense it is men's work, rather like building cabinets or fixing the plumbing in America. I do not, however, have any explicit statements one way or the other from people in Bao-an.

Two men struggle to hold onto a *kiō-á,* a divination chair, as a god comes to sit in it.

right position before an altar while incense is burned and the relevant supernatural is requested to descend into the chair. His descent is indicated by the onset of motion in the chair, particularly bouncing motion. This is occasionally quite violent, and the holders of the chair sometimes appear to have great difficulty keeping their hold on it. At length the chair leans forward and with an ear-splitting crash descends upon a table (prepared in advance with a protecting surface of wood or burlap) and traces characters upon it. These characters are considered to be written by the possessing god, and their interpreted meanings are the responses to questions put to the god by the petitioner.

Not everyone can wield the *kiō-á* effectively. One informant described it this way:

It certainly is not the case that just anyone can wield the *kiō-á*. For example, I once wielded the *kiō-á* and the god didn't come and sit in it, but when I turned it back to someone else, the *kiō-á* immediately had a god come and sit in it. . . . Naturally there are a lot of people who can wield the *kiō-á* and have it move. But there are not many who can wield it so that it writes characters on a table. For example, in our village there may be as many as a hundred people who can wield the *kiō-á* so that it will move, but there are probably barely ten who can wield it so that it can write characters. Furthermore, of these ten the majority have never studied characters and are illiterate.

I understand that if you want to be able to wield a *kiō-á* so that it writes characters, it is very easy. Ordinarily you just have to be a person who can wield the *kiō-á* so that it can move, and then practise the *kiō-á* often. Finally after you know the *kiō-á*'s nature, you can of course write characters on a table. And that is how wielding the *kiō-á* works.

As noted, it is usual in Bao-an for the wielders of the *kiō-á* to be illiterate. Indeed, some (but not all) informants questioned on the subject seem to believe that the whole procedure would lose its interest if the bearers of the little chair could read, since there would be no way to know that what was being written was not being faked. The characters traced upon the table are unclear, and a good deal of study of each character is necessary before it is "correctly" understood. Sometimes one even has to ask the god to retrace the character three or four times before an acceptable interpretation is finally proposed by the person in charge of reading what the *kiō-á* traces.[8] When at last he gives the correct reading, it is confirmed by a single rap upon the table by the little chair. But when he gives a wrong reading, the chair raps twice.

This sort of séance, as conducted in Bao-an at least, divides the act of creation among three people. By far the largest role is played by the reader, who interprets the writing of the *kiō-á*. He is limited by the glyphs that he (and literate onlookers) may be able to fit to the random movements of the *kiō-á* on the table, by his imagination in free-associating to make them relevant to the questions at hand, and by the veto power the wielders of the *kiō-á* have upon his interpretations of the characters (though not upon the free associations).

Although a *kiō-á* is perhaps most commonly used as a means of divination, it is not always so used. Many times the divine presence is desirable even when there is no need for direct consultation. We noted this in connection with the exorcism discussed above, and shall see clearer examples below.

Through the *kiō-á,* as never through the *poe,* man is in contact with and in the presence of the supernatural. In the *kiō-á* the gods may descend whenever they are needed to be present as guests, overseers, guides, or decision makers.

### THE TÂNG-KI

To the *kiō-á* we may compare the spirit mediums.[9] I have used the word *medium* because it is English. The Hokkien word for which it has been doing service is *tâng-ki* 童乩 (occasionally spoken as *ki-tông* 乩童), literally a "divining youth." [10] A de-

8. Because no mark is left on the table, one must be adept at understanding characters traced in the air. This is a skill widespread among literate Chinese, who often trace characters in the air or on a table with a finger while speaking, but it is seldom attempted with script 草 forms. It is widely believed that the difficulty in reading the characters in divination derives from their usually being script forms; Chinese gods, like American doctors, have bad handwriting. Given the incredible amount of variation in the script representations possible for any given character, it is rare that a random combination of squiggles and jots cannot be construed as *some* character.

9. There is a good deal to be said about the mediums. In the present context I include only a sketch designed to clarify what has already been said about relations between men and gods in Bao-an.

10. The Mandarin cognate would be *Jitorng* 乩童, but it is not clear

scription of the *tâng-ki* of Singapore has been made by Elliott (1955). Elliott describes particular temples maintained by *tâng-ki* for their use. Their performances are largely confined to these places, which are provided with kinds of equipment necessary to their trance performances, including particularly chairs of nails and beds of knives. Individual petitioners present themselves at the *tâng-ki* temples, where their problems are handled by the *tâng-ki* in order. When there are medical problems, the *tâng-ki* normally cuts his tongue and blots the blood upon a sheet of spirit money, making a blood charm 血符, which may be carried on the body to fend off baleful influences.

In Taiwan one can find *tâng-ki* attached to certain temples, especially small, private temples: essentially outgrown family altars in many cases.[11] Also, many *tâng-ki* go to public temples to be possessed and there answer petitioners' problems, but they are not attached to these temples any more than minstrels and soothsayers are attached to the parks and bazaars where they ply their trade. Although the Taiwanese *tâng-ki* performances are apparently less spectacular than those of Singapore (for they lack the face painting and are somewhat less bloody), they seem to be essentially similar in cities. In rural areas, however, the role of the *tâng-ki* is somewhat different, for he addresses himself not so much to individual problems as to collective ones. He becomes the oracle of the community some of the time, of individual families other times —seldom of the individual petitioner.[12]

I do not know how many *tâng-ki* are ordinarily found in a Tai-

---

that it is actually used, and I have preferred the Hokkien *tâng-ki* for the present discussion. Groot (1892–1910: 6.1269) lists *tâng-ki* and *ki-tông* also for Amoy city, adding *sîn-tâng* 神童 and *tâng-chí* 童子 as well, although apparently this last is often used for lads in general as well as for gods' lads in particular. Comber (1958: 8 f.) indicates that in Singapore the Hokkien *tâng-ki* is used, plus numerous Cantonese expressions, viz: *lok9-tung4* 落童, *gong3-tung4* 降童, and *sen4-tung4* 神童.

11. On Taiwanese *tâng-ki, see* Lin Tsair-yuan 1968: 48 ff.; Diamond 1966: 124 ff., 311 ff.; Gallin 1966: 260 ff.; Wu Ying-tau 1970: 168 ff.; Kokubu Naoichi 1962. Gallin uses the word *Tiawtorng* 跳童, used also by Wu in a somewhat more restricted sense, but he is clearly talking about the same thing.

12. For purposes of the present discussion I have ignored differences between male and female *tâng-ki*, just as the Taiwanese do. There seems to be a tendency however for female *tâng-ki* to be associated often with purely local divinities who answer individual petitions at private altars in the medium's home, whereas male *tâng-ki* seem usually to operate by visiting the family of the petitioner or guiding village affairs in the village

wanese village. In Japanese times they were forbidden to exist, and most people believe (realistically) that Westerners find them disconcerting. Further, Chinese culture itself hardly exalts them. Accordingly, a casual inquiry in a strange village will almost inevitably win the inquirer the response that there are no *tâng-ki* in the vicinity, the respondent never heard of a *tâng-ki, tâng-ki* no longer exist in Taiwan, and the like, regardless of the facts. When I arrived in Bao-an I was informed that the village had one *tâng-ki,* a certain Guo Tian-huah 郭天化 by name,[13] who presided over the rites described in the last chapter. As time went on, however, more *tâng-ki* began emerging from the woodwork (or bamboowork).

Guo Tian-huah is seventy years old and has served his god, the Third Prince, for twenty-five years or so. A woman named Guo Huey-miin 郭惠敏, about thirty, has also been subject to possession for some time, and shortly after I arrived in the village she began holding séances in her house. One village woman returned to Bao-an shortly before I left. Age thirty-three, she had been divorced from her husband and spent some time at jobs in Tainan city trying to avoid her possession, but eventually she gave in to the inevitable and came back to Bao-an, where she was initiated. One man, Guo Ching-shoei 郭清水, was possessed most unexpectedly one evening and remained in trance for eighteen hours; eventually he became a practicing *tâng-ki* about the time I left. Another man had apparently been possessed a few times in the past, but claimed he was no longer, and certainly did not practice often. Two men who had moved to Tainan city subsequently were possessed by gods there, and one of them has been so successful that appreciation gifts of gold made to his possessing deity have enriched him enough that he has constructed a new house.[14] One

---

temple. The distinction is not hard and fast and exceptions occur in both directions. The present discussion is based largely on the more common, male *tâng-ki*.

13. All personal names are real Taiwanese names, but have been scrambled to make identification impossible. Surnames have been maintained intact.

14. Some *tâng-ki*, as in Singapore, accept (occasionally demand) a fee from a petitioner. This is particularly common in cities. In the countryside many *tâng-ki* scorn both fees and various thinly disguised "gifts" and insist that it is unseemly to accept reward for doing the work of the gods. So far as I know, of the *tâng-ki* living in Bao-an only Guo Huey-miin accepts money, usually about twenty *Kuay* 塊 ($.50) per session.

man has also been possessed a few times by the spirit of his dead brother and cures illnesses upon occasion. Another young man, Jang Ding-jyi 張丁吉, was in the army when I arrived, but was subject to occasional possession and clairvoyance there. After his term of service expired he returned to the village and began, to his dismay and disgust, to engage in trance more frequently. If all these *tâng-ki* are counted, we have a total of nine *tâng-ki* living or born in Bao-an.

THE TÂNG-KI AS ORACLE

The *tâng-ki* is above all things else an oracle. He is applied to in order to put questions to his god. Normally he is the mouthpiece

TABLE 2
LIVING MEDIUMS OF BAO-AN

| *Pseudonym* | *Sex and Age in 1966* | *Year of Initiation* | *Present Residence* | *Possessing God* |
|---|---|---|---|---|
| Guo Tian-huah 郭天化 | M 69 | 1945? | Bao-an | Third Prince |
| Guo Ching-shoei 郭清水 | M 33 | 1968 | Bao-an | Great Saint |
| Guo Huey-miin 郭惠敏 | F 29 | 1966? | Bao-an | Wangmuu 王母 |
| Jang Shiow-yeh 張秀葉 | F 32 | 1968 | Bao-an (temporary) | Little God |
| Jang Ding-jyi 張丁吉 | M 23 | Mid-1960s? | Bao-an | His Highness Chyr |
| A * | M 59 | ? | Bao-an (transriverine) | Great Saint |
| B * | M 52 | ? | Bao-an | (brother) |
| Guo Dong-ming 郭東明 | M 40? | 1955–1965 | Tainan | His Highness Lii |
| — | M 38 | 1955–1965 | Tainan | (plague god) |

* Rarely performs.

of but a single deity. This is not to say that he will *never* speak the words of another god, but that it will be a rare occasion, for which some explanation will be necessary. The *tâng-ki* is a man whose natural life is thought to be short (hence the term *tâng,* "lad"), and who has been granted an extension, as it were, in order that he may serve his god. The job is not one that people enjoy, or so it is claimed. Nearly all *tâng-ki* maintain that they tried every possible inducement to persuade the possessing god to select someone else before they finally surrendered before the inevitable. The following story seems typical, although I do not have completely detailed data on all the *tâng-ki* of Bao-an. (The tale must be pieced together from discussions with several different informants, so there are occasional inconsistencies.)

About two or three years before Liberation we had a typhoon. Guo Tian-huah and his mother were buried under a wall that collapsed on them but were not hurt in the least. They thought this was very strange, so they asked a god about it through a *ki̦ō-á*. The *kiō-á* told them that the Third Prince had chosen Tian-huah as his tâng-ki.[15] A few days later Tian-huah was possessed for a time. Afterward he took to eating charms and did not become possessed again.

The Third Prince chose Guo Tian-huah as his *tâng-ki* about thirty years ago, so he has been a *tâng-ki* for about thirty years. Before he became a *tâng-ki* he was periodically possessed for several years (perhaps three or four or more). At first the Third Prince often came to make Tian-huah possessed, but whenever Tian-huah felt he was about to be possessed, he would drink charm water to keep from being possessed. After a time the charm would wear off, and then he would be susceptible again. This happened many times. . . . Sometimes Guo Tian-huah would run out of charms, and then the god would come to possess him and he would run and jump into the fishpond and in that way would avoid possession. So for two or three years the Third Prince was unable to catch him. Guo Tian-huah really didn't want to become a *tâng-ki.* Probably it was because of his fear of blood. Whenever he saw that his own hand or body was bleeding he would immediately faint.

In 1946 or 1947 the temple at Hsikang was having its triennial festival, and the Fourth Guardian of King Guo came to our village from Tai-

15. The Third Prince 三太子 is Lii Ne-chah 李哪吒 , one of the most picturesque figures of the *Romance of Cannonizations.* For accounts in English, *see* Werner 1922: 305–319, Doré 1931: 111–122. He is one of the most commonly met among the gods who possess mediums.

nan. He had only just arrived at the village temple when Tian-huah was possessed. As he felt it coming on, he immediately devoured some water that a charm had been burned over, but this time the charm was not powerful enough. After he had become possessed, he ran to the temple area and announced that he was the Fourth Guardian. . . . The Fourth Guardian is more powerful than the Third Prince, so when Tian-huah ate his charm, it didn't do him any good. The Fourth Guardian possessed him and brought him to the temple, and then said: "The Third Prince is always trying to possess you for his *tâng-ki* and you are always carrying and eating charms and not letting the Third Prince possess you. How can you have such gall? Don't you know that your natural life is very short? Don't you remember year before last when the wall of your house collapsed? Wasn't it the Third Prince that saved you? Otherwise how would you be living today? Who saved you? You know that. I don't have to tell you. Yet you are not the slightest bit grateful. The Third Prince wants you to help him. . . ."

After Guo Tian-huah had delivered himself of the words that the Fourth Guardian wanted to say, he became more violent and began striking his fist against his own face and mouth. It was to represent the Third Prince striking him, and it showed that Guo Tian-huah had been opposing his Third Prince and not obeying his Third Prince's instructions. When it was over, many people urged him not to oppose the gods and to obey their instructions. Perhaps Tian-huah himself knew he could not escape the danger, so he finally agreed. After that incident when the Fourth Guardian borrowed the Third Prince's *tâng-ki,* the Third Prince often possessed Guo Tian-huah. . . . Not long afterward we held his initiation [開 光]; [16] I don't remember the details about that.

Other informants added more details. One recalled that Tian-huah used to flee the village whenever the *kiō-á* was used lest he be possessed. Another remembered that his daughter's face became badly swollen for nearly a year in order to punish Tian-huah for his perverseness. Some people, including Tian-huah himself, attrib-

16. All *tâng-ki* are initiated, an issue I intend to take up in a separate paper on *tâng-ki*, but which need not detain us here. The exact form of the initiation seems to differ widely from place to place and circumstance to circumstance. In general, Bao-an *tâng-ki* initiations involve an exorcism, designed to evict a ghost, in case the medium is being possessed by a demonic rather than a benevolent power. They also involve providing the *tâng-ki* with instruments of mortification for the first time, and his first mortification of the flesh. Both of these points will also be considered briefly in the discussion that follows.

uted his mother's sudden death during this period to his unwillingness to become a *tâng-ki*.

It is difficult to decide what is the basis of the widespread reluctance to be a *tâng-ki*. Taiwanese who are not *tâng-ki* themselves speculate that it is because of the "inconvenience" of being subject to possession at any time at the whim of a god or because mortification of the flesh hurts (or at least the prospect of mortifying the flesh, even painlessly, is unsavory). Those who are *tâng-ki* have little to say on the matter, except to recount their trials in trying to resist this calling. Several lines of interpretation are possible. One will become clearer below when we have considered the relations between gods and ghosts in greater detail. Another argues that the reluctance is largely theatrical, like the disavowal of political ambition by ardent campaigners for governmental office (a common enough approach in the West, but one that is *de rigueur* in Taiwanese politics). A third view would make the divine calling initially one of several interpretations of a set of physiological symptoms (shortness of breath, for example) which then becomes an ever-increasing fixation on the part of the subject, terrible on the one hand, fascinating on the other. On the basis of the data at hand, I see no way to decide among these and other possible explanations.

Despite the appalling soul-searching the prospective *tâng-ki* may go through when he is initially selected by a god to follow this calling, his position in the village is, at least in the ritual sphere, extremely important, even exalted. A week does not pass in which Tian-huah, now seventy, is not called to someone's house to go into trance so that the Third Prince may reveal answers to a wide variety of questions or write charms to be consumed as medicine for the cure of illnesses of all kinds. In addition, his presence is required in all village activities of various kinds.

Because of the amount of power the *tâng-ki* is potentially able to wield, there is, of course, a danger of his being "wrong." To me "wrong" means that the *tâng-ki* is sociologically or psychologically insensitive to the needs and realities of the community, or that he is manipulating things to his own (perhaps devious) ends. To Taiwanese the idiom is different, although the principles seem the same; that is, the big danger when a new man is possessed is that he may be possessed by a ghost (*Goei*) rather than by a god (*Shern*).

Various devices are tried in order to separate godly possession from ghostly possession. Initiations of *tâng-ki* accordingly include exorcism and trial by miracles. Thus when Guo Ching-shoei was initiated as medium of the Great Saint in 1968 he was required to splash boiling oil on his face with his bare hands.[17] He suffered no harm because he was protected by his god; a demonic presence would not have been able to stand by him in this way, but would have fled in terror, leaving Ching-shoei to be burned.

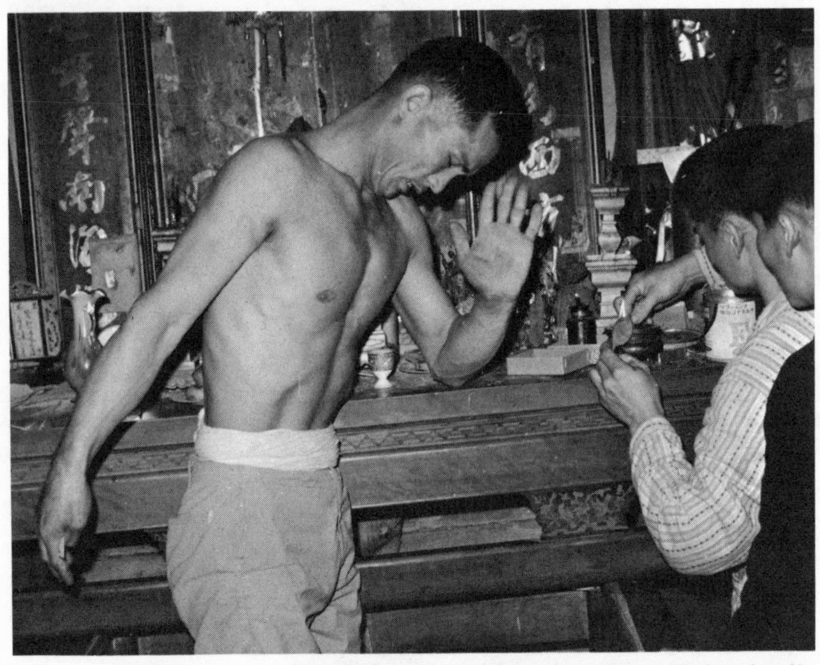

Guo Ching-shoei, a *tâng-ki,* or spirit medium, stands before his family altar in his first trance, which lasted eighteen hours.

There are such things as false *tâng-ki*, by which I mean *tâng-ki* who are possessed by no presence at all, be it divine or diabolic. These men merely imitate the behavior of possessed *tâng-ki* to defraud the public by charging for the "services" they render. They are known as "divine rascals" 神棍. In general they are urban, because it is more usual for urban *tâng-ki* to accept cash for their trance performances. Because a person goes to a *tâng-ki* he does not know only if the *tâng-ki* is recommended by friends, relatives,

17. Cf. Diamond 1966: 309.

or gods (other *tâng-ki*) in whom he has confidence, it is unlikely that he will regard "his" *tâng-ki* as a divine rascal, but it is easy to be suspicious of an utterly strange *tâng-ki*, particularly if his rates are unusually high. In rural areas the low or nonexistent fees exclude the possibility of divine rascals, it is reasoned, and the fact of possession is seldom, if ever, questioned. Whether in a given case the *tâng-ki* is really possessed is not important. That is not questioned. What is important is that the possession is benign and not malign. Once a rural *tâng-ki* is established to everyone's satisfaction as truly *beātus deum*, charges of diabolic interference are dropped and he functions as the community oracle. Should he slip, the possibility of goblins in the works is always lurking in the background to explain lapses of divine reason and to discredit an erring medium.

Different *tâng-ki* introduce slight differences in their trance performances, but there is a general pattern to which most conform. Let us start with Guo Tian-huah as an example. Tian-huah is called to come to a house that desires his services, or, upon occasion, the family that wishes him to come burn incense to the gods at their family altar and pray for a revelation; in time Tian-huah appears, unsummoned, but led by supernatural forces to the house where the revelation is to take place.[18] He usually appears after dinner, any time between seven o'clock and about ten in the evening. He sits chatting quietly in the courtyard of the house or in the central room with the host. As he begins to feel possession creeping over him he is less and less a participant in the conversation, which continues beside him. When it is noticed he is beginning to appear drowsy, a bench is set before the lower family altar, and here he seats himself, leaning over onto the table, as his shirt is removed. Shortly, perhaps within five or six minutes, he begins to shake. At first it is a slight vibration, barely perceptible. To this is added an occasional belch or gasp. Within minutes he is shaking violently and begins drumming his fingers hard and rhythmically on the table. Suddenly he breaks into loud, high-pitched, unintelligible "gods' language." He now stands over the table, and the bench is re-

18. For the peace of mind of readers who are disturbed by the operation of divine forces, it is only fair to admit that summoning the medium through prayer this way often requires several evenings before he appears, so there is time, one could maintain, for him to receive news of his call by more familiar channels.

moved. Within a minute or two the gods' language has become a variety of Hokkien. It is distorted by the imposition of melodic lines that destroy the normal tones of words, and it is complicated by the introduction of odd expressions, interrupted by belches and vocative shrieks addressed to the "little brethren," a term used by the Third Prince to address his followers. The god is now ready for questions. These are normally addressed to him by the head of the household, standing anxiously beside the family altar. After each answer has been given, the medium's flow of speech trails off and becomes a series of unintelligible mutterings, and the bystanders discuss the import of what has been revealed. Because of the distorted language, only people who have been through many séances with Tian-huah are able to interpret what he says, and they sometimes must ask for clarification.[19]

A session may last from forty-five minutes to an hour and a half. When it is finished, the god announces he is going to return 退, and the bench is placed behind the *tâng-ki*. Suddenly the *tâng-ki* reels backward onto the bench and into the arms of two men who station themselves behind him to catch him. He slumps down onto the table and slowly comes to, then retires to wash himself, put on his shirt again, and discuss what has taken place with his host over a bowl of noodles.[20]

Tian-huah claims to remember what transpires while he is in trance. Not all *tâng-ki* remember what has happened.[21] There are other differences too. Some *tâng-ki* jump around while going into trance, or have various kinds of convulsions. Some also empty their stomachs, and may salivate extensively while speaking. The speech of some is normal, even conversational, whereas others speak in cadences as Tian-huah does, or in rapid-fire falsetto. Some Taiwanese say that the reason for these different kinds of speech is that they are the voices of different gods. Thus falsetto is often

19. I tape-recorded several sessions, but my research assistant was unable to transcribe them without word-by-word assistance of village people with longer experience listening to this *tâng-ki*.
20. Noodles are seldom eaten by Taiwanese for meals, but are a frequent snack for either oneself or guests. They are normally prepared with finely chopped vegetables, pork, fish, and occasionally small shrimp.
21. According to Comber (1968: 14), Singapore *tâng-ki* never remember what has taken place. Diamond (1966: 125) notes the same for Taiwanese *tâng-ki* in her village.

associated with possession by a goddess, whose voice would naturally be higher. On the other hand, Chinese skeptics never tire of pointing out that the same god possessing two different *tâng-ki* speaks with two different voices.[22]

In a certain sense, the *kiō-á* and the *tâng-ki* can be considered interchangeable. The *tâng-ki* normally has the advantage that he speaks and is easier to understand than the bizarre characters scribbled by the *kiō-á*. However, it may go the other way about. In one *tâng-ki* séance held in a town near Bao-an no one was able to make any sense of what the *tâng-ki* revealed. Accordingly, a second séance was held in which the divination was performed instead with a *kiō-á* in hopes that what had been an unintelligible jumble of sounds from the mouth of the god's verbal oracle would be understood if reduced to hieroglyphics through his written one.

Another incident also suggests the interchangeability of *tâng-ki* and *kiō-á:* the case of Jang Wen-tong's 張文通 grandfather. Jang Wen-tong's grandfather was chosen by His Highness Chyr to be a *tâng-ki*. He did not want to do this. After a long period of trying to avoid the god (similar apparently to Tian-huah's reaction), he at last was able to strike a bargain with His Highness Chyr: Grandfather would not be His Highness's *tâng-ki,* but he promised that he would learn to read characters written by a *kiō-á* and make himself available to people desiring to have oracles read to them in this way. This compromise was accepted, and he gained great fame as a talented *kiō-á* reader.

But despite some similarities, there is a fundamental difference between the *tâng-ki* acting as the god's oracle and the *kiō-á*. Within the limits we noted above, the *kiō-á* is handled by anyone and read by anyone. Some people come to be specialists but, unlike the *tâng-ki,* they are not in trance.[23] The chair itself, not the men who control it, is the instrument of the god. Holding the chair and reading its characters are thought to require only practice, not divine inspiration, and no one who undertakes one of these jobs is liable to be suspected of being under the influence of devils and ghosts;

22. Every god speaks Hokkien, regardless of the region where he passed his earthly life.

23. If one wanted to make a comparison with the West, a *kiō-á* might be seen as more similar to a ouija board, whereas a *tâng-ki* more resembles speaking in tongues.

that is, rejected by the community as illegitimate. The *tâng-ki,* on the other hand, is always potentially suspect.

The village has control of a *kiō-á* in a way that it does not a *tâng-ki.* The *kiō-á,* after all, is manipulated by two men and read by a third. The two can confirm or deny any reading made by the third. In fact, it is fully part of the system that the reader should be wrong part of the time, and bystanders are perfectly welcome to contribute their ideas to the emerging interpretation of the message coming from the gods. There is plenty of room for the divine opinion to be a truly collective decision. In the case of the *tâng-ki,* the divine message is produced by a single man and consists of entire sentences rather than merely enigmatic single characters, so there is little room for collective interpretation. The divine message can be true or false only. The only check the village is able to put on him is to reject his claim to divine inspiration and discredit him. When the village people accepted his revelations as genuine, they are placing themselves entirely at his command.

It is therefore easy to see why it is that the *kiō-á* manipulators are so casually trained: they can be easily censured. But the *tâng-ki* is rigorously examined and highly suspect, and he requires an initiation, for once he has been created, there is no way to censure him short of destroying him.

### THE TÂNG-KI AS SPECTACLE

A *tâng-ki* is more than merely an oracle, simply another means of divination for a people already rich in methods for the discovery of unknown things. He is also a spectacle or perhaps, one might even say, a miracle. For on some occasions a *tâng-ki* engages in dramatic mortifications of the flesh.

In Taiwan mortification of the flesh is performed by means of any of five instruments (the so-called *gō-hāng-ke-si*五項家私, "five kinds of tools"). The most commonly used is a ball of nails (called by Groot a "prickball"). The usual Chinese word for this is "ball of nails"刺 球, but in Bao-an it is termed a "heavenly red tangerine"天 柑, a name that suggests its associations with religion. It normally is made from a ball of brilliant red cotton in which nails are fixed with their points protruding from all sides, secured against being pulled out of line by a network of red cording extending from nail to nail. The points of the nails extend from two to twelve millimeters beyond the cording (a couple of centi-

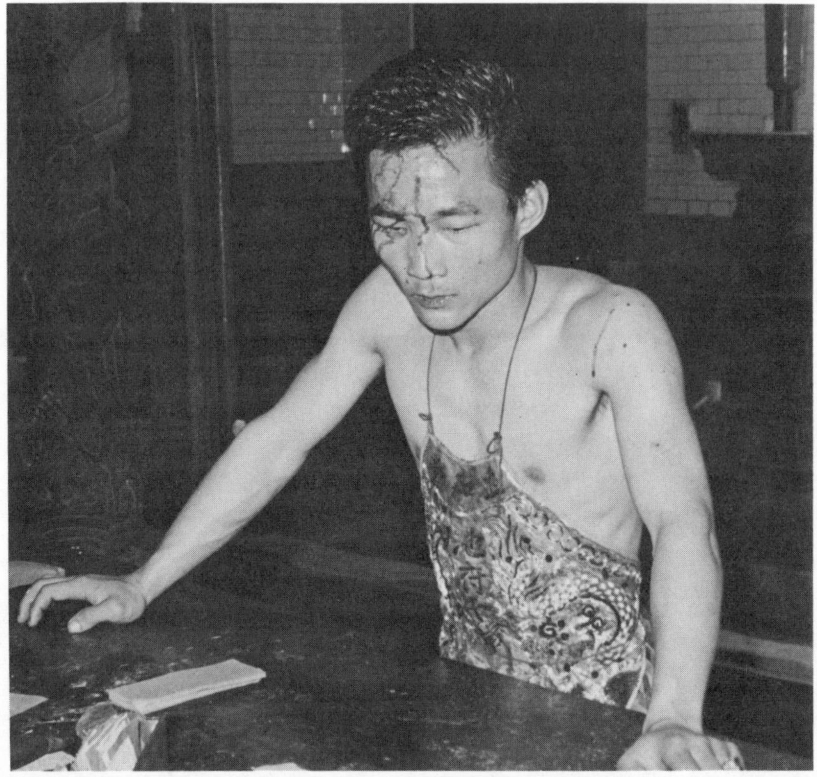

A young *tâng-ki* mortifies his flesh and offers godly advice in a city temple.

meters beyond the cotton core), and accordingly these figures represent the approximate depth of a wound that can be made with such an instrument.

A second instrument, also very widespread, is a sword 七星劍 about fifty centimeters in length. The sword is kept quite sharp, so that a cut can be produced by hitting the flesh with it. Other instruments include the saw of a sawfish 排劍, a spiked club 銅棍 made of a wooden baton in which either nails or triangular bits of copper have been mounted, and a large axe 月斧, considered to be the most dangerous of the mortification tools.

The medium inflicts wounds on himself by swinging the instrument of mortification over his head so that it lands on the upper part of his back. Some mediums also hit themselves on the forehead, causing the blood to run down their faces, producing yet a bloodier scene. Most of the wounds are superficial and heal in a few days. The rapid healing of these wounds, and the fact that they do not become infected are understood to be part of the miraculous nature of the performance.

Mortification of the flesh is the *tâng-ki*'s sign to the world that he is real. Some village people say that the *tâng-ki* himself cannot feel his wounds (and certainly he gives no indication he does). Others suspect that he can. But all agree he cannot prevent himself from inflicting them, for he is impelled to do this by his possessing god as a sign of the genuineness of his trance.

A *tâng-ki* does not mortify his flesh until his initiation. One of the prime acts of initiation is teaching the initiate to mortify his flesh.[24] In some sense, therefore, mortification is a sign that the possession is genuine, not only for the Taiwanese farmer, but for the Western analyst as well: the community does not initiate *tâng-ki* who are not adjudged to be real!

In theory a *tâng-ki* might mortify his flesh each time he is possessed. In fact, mortification is not so frequent. Mortification is a drama not necessary when a private person has called the medium to speak oracles at his family altar. The primary occasion for mortification is when the gods must be present in the village for reasons other than oracular. One such occasion was the birthday celebration we considered above. Another occasion is religious processions. At the triennial festival in Hsikang *tâng-ki* from surrounding areas turn out in force and accompany the palanquins from their home villages. It is always possible to discover when the procession is approaching a spiritually charged part of the processional route, for the movements of the palanquins become unsteady and erratic, and the *tâng-ki* begin to shake violently. The vicinity of a temple will usually invoke this response. So will a place in the road where someone has died, or an encounter with another medium or other palanquins. If the *tâng-ki* are armed at that particular moment, they begin to mortify their flesh.

When the procession approaches the Hsikang temple at the end of the day, and particularly at the end of the third day when the procession has been joined by palanquins from all of the villages it has visited and is now at its largest, one can witness *tâng-ki* after *tâng-ki* in a transport of ecstasy appearing before the temple fully armed and bleeding as he whacks at his back and forehead with

24. Cf. Elliott 1955: 61.

his weapons. He is allowed three strokes, normally, before bystanders stop him; then he jumps and shakes, holding his weapon tenaciously and recycles for another bout of whacking.

The presence of *tâng-ki* in a village brings it the prestige and awesome status one might expect to accrue to a place that has found favor and protection of the gods. It is said that in the late Ching dynasty Taiwanese *tâng-ki* might be called from one village to perform in another, and they would proceed in state along the rural byways accompanied by banners and large drums and riding in palanquins. The custom died with the Japanese ban on possession (as though possession could be legislated out of existence) and has not been revived under the present government.

Prestige accrues today to a village able to send one or several *tâng-ki* to the great festival at Hsikang. Thus when Guo Ching-shoei was suddenly possessed in Bao-an during my stay, one village man confided to me that he was able to see cunning forethought in the gods' plans for the village, for by providing a new *tâng-ki* they were giving Bao-an a chance to be that much up on a rival village at the 1970 triennial festival. Whether that was the plan of the gods or of men, there was no doubt in his mind that a rise in Bao-an's ritual position and prestige would be one effect of the new *tâng-ki*.

To return to the actual performance of mediums, the Norwegian missionary Reichelt has left a better record of a Westerner's reaction than of the performance as such (1951: 18 f.):

> . . . through the worship of local divinities of a lower moral order (at times even demons) [they] are brought into a condition of ecstasy. In this state they achieve superhuman power, as they are thought to be possessed by the divinity's spirit. It is especially the young, high-strung boys, whose nervous and emotional organization is easily affected, who are used in this sinister and repellent traffic.[25] . . . Some of these scenes are among the most unpleasant things one sees in China.

25. Tian-huah was possessed sometime in his forties; Ding-jyi, in his late teens. Guo Ching-shoei is thirty-four. Of the women, Guo Huey-miin began having "strange" experiences at twelve, whereas Jang Shiow-yeh 張秀葉 became subject to possession only after her marriage, but was not initiated until the age of thirty-three. I know of one case of a woman being possessed at age sixty. Ding-jyi is reclusive. Tian-huah is social and likes nothing better than an evening of conversation, perhaps over a snack of fruit. Ching-shoei is hard-working and hard-drinking. I am afraid I do not see a pattern emerging as clearly as Reichelt does.

It is not clear how unpleasant they are to the Chinese. In the case of Hsikang, it is this couple of hours at the end of the last day of procession, when the *tâng-ki* return to Hsikang in large numbers walking beside or riding upon the palanquins of gods from their villages, that is considered to be the peak of the festival, and their bloody exploits are recounted years afterward with an enthusiasm that does not altogether suggest revulsion. How many times was I told of the *tâng-ki* who was saved from splitting his head with an axe some years back only because a bystander, realizing the *tâng-ki* was becoming dangerously violent, pushed his arm to one side as the axe fell, so that he lost only an ear? How many times have Taiwanese told me that all of the *tâng-ki* bleed profusely before the temple at Hsikang, when in fact a few who are elderly or infirm do not mortify their flesh at all? How many times after discussing these performances have Taiwanese rural people added that it is all very *Rehnaw* 熱 鬧, a word of vigorous approval associated with an atmosphere of carnival and noisy confusion that is clearly much appreciated? This is not to say that the performance is truly enjoyed. Enthusiasm at a distance turns to morbid curiosity in face of the real thing, and the mob packs thick about the fenced-off court before the temple to watch the performance with profoundly involved but expressionless faces.

The extraordinary figure of the *tâng-ki* suggests several lines of thought about rural Taiwanese culture. It would, for example, be interesting to explore the way in which the *tâng-ki,* particularly the *tâng-ki* as a mortifier of his flesh, relates to Professor Eberhard's recent thesis about the importance of guilt among the Chinese lower classes (1967).

What is of relevance to the present discussion, however, is the social role of the *tâng-ki* in the village and how mortification of the flesh is important to that role. As is well known, one aspect of filial subservience 孝 in China is preserving one's body so that one may care for one's parents or their shades and produce children who will do the same. In the opening chapter of the *Classic of Filial Piety* 孝 經 we find the following passage: "Our body and limbs, our hair and skin are given us by our parents, and we must be careful not to injure them: this is the beginning of filial piety." [26] Hoogers (1910:6–8) cites additional Chinese sources on the same theme:

26. 身体髮膚受之父母不敢毀傷孝之始也.

A prominent feature of the subject we are concerned with is that filial piety requires, as an overriding duty, that one take scrupulously good care of one's body in order to maintain intact the corporal substance received from one's parents. Here are the curious texts which relate to this singular precept:

"As the body is made by one's parents and is a legacy of their substance, would one dare not to respect it? A man's body is as a branch from his parents, and he who abuses his body outrages and wounds his parents; he wounds the trunk from which he has sprung, and when that trunk is wounded, the branch will perish. Of all the products of heaven and earth, man is the most noble. Thanks to his parents, he is born perfect and he must die perfect if he would be called a pious son. Therefore let no man mutilate or defile his body." [27]

. . . The paraphrase of the instruction on sects of the Sacred Edicts sermonizes against foolish people who travel long distances to burn incense in satisfaction of a vow for the recovery of their parents' health, but do so at the cost of multifarious dangers to their own life and limb. They say that endangering their lives for their parents is a sign of filial piety. But, says the instruction, can you be unaware that not taking care of the body you have received from your parents is, instead, impiety? [28]

Such theories are quite alive today and are visible in the custom of punishing a child that has hurt himself before comforting him. The comfort is to soothe his fears or relieve his pain, but the punishment comes first to teach him not to damage his body. The sight is not uncommon, and the explanation is easy enough to elicit. An

27. Un trait saillant dans le sujet qui nous occupe, c'est que la piété filiale exige comme un *devoir impérieux*, qu'on ait scrupuleusement soin de son corps, pour conserver intacte la substance corporelle reçue de ses parents. Voici les curieux textes en rapport avec ce singulier précepte. «Le corps étant un legs de leur substance, fait par les parents, oserait-on ne pas le respecter? Le corps de l'homme étant comme un rejeton de ses parents, celui qui abuse de son corps, outrage et blesse ses parents, c'est blesser le tronc dont on est sorti; le tronc blessé, le rameau périra. De tour les êtres produits par le ciel et la terre, l'homme est le plus noble. Grâce à ses parents, il est né entier. Il doit mourir entier, s'il prétend au titre de fils pieux. Qu'il ne mutile donc, ni ne souille son corps . . . » (p. 6).

28. . . . La paraphrase de l'instruction sur les sectes (Augustes Edits) tonne contre les sots qui aux prix de mille dangers pour leurs corps et leur vie, s'en vont au loin brûler de l'encens pour satisfaire à un voeu qu'ils ont fait pour le recouvrement de la santé de leurs parents; ils disent qu'exposer sa vie pour ses parents, c'est montrer sa piété filale; et ne savez-vous pas, dit l'instruction, que n'avoir pas soin du corps que l'on a reçu des parents, c'est au contraire être impie? (p. 8).

example occurred on my own doorstep one day. My landlord's two-year-old granddaughter was standing on an armchair and suddenly shifted her weight too far to the back. The chair went over and the wee girl fell onto her head in a heap on the concrete porch. Her uncle immediately fished her up. She was crying so hard she could barely make a sound. He struck her hard several times. Afterward he told me this was in order to teach her not to do such a stupid thing again. A bystander offered the same explanation, and added that "probably about 60 percent" of rural Taiwanese would do this.

It becomes clear that the *tâng-ki* is deliberately flouting such rules, or is somehow outside them. We recall that he is considered to be a man who would normally die at an early age, but whose life has been "artificially" extended by a god so that he may serve as the latter's mouthpiece. His mortification is said to be caused by the god as a sign of this status. It seems to me that the reason this is an appropriate and powerful sign is that it is a directly unfilial thing to do and represents the *tâng-ki's* being cut off from the world of ordinary mortals and their responsibilities and becoming (while he is in trance) *entirely* the instrument of the god.

It is not correct to say that the filial obligations of a *tâng-ki* cease because he is a *tâng-ki;* on the contrary, a rural *tâng-ki* acts in that role only a small percentage of the time. The rest of the time he is indistinguishable from the rest of the village farmers. But during the times he is in trance, his own personality ceases to exist and he becomes the tool of his god. The drama by which this is made explicit is mortification.

### SOME OBSERVATIONS ON DIVINATION

On the surface of it, divination in the Chinese sense is an act of communication between men and supernaturals. In fact, of course, there are no supernaturals, and the conversation is destined to be a monologue. Or is it? The means of divination themselves provide at least an imitation of the gods' side, and when a *kiō-á* or a *tâng-ki* is used, there is a kind of role-playing of what the gods might be saying if there were gods. When the actors are good, and the performance is godlike, the imitation is accepted. Should they be bad and their declamations be incredible, the imitation is rejected as demonic and invalid or (rarely) as human fraud.

However the mechanics (or theatrics) of the performance be regarded, it is clear that the voice given to the gods is the crucial operator that sets the entire system of divine alliances, explanations, and miracles in operation.

If supernaturals were to be compared with the playing pieces of some kind of game, and the principles of descent, surname solidarities, natural death, and so on were to be compared with the rules, then the *tâng-ki* and other means of divination might be compared with the dice thrown to determine the actual applications of the rules in particular instances. The *tâng-ki* are the prime rural religious arbiters. It is they who diagnose a given case of familial or village disharmony as caused by ghosts; it is they who explore the family tree or the village forts for possible ghosts and their motivations; it is they who prescribe the cure. Spirit mediums drive harmful ghosts from the village; spirit mediums perform exorcisms; and spirit mediums represent the august presence of the divine at rites performed in their name. It is likely that in the past it was the spirit mediums who had the final voice in alliances between villages united with Bao-an in defeat of the Hwang, for the idiom of these wars is one of alliances between patron gods. I do not say that divine communication requires spirit mediums (though to function as the divinities do in China would seem to require communication), but in Bao-an the *tâng-ki* is the most dramatic form of communication.

The image of the dice can be pushed too far. The *tâng-ki* is not a free man, and his imitation of the gods is not a matter of his own caprice. Not only must he perform in trance (and therefore presumably not be guided by conscious desires but only by unconscious directives), but he is subject to charges of being possessed by ghosts rather than by gods should he become incredible. He is a religious arbiter to be sure. He can bring order out of confusion by making a decision with authority vested in no one else. But his authority belongs ultimately to the community, which trusts and initiates him when it could as readily suspect and exorcize him. He is not the master of the village populace; he is their jade chop.

At the beginning of this chapter I justified the interruption of our flow of thought by pointing out that such frequent reference must be made to divination in a discussion of rural Taiwanese life that it is best to include an excursus that makes its working more explicit. The ubiquitousness of divination among the Chinese has often been noted by Western writers; its importance in family and community decision-making has not. And its relevance as a mode of developing and maintaining group concensus (which in its most extreme and dramatic forms seems to be its main function) seems never to have been discussed. Is the phenomenon uniquely Taiwanese? Are nine *tâng-ki* tracing their origins to the same village far too many? Or have *tâng-ki* been for decades or even centuries primary devices for coordinating and directing rural efforts in the southeastern Chinese countryside?

My suspicion is that the importance of divination is not peculiar to Bao-an, or to Taiwan, or to this century. It seems possible that divination, and particularly divination through trance behavior, may be responsible for a great deal more Chinese decision making than we normally imagine and might even be a factor of importance in understanding, for example, the galvanization of the countryside during revolutions or secret-society rebellions, or the patterns of alliances between and among villages throughout south China during periods of local raiding and warfare. So far this is only a suspicion, but I know of no evidence to contradict it. These and other questions are raised by the existence and importance of *tâng-ki* in Bao-an. Divination is more than superstition.

# Chapter 5
## *The Family*

At this point our attention shifts from Bao-an village to the individual families that make it up. First we shall examine certain ritual manifestations of the family that are quite similar to the ritual manifestations of the village. Afterward we shall turn our attention to other aspects of supernaturalism that are unique to the family situation itself. Before we start, however, a preliminary word or two about the family is in order. There is no need to say very much on the subject.[1] Most of the features involved directly with our discussion of the family's supernatural aspects are rather outside the range of normal family functioning (which is one reason they are related to the supernatural in the way they are), and they will be discussed in their appropriate places as we come to them. The most that is usefully essayed here is a brief sketch of the definition of a family and some of its characteristics that Taiwanese themselves see as most important.

### IMAGES OF THE FAMILY

In general a family 家 in Taiwan is patrilineal, patriarchal, and virilocal. It includes a father and his sons, plus all the wives, unwed daughters, and unwed sisters of these. The old father is normally the family head 家長, in whose name the business of the family

1. Such observations as I had occasion to make about Bao-an families do not convince me that they differ in any marked degree from families of other rural Taiwanese described by writers in English, Chinese, and Japanese who were concentrating on family matters. For a bibliography of 262 items recently published in Taiwan, *see* Tsay Wen-huei 1967. Of material in English, the most readily available is S. H. Chen 1956; Cohen 1967, 1968, 1969; Diamond 1969; Gallin 1960, 1963, 1966; Marsh and O'Hara 1961; Pasternak 1968; A. Wolf 1964, 1966, 1968; M. Wolf 1969, 1970; and Yang 1962.

is transacted, and who in theory has authority over all the other members.[2]

Western writers have developed a number of terms to distinguish various compositions of the Chinese family unit. The terms do not represent different types of families so much as different stages in the family cycle. If the family consists merely of a man and his wife and children it is a *conjugal* family.[3] By the time one of the sons has married and had children, the family has become a *stem* family. If later on a second or subsequent son is married as well, it is *joint* or *extended.* (Both terms are used.) If the old father then dies, it may come under the direction of one of the brothers. This too is joint (or *fraternal joint*). If it then goes on for several generations without splitting into smaller families, it turns into what the Chinese call a "large family"大家, not because of its size—for it is not always large—but because of its complexity.

The Chinese themselves have no such elaborate nomenclature. A family is "large," or it is "small." Those families that are not large (joint) are small. Nearly all Taiwanese families are, in Taiwanese eyes, small.

What is more important to the harmony of day-to-day life than the conjugality or jointness of the family is who its members are, what its resources are, and whether given these people and these resources the family is able to get on harmoniously, for normally the family lives as a unit. It maintains physical quarters that all members acknowledge to be home (expressed in Chinese by the same word as "family"家). In theory, and ordinarily in fact as well, it has also a common budget, to which the incomes of individual members are contributed and from which expenses are met.[4] The "farming family" is the rural landholding unit in Taiwan today, and limits

2. In most matters, decisions of family policy or action are communal efforts, with adult sons taking the principal role. The process of decision making is not complete, however, without the agreement of the family head, and this old gentleman has the authority to throw the decision any way he thinks best. One Bao-an man was a local politician of great popularity. During a dispute on village road paving his father compelled him to take a stand strongly in opposition to popular opinion. This seriously endangered his political career for a time, and the loss of prestige and support this brought about took the best part of a year to recover.

3. In these usages, I follow Lang 1946.

4. An exception is money given to a bride in connection with her marriage. *See* Cohen 1968.

upon the amount of land that may belong to one owner apply to the family as a corporate unit. Individual property is ordinarily ill-defined within the family (although usufruct may be fairly specifically assigned). Even disaster, as we shall see shortly, is the joint property and responsibility of the family.

The social boundaries of the family are ritually set forth in terms of commensality, or, more exactly, a common stove or other cooking facilities. When a family becomes too large, or the economic contributions of individual members become so uneven as to cause interpersonal friction, or when sisters-in-law or brothers do not get on well together, the family may split into two or more families. Splitting the family 分家 is always an explicit act. It means dividing the inheritance and making each of the dividing groups of family members independent of the other groups. Ordinarily that is all. The divided families oftentimes (even usually) continue to occupy the same quarters they have been occupying, and if the house is physically adequate, several such families, each one growing gradually toward division itself, may occupy the same building, which for this reason is called (in English) a *compound*. In Bao-an, as we have noted, there seem to be fewer families per compound than in some other areas of Taiwan, but this says nothing about splitting of families. The casualness of the split in terms of physical distance and interaction should not lead us to suppose that it is not important. It seems to provide the psychological distance necessary for many personal antagonisms to be relieved of some of their bitterness, as well as changing the economic base on which each of the resultant families is able to operate. Splitting the family is typically (probably universally) represented in China by dividing the cooking facilities. One family, one stove. We shall see below that there are other ways, too, in which the family unit is symbolized in Taiwan.

Taiwanese have a clear and rather absolute notion of what a family ought to be. It is said that a family ought to be "round" 圓, or complete. The imagery of roundness occurs in artistic motifs and in verses pasted to the door of the central room at New Year. It occurs in food, when festival foods made for familial occasions such as New Year are made in round shapes. These would excite no comment perhaps at other times. In the context of New Year festivity their roundness becomes one of their most important features. In conversation, too, Taiwanese speak of the family ideal as roundness.

And what is roundness? We saw earlier that the theology of the soul and its fates is closely related to the continuity of the descent line. In roundness we find the familial aspect of the same point of view. A round family is one in which the descent line is being carried on. Roundness means all men find wives, and all women have husbands to whom they bear sons. It means that children do not die, and that old people remain alive and healthy to a hoary old age. Roundness suggests a unity of the family circle, but it seems to imply as well that the family is successful in fitting to a structural ideal of flawless Chinese patriliny.

There are, of course, problems. Some women are without sons. Under classical law, failure to bear a son was grounds for divorce. Some children die before they are of age to produce offspring. They are buried unceremoniously and unmourned.[5] The older generation at times does not live to great age, and their families lack the honor paid to the very old. What does one do in face of these facts of life?

What nature cannot do is done by art. The death of parents does not preclude their participation in the family through their tablets. The death of a husband does not weaken his wife's claim to a position in his descent line. The failure to have children is correctable by adoption, even postmortal adoption if necessary. Social fictions compensate for fickle biology. This point is crucial, for it underlies

5. Sons who do not produce offspring, whatever their other virtues, are not properly fulfilling their function as children. The same world view that inspired the famous female infanticide of dynastic times decrees that in contemporary Taiwan dead children are not honored with a coffin but are buried in a rough box. Nor do their families follow this box to the grave in a wailing funeral procession of the kind that is an essential part of the funerals of others. Only their younger siblings are allowed to accompany the body to the grave, where it is interred by neighbors while a single priest recites a simple liturgy. Although the loss of a child is felt emotionally to be a tragedy, there always lingers a sense in which it is not quite respectable for it to have died without having done its duty to its elders by supporting them in their dotage and giving them a good burial and descendants to worship their spirits. Not only is the child pathetic in dying without offspring to serve its ghost, but it is unfilial, and the family that produced it is stained with the sin of its product. In the writings of Mencius (IV. i. 26) we find the oft-quoted dictum: "There are three things which are unfilial, and having no progeny is the greatest of these" 不孝有三無後為大. This line is known to virtually every Chinese, and it is so often cited that there can be no question of its importance and correctness in the Chinese mind even today.

much of the logic of what is to follow. Let us consider the question of adoption.

When a married man lacks a son, who can carry on his descent line and provide him with sacrifices after his death, a son may be adopted in any of three ways. One way is to adopt a son from another family that has more than one. When possible, arrangements are made to adopt the son of a kinsman who is favored with several. When this is not possible, negotiations may be undertaken with others which often require a cash outlay. The adopted son becomes in every respect the son of his foster father. His surname is changed to that of his foster father's line; he inherits from his foster father and not from his biological father; and his loyalties and obedience are expected to be to his foster father. Should subsequent sons be born by nature to the foster father, the adopted son is their elder brother.[6]

There is another way to adopt a son, and that is to adopt the husband of one's daughter, making the adoption one of the conditions of the marriage. This man is added to his foster father's household as a son, and the children of the marriage are the lineal descendants of their mother's father, their father's father-in-law (or, if we accept the changes in status created by the adoption, of their father's father and their mother's father-and-father-in-law).[7]

There is also a third way to adopt a son. Or, more exactly, a second way and a half, for one does not end up with a son, but a grandson. An agreement is made when one marries out one's daughter that her first boy child will bear her father's surname and will have the responsibility for seeing to the sacrifices after the father's

6. I expected to find a certain amount of antagonism between such sons, because the younger knows that had his father not hastily adopted the elder he would himself have been the number-one son. I am not convinced that antagonism does not exist between such sons more often or to a greater degree than between other sons, but, on the other hand, it is by no means evident that it does. The question warrants study by someone in a position to do psychological testing of latent attitudes among Chinese brothers, for it has important implications for the degree to which a known and self-known social brother is an acceptable equivalent for a brother who is also from the same womb. And how does all this relate to the famed Chinese sworn brotherhood? Offhand I suspect that Chinese are more satisfied with social fictions than Americans, say, might be, but that is a guess.

7. It has always seemed to me that this ought to smack of incest. In fact it does not. A man is marrying not his sister, but his wife. It just so happens that they come to share a father in the process.

death. The existence of this possibility (and of certain variants of it) is revealing, for the fact that such an arrangement is allowable shows clearly that what is important is not a son, as such, but a descendant. The point of preoccupation is carrying on the descent line, providing descendants for all people, making all families round.

Roundness is not the only trait a family ought to possess. Roundness is a matter of structure, rather as joint-ness or stem-ness are matters of structure. And as everyone knows, content is important too. There is another word used for the content or quality of family life at any particular moment, and that is "harmonious"平安, sometimes translated as "peaceful." The gloss is deceptive, for the Chinese word implies a good deal besides peace or harmony in any English sense. A harmonious house is one that is functioning the way a household is supposed to function. It is round, to be sure; that is almost a prerequisite for harmony. But it is more than that. No one is sick in a harmonious family. There are no financial reverses. Sons are not killed in war. There are no major accidents. Crops are not destroyed by insects, floods, or drought. There are no domestic quarrels, nor jealousy between brothers, nor friction between daughters-in-law and their mother-in-law. A family that is "inharmonious" 不平安, on the other hand, is cursed by disaster. It is a household in which family members are quarrelling, or in which there are grave financial difficulties, a place where luck is generally bad or where (most commonly) there is sickness or death. Individuals, too, are harmonious or inharmonious. So are villages, or even nations. But by far the most common prayer in Taiwan is for the harmony of the family家庭平安. The phrase is not only constantly upon the lips of the populace, but is printed on door frames, on charms, on wedding cakes, and on walls of houses. It is a prayer addressed to ancestors and gods, and a plea presented to ghosts.

The fortunes of no man are separate from those of his family. At times it seems as though even personal glory is "planned" by the individual's family. Most Bao-an people with whom I discussed the matter told me that an ideal family would have three sons and two daughters. Of these sons one would be a farmer, for that is the Bao-an way of life. The second would be a merchant, for in that way the family would be enriched. The third son would be a high official, perhaps even elected the governor of Tainan county or made provincial governor of Taiwan. It was not the sons who expressed such ambitions to me; rather they came up in the course of discussions about an ideal family, mostly conducted with women.

Personal misfortunes, similarly, are inseparable from the fortune of the family as a unit. Taiwanese interpret sickness of a family member as an instance of family inharmony. But it can be more than that. Repeated sickness or prolonged sickness or sickness of several members of the same family is not simply an instance of inharmony any more, not simply a personal misfortune which interrupts the harmony and smooth functioning of the home temporarily. It comes to be seen as a *result* of some more basic inharmony that has infected the family. This is a point that will become crucial in the matter that follows, for the symptoms of illness are now also the symptoms of something the matter with the fortunes of the family as a whole. Not only is a family inharmonious because a member is sick, but the member is sick because his family is inharmonious; that is, because in some other and more profound way his family is failing to meet the ideal, harmonious model. It is at this point that supernatural explanations become important, which we shall examine below.

## THE FAMILY ALTAR

Every house (not necessarily every family individually) has a family altar, which is the spatial focus of its religious activity. This stands in the central room of the house, opposite the principal door. The normal family altar consists of two parts: there is a long, high, narrow table placed against the wall and bearing the sacra of the household. This is called the "red approach table"紅格桌, although "table for approaching the gods" would perhaps be a better translation.[8] In front of it is a lower table, square on top, and cubical in general appearance. This is called a "table of the eight immortals"八仙桌. The table of the eight immortals may be used for eating dinner, for stacking things one has been carrying, for doing schoolwork, and for a multitude of other general purposes. It is also used to hold sacrificial food during sacrifices. It is a kind of service table. The red approach table, on the other hand, is a far more sacred object, on which one does not carry out activities other

8. Red in China, as elsewhere, is a felicitous color, often associated with the gods.

than worship and does not normally store goods, and which one does not readily move about the room. When sacrifices take place outdoors for some reason, neighbors will sometimes carry their eight immortals tables outside to make temporary altars there. It would be unthinkable to move a red approach table from the house for this purpose. In English we use the term *family altar* for both tables. This usually does not cause confusion, but it is usually the higher one that is referred to, or the lower one only in its religious aspects.

The red approach table is divided into two zones. One of these, the area at the left, is devoted to ancestral worship; all the rest is devoted to worship of the gods. At the left rear are the ancestral tablets. In many cases a portrait of a recently deceased family member hangs on the wall above these. In Taiwan these portraits are inevitably done in black and white and convey an impression of charcoal portraiture in very stereotyped poses. The association with the dead is clear, for such portraits are made only for the dead. I find them morbid. In front of the tables is an incense pot, and often one finds here a pair of *poe,* which are thrown in order to communicate with the ancestors.[9]

Behind the center of the altar is a hanging that shows various Taiwanese gods. Presumably at one time such hangings were painted. Today they are printed, at least among farmers, and in most fashionable houses they are made of brilliantly colored glass.[10] If the family owns a joss, it is placed immediately in front of this. In front of the hanging—or if there is a joss, then in front of the joss—there is an incense pot, usually similar to the pot in front of the ancestral tablets, but larger. Before this there is a small platform on which offerings can be placed. To either side of this are candles

9. The distinctness of the two cults of the altar is made the more explicit by the custom that the ancestors always use a different set of divination blocks from the gods. About the only question addressed to the ancestors, however, is whether they have finished with the sacrificial food.

10. These hangings (known locally as *pùt-chó·-chhat-á* 佛祖漆仔) typically portray Guan-in at the top, attended, and beneath her the Queen of Heaven or sometimes the Queen of Heaven and Guangong. At the third and lowest level are the earth god and the kitchen god. Although this particular combination is perhaps distinctively Taiwanese, little else can be said of it. These gods do not necessarily represent the most important gods of any particular community (let alone household). The scroll seems to function primarily as a felicitous decoration. The images printed on it do not function as specific objects of worship or seats for the occupation of visiting divinities.

(today often electric candles) and glass vases for flowers. Often a pair of divination blocks will be found here too.

On the wall beside the hanging of the gods, charms may be pasted to ward off disasters that might befall the house. At the rear of the altar, near the joss if there is one, there are often various other objects brought home from a famous temple or shrine, from a religious festival, or even from a very humble home-altar temple of some purely local god in another town who cured a disease for one of the family members. These objects (which I have found it convenient to call collectively "fetishes") are worshipped with the gods, and their presence is thought to bring harmony to the house. Flags are a usual form; so are tall, narrow tablets with a dragon pictured on them. But there are others as well.[11] One of the most common fetishes in the Hsikang area is a papier-mâché carp sold at each triennial festival by the Hsikang temple.[12]

At the far right end of the altar certain materials of worship are often stored, such as boxes of firecrackers or packages of incense. Sometimes one also finds certain souvenirs of family history: a glass ornament given by a friend when the house was built, or a tablet, enshrined in a glass box, commending a member of the family on his excellent public service record. When the family seldom uses the eight immortals altar for other purposes, the worship materials may equally well be stored there, and so may these items of sentimental, rather than religious, importance.

These two areas of the family altar (the left end and all the rest) represent two distinct cults. One is the cult of the gods; the other, the cult of the ancestral dead. We turn now to consider these two cults, beginning with the ancestors in this chapter and continuing with the gods in the next. Then we shall move on to a third group of supernaturals who are *not* represented on the altar: the ghosts, for these are in some ways the most important other-worldly folk of all.

11. Differences seem to depend principally upon price, and a single shrine normally has fetishes for sale at a variety of prices. Profits from the sale of these contribute to the support of the shrine and its festivals.

12. Geomantically, the site of the Hsikang temple is associated with the carp, and the fish has come to represent Hsikang. When I left, work was in progress on the construction of an enormous concrete and glass image of a carp crowning a multistoried pavilion rising from a rear court to become the highest point of the temple roof.

THE ANCESTORS

Just as the ancestors receive far less than half of the family altar for their sacrifices, the rest being given over to worshipping the gods, so also the ancestors receive much less attention than the gods.

In Ching times, and occasionally in the postwar period, ancestors have been represented on individual wooden plaques, ranging in height from about fifteen to thirty centimeters or even taller, and a few centimeters wide. Some bear the name of the deceased carved on the face of the tablet, whereas others have the name written with a brush on a small indentation in the front of the tablet, and are fitted with a sliding panel that conceals the indentation from sight. So far as I know, these were interchangeable styles during the late Ching, and the difference was a matter of budget and taste. During the Japanese period the manufacture of plaques was apparently prohibited, and in some instances tablets of this type were seized and destroyed by the authorities, although many were hidden and brought forth once more after the withdrawal of the Japanese government. In Japanese times the prevailing style, of necessity, was the Japanese ancestral shrine, a small black and gold cabinet with two doors on the front of it in which the tablets as such are small wooden slips, one for each ancestor.[13] An entire lineage can be kept in a single shrine, as the slips are simply placed one behind the other. The majority of the ancestral tablets in Bao-an are still of this type, although Japanese-style shrines have all but disappeared from the market. After the war the slips of wood used during Japanese times found their way into a new style of shrine made to contain the wooden slips in a rack on the back of a squat commemorative tablet. The commemorative tablet normally stands in a wooden case with a glass front panel, and access to the slips is had by removing the glass panel and taking out the tablet rack. The slips of wood themselves are concealed from view when the rack is in its wooden case. Such an object allows for the preservation of the sacred slips of wood (which even though they were a Japanese introduction came in time to be regarded as just as valid as the old tablets apparently), while at the same time being neither "old fashioned" nor Japanese.

Many families have an entire collection of various different kinds

13. The actual variety of tablets in Japan is apparently much greater than this. Cf. Smith 1966.

of ancestral tablets and shrines, depending upon the vagaries of political control of the island at the times of various deaths in the family and upon their success at concealing the pre-Japanese tablets from the Japanese officials. In one family a duplicate slip was made for a certain ancestor in case his original plaque should be confiscated. Today both the plaque and the slip can be found on the altar. The slip is what is worshipped, but the plaque is kept because "after all that trouble to keep it away from the Japanese we are not about to throw it away!"

As objects of worship, the ancestors are not a very inspiring crew. Maurice Freedman (1966: 151) speaks of "what, in the light of comparative ethnographic evidence, appears to be the relative ineffectiveness of Chinese ancestors, their general air of benevolence, and doubtless too the lack of strong feelings of hatred or guilt toward them on the part of their descendants. . . ." He points out that punishment by one's ancestors is rare in China. So long as they receive their sacrifices, they seem contented and beneficent, protecting their offspring with such power as is available to them from their influence with gods. Unlike ancestors in many parts of the world, Chinese ancestors are not moralistic arbiters of their descendants' behavior.

The worship of these beings is tied up with notions of memorializing the dead and providing for their continued comfort after death, as we have seen. But in China, as elsewhere, the ancestral cult inevitably becomes involved in a variety of ways with relations between and among families, compounds, and lineages.

Freeman (1958: 46 ff.) describes one kind of pattern that apparently prevailed in southeastern continental China. He distinguishes domestic ancestor worship from the worship of ancestors in ancestral halls. A tablet would normally begin its career on a domestic altar. Then, as the descendants split their families and split them again, it was moved to a common ancestral hall of greater accessibility. When in time this hall filled up with tablets—and it is tempting to speculate that human relationships were as important as lack of physical space in determining when this state was reached—a new hall would be founded by each of several different sections. Each section would take the tablets of their most recently deceased ancestors and install them in a new building, considered to be founded from the old. Freedman relates this to the foundation of these sections as intermediate segments between family and lineage, whose emergence depended upon the endowment of independent ancestral halls. He also notes a contrast between these segments on the one hand, in which benefits and responsibilities of the ancestral hall were rotated through the participating units of the segment, and the maintenance of the domestic cult on the other hand, in which a principle of primogeniture prevailed in the assignment of privileges, benefits, and obligations associated with the cult.

A contrasting relation between ancestor worship and familial functioning is described by Myron Cohen (1960). Cohen suggests that in the Hakka village of Yen-liao, in Pingtung, Taiwan, the separate ancestral halls are unnecessary because "domestic worship is merged with that at the level of the compound. A founder of a compound, as noted above, may build a hall [i.e., a central room] and place tablets within it. Until such time as his family divides, of course, worship of this sort may be considered domestic. Thereafter, however, there is no proliferation of tablets corresponding to increasing numbers of families. In any given compound, there can be only one set of tablets, located in the *cheng-t'ing*" (p. 170). As families divide they may outgrow the original building complex and begin a new one. This typically contains a room that could function as a central room (Cohen's *cheng-t'ing*) but does not, for apparently no altar is installed in it, and worship is continued in the central room of the original compound. Many tens of years pass before independent worship is established in the new compound.

Bao-an follows neither the southeastern Chinese pattern described by Freedman nor the Hakka pattern described by Cohen. In Bao-an it is possible for ancestral tablets to be kept in one central room, and it is possible for them to be passed down by a principle of primogeniture. But this is only one possibility. It is equally acceptable for the tablet of an ancestor to circulate among a group of brothers, say, usually spending a year in each household.[14] The house is selected by lot or by following a regular cycle of rotation.[15]

14. When a family divides before the death of the paterfamilias, this gentleman may or may not remain the head of one of the units. In event that he doesn't, the same options apply to the care of the parents; that is, they may be cared for by a single son and financial adjustments be made for this, or they may be circulated on a regular cycle among their children.

15. For this reason a single collection of tablets does not necessarily account for all ascendant dead.

In other cases it is acceptable for the tablets of the parents to find their way to the most elaborate family altar and to remain there by common consent. Unlike the Hakka case (but like the circumstances described by Gallin [1966: 239] for Hsin Hsing), individual households within a compound might also have individual altars (usually shelves on one side wall of the household's principal room) on which gods that other families in the compound do not worship may be kept, and on which ancestors that are common only to themselves may be represented in tablets.[16]

There are few separate ancestral halls in Taiwan, and none in Bao-an or used by the people of Bao-an. One village friend of mine assured me that the Guo who migrated to Bao-an from Hsuehchia to the north had an ancestral hall in that town. Arriving in Hsuehchia, I discovered that the only ancestral hall locally known was a recently built communal one serving five surnames in which generalized ancestral rites might be held, but which contained no tablets. None of these surnames was Guo. At length one old man was able to think of a connection between Hsuehchia and the Guo of Bao-an, and he led me quite a long way to an outlying cemetery where two bone pots protruded slightly above the surface of the ground, heavily overgrown. These were graves, he said, which people from Bao-an used to come and worship at the *Chingming* 清明 festival.[17] When I returned to Bao-an I faced my original informant with this. He admitted then that he had in fact never seen the ancestral temple, but had heard there was one and assumed it was his. The anecdote is revealing in that were the ancestral temple a truly important institution in this area, one might expect a man over thirty to be better informed about "his own" than this!

If Bao-an does not make use of ancestral halls, and if the tablets are not carefully maintained in a single central room serving many families or even many compounds, what becomes of the older

16. The term *ancestor* is a bit misleading. All of the agnatic dead may be found among the tablets. Some of these may be sons of the living household head. We shall see later that these are provided with adopted descendants in order to render them ancestral. It often happens therefore that a fairly young family may have its own ancestral plaque or two.

17. *Chingming* 清明, "clear and bright," is the annual festival of the cleaning of the tombs. Any standard book on Chinese festivals contains a description of *Chingming*. Some of the most interesting are Groot 1886; Bredon and Mitrophanow 1927; and Tun 1900. For Taiwan, *see* Saso 1966; Ngô 1955; Her Lian-kwei 1955; and Lin Tsair-yuan (forthcoming).

ancestors? The answer seems to be that they are abandoned. This becomes clearer if we distinguish two kinds of ancestor worship. One we might call individual ancestor worship. This is directed to a particular ancestor, and is usually performed on the anniversary of his death, and sometimes also on his birthday. The other kind might be called general ancestor worship. This latter type is worship to all of the tablets of the dead on one's altar. Worship of this kind occurs at the *Chingming* festival and at certain crisis rites, such as marriages. The distinction is important, because informants assert that only certain tablets are worshipped, whereas others are not. What is meant is that only some tablets are worshipped individually. Collective worship is always addressed to all the tablets on the altar.

For those ancestors who are individually worshipped, sacrifices are provided not only by the family that maintains the tablets, but also by other, immediately related, descendant families, and there are examples of as many as eight households joining together in worshipping a great-grandfather.[18] This, however, is not common. In general, those dead are honored by individual sacrifices who are remembered by the living. Thus, to take an extreme case, there are several families in which worship is directed to the father of the paterfamilias, but where his grandfather, though represented by a tablet on the same altar, is not worshipped.

There is reason to suppose that this situation of more tablets than sacrifices is very widespread. Some families allowed me to examine their ancestral tablets, and some did not.[19] Many who would not allow the tablets to be examined recited the information that would be found on them. However, when a few families *both* recited the information *and* allowed me to examine the tablets, there were in nearly every case more names on the tablets than had been remembered, and there is no reason to suppose that the same trend would not continue if one could examine all the tablets in the village and interview all the worshipping families.

18. If distance makes attendance at such a sacrifice too difficult, one acceptable alternative is for the distant branch of the descendants to make a duplicate tablet for its own altar, where the cult undergoes a history as separate from the original tablet as would be the tablet of a totally different ancestor.

19. Except for the style of individual plaques on which the name is carved on the outside, it is impossible to examine the tablets without moving them, and moving them is potentially disturbing to the spirits, in some minds, and a breach of etiquette toward them to almost all minds.

Some families, more enthusiastic about worship than others, honor a great many of the dead with individual death-anniversary rites. But oftentimes they do not know whom they are worshipping. Pasted to the wall in the vicinity of the altar one often finds a piece of red paper with a series of dates marked on it. These are dates of death of ancestors represented by such of the tablets on the altar as are individually worshipped. They are therefore the dates when sacrificial food must be prepared and laid out on a table before the ancestral shrine. The names of the ghostly recipients are irrelevant to the performance of this duty, and need not be recorded.

There seems to be no explicit principle by which a tablet is declared at a certain time to become void. Rather it degenerates into irrelevance as the family members who knew the deceased become fewer or vanish, as memory dims, and as the decision to conduct worship is put into the hands of family members with less interest in ancestral worship as a formal religious expression. Thus in one household the family altar contains tablets for the parents of the household head, worshipped with great regularity; but there are also some older tablets of ancestors who died in 1887 and 1867. Their names and kinship relationship are no longer known (although the names are written on the tablets and are therefore recoverable information), and the family "worship them on their death anniversaries, unless we forget; and then we don't."

In Bao-an, it seems, one finds little or nothing of the use of ancestors to distinguish segmenting clans, as Freedman has described for Fukien and Kwangtung. Their worship seems to be purely commemorative of their individual persons, and when they are forgotten as individuals by the household head and other older people, they tend to lapse into oblivion. There are traces left of the ideology that dictates one must worship a line in perpetuity, as we shall see, but these feelings ordinarily do not seem strong. It was never with a sense of shame or reluctance, it seemed, that people told me they no longer worshipped old So-and-so; it was merely a statement of fact. And for those who do carry on individual worship for a larger number of ancestors or a larger number of generations, it is mechanically done by the women of the household with reference to a chart showing only the dates for the rites.

One group of five sons held the most elaborate funeral Bao-an had seen within memory for their elderly father after his death. The many ancestors recorded on their tablets attended many of the funeral rites in the form of small paper statues. But at the end of the funeral the ancestral tablets (like the paper statues) were burned, and no record was kept of their names. The old father was now the founding ancestor, and all that was recorded of the previous history of the family was the number of generations represented by the plaques burned. This act was considered odd by most village people, and no one was able to explain it to me, but nobody seemed upset by it. Apparently the older plaques were simply irrelevant, and were done away with.

This decreased emphasis on the ancestral cult (if indeed there ever was much emphasis on it among Taiwanese [20]) does not imply a decreased interest in the dead. On the contrary the immediate family dead are folk of great importance, as we shall see. Nor does the fact that ancestors in time lose their individual worship negate their requirement for worship in earlier years. On the other hand, reasons are easily adduced why worship need not be perpetual. One village informant suggested that older tablets did not require worship because the people whom they represented had already been reincarnated. Elliott (1955) cites a case in which a séance revealed the recently dead to be waiting briefly while his application for reincarnation cleared through a tangle of celestial red tape.

There are constructs, in other words, which provide reasons, if reasons are necessary, for the dead to stop needing their tablets. The morality of filial subservience and the theology of feeding the manes may provide an ideology for maintaining ancestral worship where it is also utilized by the living in the segmentation of clans or otherwise. But other doctrines such as reincarnation or deification of the dead (which we shall discuss below) allow these principles to be laid aside after a time in Bao-an and probably among Taiwanese generally, where principles of clan organization and segmentation do not seem to function as they do on the mainland.

20. We recall that Freedman associates the ancestral cult with corporate lineages, and that this kind of lineage structure was apparently lacking in Taiwan from the beginning. If we find both of these arguments convincing, it is not difficult to see why the ancestral cult should receive little attention in Taiwan, and we would predict that this has always been the case.

# Chapter 6

## *Divine Guardians of the Family*

Gods, it will be recalled, are important because they are allies against oppressive forces, be they competing villages or malignant spirits. The gods are not always willing allies, and ordinarily they must be cultivated before one makes extensive demands upon them. In Mandarin a folk expression enjoins men not to "ignore worship ordinarily and pray only when disaster strikes" 平時不燒香 臨時抱佛脚. Worship in general is considered a good thing, and in larger towns many elderly women go daily to a temple to burn incense. They often have little notion whom or what they are worshipping, but merely "take incense and worship with the others" (*giâ-hiu*$^{n}$ *tòe-pài* 抬香隨拜) in pious ignorance.

SUPERNATURAL PROTECTORS OF THE FAMILY

The more shrewd, however, consider subtler strategies to assure themselves of supernatural support. One official of the Nankeunshen shrine at Peimen, one of the major shrine centers in Tainan county, suggested to me that one should not worship too broadly, but rather concentrate one's adoration on one or a few divinities. The rationale was simple: if you worship a great host of gods, he explained, then when you bring one of them a problem he will just say, "you often worship old So-and-so; why not bring this problem to him instead of bothering me with it?" But if you worship only one or a few gods, it is harder for them to shift the responsibility for helping you to their codivinities, and it is easier for you to get action.

There is another reason too, equally pragmatic but less calculated, why Taiwanese tend to have favorite gods. When catastrophe strikes one appeals to a god. If nothing happens, one appeals to another god, or visits a different temple. Ultimately, relief comes, and one has then a sense of having discovered a system that works. Everyone has his preferred mediums, preferred gods, preferred temples, on the basis partly of his own experiences, and partly of hearsay about the experiences of others. Preferences change. Fashions come and go. Perceptive spirit mediums become successful, while their clumsier confreres are declared the tools of demons or simply are possessed less and less often until they are no longer mediums. Rich and impressive temples become more rich and more impressive, while blundering false starts in front parlors are ignored and revert to family altars, and shrines grown unfelicitous are used to store grain or to quarter soldiers or teachers. The system is by no means static.

It is not unnatural in such a system that certain people, and certain families, should find that they have good success in appealing to a certain god, and that they should develop with him a relationship of patronage. In many cases a joss is carved in which form the god is present in more directly palpable form. A joss might be collectively owned, as those belonging to a public temple, or privately owned by an individual household or a group of households. It forms a dwelling for the god when he is called into it for extraordinary worship or divination. Household josses stand in state near the center of the family altar, often upon a small dais formed of sheets of spirit-money, and are objects of great reverence.

The possession of a joss marks a special relationship of reciprocity with the god it represents, entailing both a responsibility on the part of the god for the general welfare of the family that has acquired and maintains the statue, and a responsibility on the part of that family to worship the statue at regular intervals.

The exact interpretation of these responsibilities differs from individual to individual. For some, great care must be taken of the joss to guard it against damage. It is enthroned atop an elaborate family altar with the finest quality fittings, and the altar is decorated with fresh flowers, and hung with a bas-relief embroidered altar cloth. For others the joss is a thing to be used, and the owner is willing to lend it to other people so that they may hold divinations with it in their houses. What is important is not the majesty of such a joss, but its efficaciousness. In some cases the worship of the joss is confined to the household that owns it and is a comparatively simple affair involving a few plates of food placed on the family altar. In other cases groups of families, organized in a variety of ways, join in the adoration of the god. They may be loosely designated by the term "god-association"神明會; however, because the term covers many more elaborate groups, as well as the sorts of associations that occur in Bao-an, I prefer the term "god-worshipping group" for present purposes.

God-worshipping groups are of particular interest because with their greater resources they provide fuller ritual expression than do individual families of the patron-client relationship that characterizes the Taiwanese view of the supernatural. In Bao-an such god-worshipping groups are few, and typically they are small. Many include only two families, or the families housed in a single building. The eight largest groups total 57 to 59, or about a quarter, of Bao-an's 226 households. But membership patterns change and

TABLE 3
BAO-AN GOD-WORSHIPPING GROUPS

| *Group* | *God* | *Number of Households* | *Distribution of Surnames (Households)* | *Total Households of This Surname* |
|---|---|---|---|---|
| 1 | His Highness Chyr | 13–14 | 12 Jang | 14 |
| | | | 1 Shieh | 2 |
| 2 * | His Highness Lii | 3 | 3 Lin | 7 |
| 3 | His Highness Wu | 8–9 | 6–7 related Guo | 164 |
| | | | 1 Shyu | 11 |
| | | | 1 Chern | 1 |
| 4 | King Guo | 8 | 8 related Guo | 164 |
| 5 | King Guo | 3 | 2 related Guo | 164 |
| | | | 1 unrelated Guo | 164 |
| 6 | Mhatzuu | 3 | 3 related Guo | 164 |
| 7 | Great Saint Equal to Heaven | 9 | 8 Shyu | 11 |
| | | | 1 Guo | 164 |
| 8 | Great Saint Equal to Heaven | 10 | 4 related Guo | 164 |
| | | | 4 unrelated Guo | 164 |
| | | | 1 Shyu | 11 |
| | | | 1 Lii | 2 |
| | | | 1 Hwang (formerly) | 11 |

* This group had become extinct by late 1966.

this figure can be only approximate.[1] Let us turn briefly to these eight groups (arranged by the names of their gods), and examine especially the ways in which their members are related to each other, and the kinds of considerations that cause a household to join one group rather than another.

*Group 1* is the cult of His Highness Chyr池府二千歲, one of five sworn brothers worshipped widely in southwestern Taiwan.[2] The statue of His Highness Chyr worshipped in Bao-an is reputed to be a century or more old. It came to the village with the ancestors of most of the present Jang households. Just as there are several different groups of Guo in Bao-an, so there are at least two groups of related Jang households, plus a couple of unrelated, single households of that surname. There are two Jang households in Bao-an who do not participate, but in general His Highness Chyr serves as a Jang god, uniting most of the Jang households in the village, whether or not they are related. In many ways His Highness Chyr is being used as a surname-group god, much as King Guo is used by the far more numerous Guo. Worship of His Highness Chyr is not compulsory for all Jang, and the presence of one or two village households named Shieh among the alleged regular worshippers indicates that it is not confined to the Jang. Still and all, the correspondence between surname and god is fairly good. We shall consider below some of the uses to which this cult is then put by the Jang.

1. I have reason to suspect that participation might be wider than I recorded, because most of these data were gathered toward the beginning of my stay, when some informants were inclined to be cautiously noncommital. A more detailed discussion of this problem and of the composition of these groups will be found in Jordan 1969: 166–183, 285–289.

2. There are no widespread traditions of their earthly lives. They tend to be worshipped singly, or in a group of the first three (surnamed Lii, Chyr, Wu 李 池 吳 ) or of all five (the final two surnames being Ju and Fann 朱 范 ). Taken together, they are known as the Five Highnesses 五 府 千 歲 There is little functional differentiation between them, except that the fourth, Ju, is considered somewhat irritable, and Fann is thought to specialize to some extent in medicine. Their major centers of worship in southwestern Taiwan are in Matou and at the shrine of Nankuenshen at Peimen. *See* Chern Ren-der *et al.* 1963: 10; Jenq Sheng-chang 1967: 110. Wider Chinese tradition designates these beings as gods of pestilence (Liou Jywann 1963), signalling this status by the frequent use of the title "prince" 王 爺 . Local people discount such accusations, and at least one Hsikang exegeticist insisted that the title could be used with any divine being one

*Group 2*, now extinct, was until recently a cult of His Highness Lii 李府大千歲, the "elder brother" of His Highness Chyr. Extinction of a cult, although normally not recordable, is probably not uncommon, and certainly one comes often enough upon private josses no longer worshipped. A statue that is not worshipped loses its power. It "no longer has a god." Seen the other way about, a statue that does not manifest its power by seeing to the successful accomplishment of the aims that inspire people to worship it ceases to be worshipped. The point is important, for it means there is a theological reason for cults to come to an end as well as for them to be founded. There are several unworshipped josses in Bao-an. The joss of His Highness Lii is of interest primarily because of its association with the Lin 林 families. The worshipping group included in the very recent past the households of two brothers, sons of an only son, plus the wife and children of a third brother's son.[3] These three households never were able to enlist the interest of the other four Lin households in Bao-an. Unlike the Jang of Group 1 (or the Shyu of Group 7), who seem to be successfully using their cults as instruments to achieve surname solidarity, the Lin achieved little unity this way. The remaining four Lin households did not and do not participate in any god-worshipping groups.

*Group 3* worships His Highness Wu 吳府三千歲, a sworn brother of Their Highnesses Chyr and Lii. The statue of His Highness Wu worshipped in Bao-an was ordered carved by the grandfather of the present owner sixty or more years ago, and the worshippers of this statue are his descendants. But there are certain differences between the group of people who worship the grandfather and the group who worship His Highness Wu. When Wu is worshipped, a neighboring Shyu and a neighboring Chern household ordinarily join, and one related household, which has moved across the river, does not participate. When the grandfather is worshipped, on the other hand, the Shyu and Chern do not join, and the transriverine family until recently sent a representative with

---

wished to honor with it, even to Guan-in herself, and proved nothing. Many other "princes" are worshipped in Taiwan, above all in the southern half of the island. *See* Liou Jy-wann 1960: 67–71.

3. The son was reported to be a ne'er-do-well who moved out of the village to the city and never reappeared. A fourth brother, like the third, had died, and his widow remarried out of Bao-an.

sacrificial food for the offerings.[4] Shyu and Chern do not join in the ancestral worship of the grandfather because he is not *their* grandfather. Not only is no real purpose served by worshipping other people's grandfathers, but it is bad form should one try.[5] In worshipping His Highness Wu, however, they are welcome to join. The owner of the Wu joss is a well-liked old gentleman, a former mayor, and fairly well-to-do, whose voice is heard in the settling of village affairs, and who is accordingly pleasing and important to associate with. The group does not seem to be used to extend the influence of this man by deliberately attracting neighbors to share his cult (and indeed when he enumerated the members of the group, he did not include the Shyu and Chern who participate), but neither is it restricted by revulsion at his personality.

*Group 4* is one of two groups worshipping King Guo. There are at least six josses of King Guo in Bao-an (each of a different "guardian"). Four of these are objects of worship in their own households only. Two are worshipped by larger groupings of households, all named Guo. In the case of Group 4 all participating households are related, and indeed the group is identical with the group of households who would, on other occasions, worship the same grandfather. We shall come back to this.

*Group 5* is the second cult of King Guo (this time in his manifestation as Seventh Guardian). The cult is maintained by one of two brothers or the son of a deceased third brother (who is the head of a household containing also his own brother). A fourth brother, also deceased, left a son who claims not to participate, although he lives in the same house in which the statue is normally kept.[6] They are joined by a widowed neighbor woman, unrelated but also named Guo, with her household.

4. In 1967 even this was considered too much of a burden, so a duplicate ancestral plaque was made and placed in the transriverine house, obviating the tedious trip across the river, and of course subverting the rite as an expression of unity of the group of descendants. This was fitting enough, in its way, for spatially at least they are indeed no longer unified!

5. A classical text of possible relevance to this opinion is the statement of Confucius in *Analects* (bk. II, chap. 24): "The master said: Worshipping spirits [*Goei*] who are not one's own is flattery" 非其鬼而祭之諂也. No one in Bao-an ever quoted this to me, however.

6. I am suspicious of this. It is possible that the informant did not properly understand the question, or that the ethnographer did not properly ask the question, or that the ethnographer did not understand the reply correctly, or any combination of these.

*Group 6* is the cult of the Queen of Heaven 天上聖母, known popularly as Mhatzuu 媽祖, whose worship in Taiwan is so widespread that she is virtually the patron of the province.[7] During the Japanese administration the government resolved to burn the large, ancient, and infinitely venerable statue of Mhatzuu which is the primary object of worship in the Hsikang temple. By a ploy, Guo Maw-der 郭茂德 of Bao-an managed to steal this statue and hide it in his house, where in secrecy he cared for it until after the island had been liberated from the Japanese and freedom of religion was possible once again. During this time he developed a great attachment to the goddess, and particularly for the exquisite old statue of her that he had been so carefully protecting from harm. As a condition for her return to her temple in Hsikang, Guo Maw-der managed to receive in exchange the permanent loan of a smaller statue from the temple. It is this smaller (but still large) joss that stands upon his altar to this day.

The statue is the object of group worship on a regular basis, but the group is not large. It consists of Guo Maw-der's household and that of his brother. Since his brother's second son has established a second household, his participation makes the total group come to three households.[8] Another brother of Guo Maw-der has moved to Kaohsiung and does not participate. Two others are deceased, both leaving widows. One widow has moved from Bao-an, whereas the other remains and could participate if she chose, but she does not. Nor do his immediate neighbors join Guo Maw-der in his worship of Mhatzuu. Guo Maw-der's unpredictable manner and dogmatic opinions about ritual (and about most anything else!) frighten many people away from close contact with him, and it is easy to understand why the group remains small—only two brothers and their offspring.

*Group 7* is a cult of the Great Saint Equal to Heaven 齊天大

7. Numerous articles exist on Mhatzuu. *See* Liaw Yuh-wen 1967: 69; Lii Tian-chuen 1956: 212; Chern Ren-der *et al.* 1963: 13; Jenq Sheng-chang 1967: 76; Shieh Jin-sheuan 1954; Jiang Jia-jiin 1957: 136 and 1959: 26f. In English, *see* Doolittle 1865: 1.262–264.

8. This particular pattern of family division, in which the eldest son and sons yet to come to majority remain in the household of the father, while a second (and sometimes younger) son founds a separate household, is not particularly uncommon, although naturally splitting the family after the father's death is considered more graceful. *See* Gallin 1966: 142–145.

聖.[9] It is composed of two groups of families surnamed Shyu 徐, plus a widowed neighbor of one of the families. Not all Shyu participate, however. Three families exclude themselves. One joins with some nearby Guo families in Group 3. Another has moved across the river and no longer returns to the group in Bao-an to worship. A third is simply "too busy" to join. But there is a close enough correspondence that many people have come to associate the surname Shyu with the Great Saint.

*Group 8* is a second cult of the Great Saint Equal to Heaven. We recall that Bao-an is located just north of the Tsengwen Chi river. The river varies considerably in depth and width depending upon the rains, and in 1932 it was confined to a wadi between two dikes in an effort to control floods. The wadi is itself almost exactly a kilometer in width at Bao-an, and there is at least another 500 meters of distance in travelling from Bao-an to the dike that defines the northern boundary of the wadi. Because landholdings are typically widely distributed rather than clustered together, and because additional land became available for sale in Taiwan after the land reform of the early 1950s, some families found that the bulk of their land lay to the south of the river, at an uncomfortably great distance from their houses. Accordingly, beginning about fifteen years back, several families have moved across the Tsengwen Chi into permanent houses almost directly across the wadi from Bao-an in a settlement called River Bank Hamlet 溪埔寮, or, more colloquially, South-of-the-River 溪南. Some of these households had been members of god-worshipping groups in the larger Bao-an settlement, but withdrew from them when they crossed the river.

Several of these South-of-the-River families are related to each other, but by no means all of them are. Nevertheless, ten families of the seventeen settled in the transriverine area participate together in a single cult. The owner of the joss, and organizer of the cult, is named Shyu and is the head of the only Shyu household in South-of-

9. The Great Saint is a deified monkey, and bears an alternative Chinese title, the Monkey Lord Suen 猻猴公. Although he is always portrayed as a monkey in paintings and statuary, his simian character seems to have no effect upon his functions as a Taiwanese deity. The most readily available English accounts of the Great Saint are Werner 1922: 325–369 and 1932: 462–468; Christie 1968: 123–130. His story is best known from the novel *Journey to the West* 西遊記, a portion of which has been translated into English by Arthur Waley under the title *Monkey* (Wu 1943).

the-River. In Bao-an proper the cult of this same god, the Great Saint, is virtually a Shyu monopoly. In the transriverine settlement, on the other hand, the cult is area based. In addition to the single Shyu household that maintains the joss, a core of four related families (named Guo) might be thought to make up the core of the cult. Four other Guo families, unrelated either to the first group or to each other, also participate. Another family, named Lii, occasionally joins. A family named Hwang previously participated, but claims not to do so any longer. An additional seven households settled in this area do not join, at least by their own accounting. One of these is Christian, the only Christian family in Bao-an.[10]

Group 8 seems to be made up of the majority of the households in South-of-the-River, and to be based almost completely on physical proximity. It is probably fair to say that it is composed of people who miss the worship groups in Bao-an, now too far away to attend easily, and are pleased, or at any rate satisfied, to substitute a local group. It is probably also fair to say that the relevant ritual solidarity in the transriverine settlement is between neighboring households, and that the foundation of a new cult simply represents the facts of life in a new setting. Theologically (establishing a reciprocal obligation with a god) and socially (doing so with one's neighbors in a new settlement), the cult makes sense.

My vision of these god-worshipping groups as informal groupings of households established in order to set up a reciprocity relationship with a god is not all there is to say, nor the only way to see them. Norma Diamond (1969: 68) reports extremely similar groups in K'un Shen, a village about twenty kilometers from Bao-an, on the seacoast within the Tainan city limits. However she interprets them as lineage[11] groupings which "function mainly as

10. The family has been nominally Christian (Holiness Church) since the head of the present household was converted about forty years ago. They are in general rather defensive and unwilling to discuss the matter, and accordingly are not a significant force for the christianization of the region. The effect of a more recent or more enthusiastic convert in the village might be different, of course.

11. Diamond speaks of "the patrilineage or *tsu* (in Taiwanese, *co*)." This is incorrect. In Mandarin, the characters for ancestor and lineage differ only in tone. Since Diamond does not mark tone, she has apparently confused the two (spelling both *tsu*), and then given the Hokkien reading for *ancestor* and glossed it *lineage*. The same error occurs in her dissertation (1966: 385). The correct words are: ancestor 祖 *Tzuu/chó·;* lineage 族 *Tzwu/chók.*

religious cults, which have become potentially open to those outside of the descent system. . . ." The similarities between her "patrilineages" and what we have here called god-worshipping groups are legion:

> . . . membership is not strictly limited to those tracing descent from a common ancestor. . . . Ancestral worship is not a concern. . . . Property, if it exists, consists of a god figure, representing the patron god of the group, along with a few items for his altar such as an embroidered cloth or candlesticks. . . . There are periodic meetings of the *tsu* [lineage], but these meetings are not limited to the males of the group [as in classical Chinese lineage ancestor worship], nor are they a group commemoration of ancestors. Men, women born into the group or married to a member, and children all participate in the celebration for the patron god at these times. In content and form, these meetings differ little, if at all, from cult gatherings for Taoist or Buddhist gods, or from the ceremonies held at the village temples in honor of the gods' birthdays. They are in the same pattern, the main difference being that recruitment of participants is heavily dependent upon kinship lines (p. 68).

Although I cannot speak for the people of K'un Shen, it would appear on the face of it that we are dealing with the same phenomenon we find in Bao-an. As we have seen among the Boa-an groups, however, denatured lineage activity has little to do with the matter. We saw that the joss of His Highness Wu used by Group 7 was acquired a scant sixty years ago. We saw that the group in South-of-the-River was founded after the war with no reference at all to kinship ties, except insofar as a household participates as a unit. But the firmest evidence is from Group 4. In Group 4 the participants live in three adjacent houses and correspond with those families who would join in the worship of a common grandfather. However, a few houses away live nonparticipants who trace their ancestry to that grandfather's grandfather. Accordingly if the participants wished to consider Group 4 a lineage worship group, it would be entirely possible for them to go up two more generations and enlarge the group to more members and greater glory by including these nonparticipants. Group 4, however, is built on different principles and with different objectives. Its founding was described this way by one village man in a letter I received after my return to the United States: "The matter is fantastically simple: . . . Guo Maw-jou

[郭茂州] often goes to the Temple of King Guo in Tainan to help out. He is a great believer in King Guo, so he brought home a statue of King Guo from the Tainan temple to worship. There is no history of transmission from their ancestors." The worshippers of this statue include everyone living in Maw-jou's own house and the houses to either side.[12] Whether we wish to say they are included as neighbors or as relatives is a matter of choice, but they have clearly been recruited to a recent cult on the basis of a principle different from (or more limited than) membership in a common descent line. And they have been recruited by one of the younger household heads of their group, not by their senior members.

To return to the more general case, the matter of recruitment of worshipping households should be clarified. God-worshipping groups seem to be recruited on a number of different principles and to be used for a wide variety of kinds of solidarity, but always in the basic religious context of establishing relationships of reciprocity with a god. Some groups seem to recruit their member families entirely on the basis of kinship, as for example the cult of King Guo (Group 4). Others recruit more widely. The cult of the Great Saint (Group 8) unites most of the transriverine families in the ritualization of a group clearly based on locality. On the other hand, the cult of His Highness Chyr (Group 1) is so closely tied to the Jang surname group that it seems in every way to be a miniature version of the village-wide King Guo cult, based on surname and village affiliation. The point of all this seems to be that when josses are carved (presumably for pious reasons rather than strictly social ones), they can provide the basis for group worship. At the minimum, the worshippers may be limited to the household of the owner of the joss (and I have not called such arrangements god-worshipping groups). Going beyond this, one founds a god-worshipping group by including one's immediate kinsmen; but there are other solidarities, too, which the group is available to express, be they local, personal, intersurname group, or what have you. It seems as though where there are solidarities to be expressed ritually,

12. Briefly, Maw-jou's house includes households 户 of Maw-jou, his Br, his Fa (with one of Maw-jou's brothers), and his FaBr. The residents of the house to the east are the families of two sons of another FaBr, and those of the house to the west are two FaFaBrSo with their families.

the god-worshipping groups provide a convenient language for this expression.

For this reason there is nothing tidy about them. They conform to a variety of models, and recruitment to them follows any of at least four principles (kinship, residence, surname, personality), often simultaneously, according to whatever seems a reasonable principle of inclusion in a given instance.

In addition to some kind of vague "group solidarity," which we may assume is involved by common special allegiances to certain gods, the form of the rites the group performs dramatizes certain facts, not about the groups, but about the participant families taken individually.

God-worshipping groups worship monthly or every two months, usually on a set day. Thus His Highness Wu (Group 3) is worshipped every two moons on the 24th, 25th, or 26th day (depending upon convenience and the almanac). The Great Saint (Group 8) is worshipped on the 15th day of each moon. The pattern of worship is quite standard and conforms to the following description based on a performance of the worship for His Highness Wu early in 1967.

A table is placed in the middle of the courtyard of the house, and a couple of benches are placed beside it to provide additional space if necessary. The table provides an extension of the lower family altar and allows the bulk of the sacrificial food to be placed in the more roomy courtyard of the house. Cups of wine are arranged along the front side of the lower altar and table. (For convenience we can consider the house a stage with the audience located where the front gate is; the front is the downstage side.) Either three or five cups of wine might be used on each table.[13] Late in the afternoon other families of the group begin arriving. The time varies, depending upon the time of year; the objective is to finish the worship at about dinner time so that it is convenient to take the food home and reheat it for dinner with minimum disruption of the daily

13. Three or five are used in the worship of gods, seven or nine for ancestors. There is no doubt a reason for the selection of these numbers, but people I asked in Bao-an were able to tell me nothing about it beyond "that is how it is done." *See* Lin Tsair-yuan 1968: 40–48 for instructions relating to home worship. This work, of which only the first volume has so far been released, promises to be one of the most valuable sources on Taiwanese customs.

routine. Each family brings two baskets of food. In one of these is the family rice bucket, and this is the only dish rigorously insisted on. Other dishes may be whatever one chooses, although, if possible, it is good to supply a platter of "five meats" [14] at least some of the time. Typically, better food is prepared than for usual meals, and more time is taken in its preparation; but for ordinary monthly or semimonthly worship there is no ritual food as such that must be prepared.

Each arriving family sets its baskets down in two or more rows running downstage from the outdoor table toward the gate and brings one dish to set on one of the two altars, inside or out, to represent the remainder in the baskets. The food is usually brought by one or two women of each participating household accompanied by a host of children. Sometimes the children alone carry out the duty. After the bearer has placed his baskets and put a bowl of food on one of the altars, he lights a handful of sticks of incense, bows before the high altar, where the statue of the god sits upon his tiny dais, and then places the sticks of incense in the dishes of food he has brought. It is not essential that every dish bear a stick of incense, but most of the dishes on the altars do, and *every pot of rice must bear incense*.

After this a few sheets of spirit money are burned. Spirit money is sold in small bundles, and ordinarily one bundle is burned at this time. Several additional bundles are handed over to the children, who busy themselves stacking the bundles in the doorway of the courtyard where they will be burned in small bonfires at the end of the rites.

The normal time during which the food is left on the tables and in the baskets for the use of the god is the time required for three sticks of incense to be burned successively. In fact, it is slightly shorter, because each stick of incense is supplemented by a new one slightly before it is completely burned out. This is merely an appropriate time, however, not a necessary one, and long before

14. Any five of pork, chicken, duck, goose, goat, fish, eggs, or tofu may be used for this purpose. On the "five meats" *see* Lin Tsair-yuan 1968: 40–48; also Saso 1966: 78n. Three meats, although less "attractive" of course, can also be used. In the Wu cult, the host household sees to it that meat is always provided. A Taiwanese proverb, quoted by Saso, is also repeated in Bao-an: "If there are not three, there is no rite" (*bô sam, put sêng lé* 無三不成禮).

the third stick has been consumed one of the attending women will throw divination blocks inquiring of the god if he has finished eating. If he indicates he has not, more incense is burned, and everyone waits for another ten minutes or so and then asks again. When at length he indicates he has finished, the bonfires of paper spirit money are ignited. When the flames have begun to die down, a pitcher of water is fetched and a circle of water traced on the ground about each fire. At this point the rite is at a close. The children are summoned to bow at the altar, which is accomplished with great speed and often hilarity; then unconsumed stubs of incense sticks are removed from the food and dumped unceremoniously upon the dying flames of the money fires, and food is hustled back into the baskets to be brought home once more, that the family may dine on the god's copious leftovers. One of the young boys of the household performs a final ritual act, throwing lighted firecrackers into the early evening air beyond the gate to mark the conclusion of the worship. First a single cracker, then a second single cracker, then a bundle of small crackers that explode not quite simultaneously, and finally another single cracker.[15]

This act of worship fulfills the human obligations toward the divine patron of the god-worshipping group. The god takes pleasure in eating the dainties set before him and derives strength from them. He is also enriched by the money. Indeed, at a worshipping session for His Highness Wu shortly before the Hsikang festival in 1967, extra quantities of money were burned. It was reasoned that as the festival was coming up the gods as well as mortals would have additional expenses, and the extra spirit money was intended as a contribution toward helping the god meet those expenses.

With respect to the relationships between the humans who are participating, some other points are important. One of these is that the worship begins as the first sticks of incense are lit and placed in the first pot of rice. Typically, this is done by the host household, owners of the statue. The rite does not depend on any particular group of households for its accomplishment. Other member households do not join the rite before it begins, necessarily, but as it progresses. There is accordingly no "necessity" in the logic of

15. Informants insist that any ordering is satisfactory, and when goaded by the ethnographer will use other orderings, but this one is usual when they are left alone.

the act of worship itself for any particular members to attend it. If they feel an obligation to do so, it is because they wish to continue a close relationship with the particular god or with the other members of the worshipping group. The rite is accordingly adaptable to accommodate any combination of households that wish to participate, recruited on any basis.

The second point is that it is families which participate, not individual worshippers. The particular constellation of people from a household who attend is irrelevant. But the household, to participate, *must* be represented by the sacrifice of its rice pot, which must be sanctified by bearing sticks of lighted incense. The symbolism involved in this is heavily loaded with meanings. Let us begin by looking at the rice.

Rice is the prime food in this area. When it cannot be afforded, sweet potatoes are substituted, but it is a mark of the prestige of rice that the substitute would not be offered to a visitor. In a culture that feeds its children when they are afraid, and whose etiquette demands that guests be constantly plied with food, tea, and cigarettes, the importance of a pot of rice is yet more formidable. The verb *to eat* in Chinese 吃 cannot stand without an object. In the absence of some specific object (noodles, pork, candy, pineapple), a dummy object is substituted: rice吃飯. The usual greeting to a friend in Taiwan is "Have you eaten (rice) yet?" (*lí chiah-pn̄g bōe?* 你吃飯沒?), to which the reply is either "Not yet" (iā bōe 也沒), or "I've eaten to fulness" (*góa chiah-pá-a* 我吃飽了).

The "potness" of the rice in the present instance is also important, probably more important in modern Taiwan than it might have been in the past or in other parts of China. The reason is this: throughout China the division of a family into two or more families is symbolized by the establishment of a new stove. In theory at least, no two households may share a stove. We recall that in Taiwan the unit of landholding is the household 户 (which corresponds for practical purposes exactly with the family 家). Because the amount of prime land any household may hold is limited by law, some families split prematurely on paper. (It would be convenient to say they split their household and not their family, but usage is not that tidy.) This introduces a gradation between unified household and divided household, because it is necessary to maintain certain divisions before the law which may or may not be very heartfelt. The stove for this reason is not so reliable a symbol of these divisions as it once was. The division of the family is symbolized last, apparently, in its ritual participation. Providing a pot of rice in a god-worshipping group for one family and two pots of rice for two families is one such context. Offering cakes to the Jade Emperor in the early hours of New Year morning is another.[16]

We have noted that the unit of participation in the god-worshipping rites is the family, that is, the unit attached to a rice pot. Individuals do not participate or refuse to participate as individuals; that is ritually unexpressable. It is the family which sacrifices to the god, and the family which the god undertakes to protect. Only in the limiting case in which a family has but one member is individualism involved, and then only in the guise of familism. For the same reason it is the family which by this act of participation is aligning itself with other participating families, and the relationships of individuals in one family to individuals in the other are relevant only if they are so friendly or so hostile and the individuals so placed in the authority structures of their respective families that they can initiate or terminate the participation of their whole families in the group. The family is represented by its rice pot, and the rice pot is there or it is not: it cannot be half there, or all there but one. The manipulation of rice pots is less flexible than the manipulation of human bodies; and it is less fickle. To the extent that the communal participation in these rites engenders willingness to cooperate in other ways, it would tend to stabilize interfamily solidarity.

But presenting the family as a unit before the gods does not merely obliterate ritual individualism vis-à-vis the other participant families. There are certain effects upon the family itself. It is not clear in the Chinese case that praying together means staying together, as Americans are continually instructed, but it *is* important that the divine protection sought by collective sacrifice is protection

16. Descriptions of Chinese New Year are too numerous to cite. For Taiwan, *see* Saso 1966: 14 ff.; Nĝ 155: 1 ff. in Hokkien, 7 ff. in the English edition. For Fukien, *see* Groot 1886: 3 ff. Although these are difficult data to collect systematically, they seem more reliable as guides to "real" or "complete" family division in Taiwan than the stove is. Tax inspectors can see stoves. Only ethnographers stumbling about in the chill air of the New Year morning see the Jade Emperor's offering cakes!

of the family unit. It extends to individuals only insofar as the afflictions they suffer are understood to be afflictions also of the family.[17] Thus the insistence upon the family as the unit of participation makes the family the unit of divine assistance as well. The security provided to the individual by the family is expressed, and it is enhanced, in these rites, for it is the family which may receive the god's assistance.

Rites of worship conducted monthly or every two months are not the only ceremonies performed by the god-worshipping groups. Each god has a birthday, and depending on the finances and enthusiasm of the membership of the group each year, this celebration is more or less festive.[18] At minimum, the birthday celebration might be nothing more elaborate than the usual worship activity. In order to make it more elaborate (more "festive"熱 鬧or "better looking"好看 the Taiwanese say), various elements might be added to this. A punch-and-judy show is usual.[19] The stage is set up at the outer (downstage) end of the courtyard of the house so that the god seated upon the family altar in the central room can enjoy the play. He has better luck than the ethnographer if he can see it above the heads of the people who fill the courtyard in front of him to see it, but it is in any case performed for his pleasure and amusement.

A second element that might be added to the divine birthday celebration is an exorcism of baleful influences from the houses of the participating families. This is accomplished by a hired *âng-*

17. As we have seen, individual disaster does often turn out to be interpreted as familial misfortune.

18. Because Chinese count their age from lunar New Year, birthdays have nothing directly to do with age, and the problem of how old the god is—the usual reaction of Americans when informed of gods' birthdays—becomes irrelevant.

19. For some reason, the villages in the vicinity of Bao-an show a fondness for punch-and-judy performances far in excess of what local custom allows in, say, the Peikang area. Punch-and-judy is a way of rendering private religious rites festive, and is virtually universal in weddings of Bao-an men. The normal theatrical company required is three or four men who perform on a collapsible stage constructed over three locally supplied oxcarts. In years past such a company required musicians as well, but today music is supplied from two phonographs, amplified through massive loudspeakers to a volume it would be difficult to describe, and supplemented by bells, cymbals, and explosions of gunpowder. American movies seem to provide many of the musical compositions on the records. The plays, however, are traditional, although details are improvised.

*thâu-á* priest with participation by one or more gods represented either by *kiō-á* or *tâng-ki*.

Here is how the Jang households of god-worshipping Group 1 conducted the birthday celebration of His Highness Chyr on the 18th day of the sixth moon of the Year of the Ram (25 July 1967 by Western reckoning). Late in the afternoon of the previous day (the 17th) the "portable" village josses were tied securely into the Bao-an palanquin, which was packed aboard a rented truck together with a large ritual umbrella (which always precedes a palanquin in a procession), a few baskets of food offerings, a great deal of spirit money, and twenty-five or thirty men and boys (selected by no principle I could discover). The expedition was bound toward the shrine of Nankuenshen near Peimen, where His Highness Chyr is worshipped. The object was to make camp at the shrine until midnight, and then to offer sacrifices to the god in the early hours of his birthday morning.[20]

The palanquin of josses returned to Bao-an about three o'clock the morning of the 18th, and the josses were carried back to their individual households. His Highness Chyr, as an important god, had been congratulated on the occasion of his birthday. It remained to congratulate him as the patron god of the Jang of Bao-an.

On the afternoon of the 18th, the portable josses were to be found on the family altar of one of the Jang houses. (The location of the rites rotates through the Jang group.) Several participating Jang households brought their lower family altar tables with them, which served to provide table space for offerings. Two of these were added to the family altar inside the central room of the host household, forming with the host's family altar a compound altar the size of three small altar tables. On this were spread rice-flour tortoises. One of these was an enormous confection, perhaps thirty centimeters in diameter, painted with pink features (including curly eyelashes). Surrounding him were smaller rice-flower tortoises, also bearing details painted in pink.[21] These tortoises are a

20. The lunar calendar is the primary means of calculating dates in rural Taiwan, despite the use of the solar calendar in government, educational, military, and semiofficial contexts. For some reason, however, hours are calculated in the Western way, and except for purposes of astrology, the old system of a twelve-hour day has been abandoned. The new day therefore begins at midnight, rather than at eleven o'clock P.M., as it normally would under the traditional Chinese system.

21. The tortoise is a symbol of longevity and stability. On the tortoise in Chinese iconography, *see* Duh Erl-wey 1966: 73–114.

felicitous sacrifice, entirely appropriate to the god's birthday, but at the same time they represent a portion of his wealth in Bao-an, for at the end of the rites, members of the worshipping group take them home (with the god's permission, revealed through *poe*), where they are eaten as a sweet. The effect of this is to bring harmony to the house. The next year, however, each eager devourer of the god's confections must present two tortoises by way of return. It does not seem to occur to people in Bao-an that if in fact this were to happen for very many years running, it would rapidly involve too many felicitous tortoises. In fact, various other arrangements are made, including returning money the following year rather than pastries, which may be lent out again to be returned with interest a year after that. What prevents massive accumulations of money is probably the fact that the capital is used to help support such activities as birthday celebrations with punch-and-judy troupes and chanting *âng-thâu-á* priests. The system can be a source of credit, however, and in the past it possibly served that end more importantly than it does today.

Before the house four more family altar tables were placed. One of these held sacrificial food of the host household. The others held offerings of other households. Because it was the birthday of the god, the ranks of worshipping families were swelled by additional village families, and the baskets were laid out in four columns between the outdoor altars and the front of the courtyard, and represented a total of forty-two visiting households.[22]

The food offerings of the normal worshipping-group participants were not separated from those of the once-a-year families, but the spirit money fires were. There were in total fourteen fires. One of these served to burn a handful of spirit money offered by each family on arrival at the event (for the worship was essentially identical with ordinary god-worshipping group rites described above). The worship of the host family began and ended a few minutes earlier than that of the other participating families, and accordingly one money bonfire was reserved for their spirit money after their rites ended. One fire was for public use at the end of the rites, and was situated at the foot of the yard. In the vacant space between

22. The representatives of these households were in many cases children, who rapidly joined throngs of other children come to watch the punch-and-judy. It is therefore impossible to say which additional families were represented.

two rows of baskets the eleven remaining fires of spirit money were laid out for the use of the eleven nonhost families that were regularly members of the normal god-worshipping group.

In this way three statuses of participant families were distinguished: that of the host family organizing the festival that year, that of other households who were regularly in the service and protection of His Highness Chyr, and that of all other households, participating on a temporary basis only and involving themselves less intimately with the god.

The worship began late in the afternoon and was accompanied by a punch-and-judy show. The host family finally ignited its bonfire of spirit money about seven o'clock, and the remainder of the fires were lit about twenty minutes later. Then the visiting families gathered their food and headed home, and the puppeteers stopped for dinner.

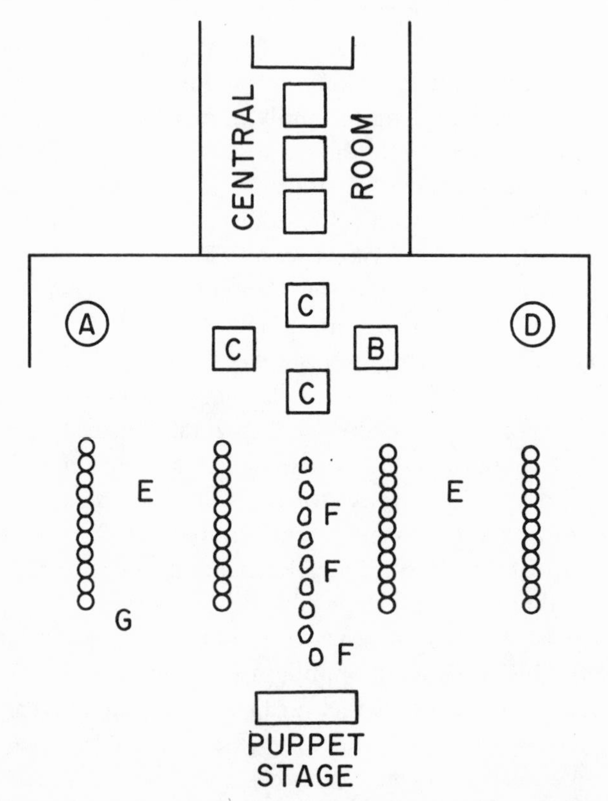


A. Pre-rite fire. B. Host's sacrifices. C. Other sacrifices. D. Host's fire. E. Four columns of food baskets. F. Group members' fires. G. Public, post-rite fire.

For the Jang, however, the evening had barely begun. Shortly before the worship had ended, the *âng-thâu-á* arrived from Hsikang and began chanting incantations over the tables of offerings. When the offerings of food were ultimately withdrawn, the *âng-thâu-á* busied himself with the preparation of purification oil for exorcism by "passing through oil," of the same kind we spoke of earlier in connection with village purification rites.

While the oil was being prepared in the central room of the house, two divination chairs were being tightly held by two pairs of bearers outside, and a drum and two cymbals pounded in a steady rhythm beside them to call down the gods. The first spirit to come was that of His Highness Chyr himself, and the chair bounced crazily to indicate his presence. Then Guo Tian-huah, the *tâng-ki* of the Third Prince, was possessed. At length the second *kiō-á* was possessed, and this presence announced he was also the Third Prince.[23]

When at length the oil was prepared, it was successively fired by the *âng-thâu-á*, and momentary columns of flame and smoke soared several feet into the air, through which each of the josses on the altar was passed and each of the pieces of altar paraphernalia (except those objects used in the worship of ancestors). In this way they were purified of any possible contamination by malign forces. The oil was fired separately for each object, and the room rapidly filled with oily black smoke. The *tâng-ki* meanwhile had called for his ball of nails and had mortified himself with it. Now he stood in the background dangling the ball of nails in one outstretched hand, muttering, bleeding, and shaking, flanked by the eagerly bouncing *kiō-á*. And thus did the gods oversee the purifi-

23. The Third Prince, Lii Ne-chah 李哪吒, is third because he is a third son. To the best of my knowledge his elder brothers were never canonized. There is therefore no First Prince or Second Prince. Recounting the possessions at Chyr Fuu's birthday celebration later, one informant seemed disturbed at the double representation of the Third Prince, and proposed that the First Prince himself must have possessed the *kiō-á*. Had he been speaking of one or another of King Guo's Guardians, it might have been credible. For the Third Prince, however, the statement was meaningless. I suspect that the double representation probably resulted from the illiterate wielders of the *kiō-á* inadvertently writing figures that were easily interpretable as two or three of the simple characters that make up the title of the Third Prince 三太子 when asked for identification. The *âng-thâu-á* who read these simply allowed the point to pass. The important thing was that divine power was concentrated on the place, and that His Highness Chyr was himself one of the attending divinities.

An *âng-thâu-á* or "redhead" Taoist priest, blows rice liquor into a pan of hot oil with a burning wick to purify the room with flame and smoke.

cation of the host's central room, by rites virtually identical to those we saw used earlier to purify the village temple.

When the central room and family altar of the year's host family had been purified in this way, the equipment was carried in procession to other households. First came the *tâng-ki,* leading the group. There happened to be an electrical failure on this particular evening, and his way was lighted only by flashlights and by the eerie and uneven light of the burning wick of the purification oil. The elderly *tâng-ki* had taken out his dentures before going into trance, and his cheeks sank into deep hollows. Now, shaking violently, flailing his ball of nails, and staring vacantly and intensely into the darkness, he looked more like a refugee from the world beyond than a link of communication with it.

Behind him came the pan of oil, hanging from its pole; next, the *âng-thâu-á* with his bottle of rice wine and the two *kiō-á,* bouncing evenly up and down as they dragged their bearers through the warm night. At the rear came masses of children and onlookers. Alongside, before, and behind stumbled the ethnographer.

This odd and holy procession visited each house in which one of the participating Jang families lived, and purified its central room by firing the oil, momentarily illuminating the entire house with a great column of flame, and leaving behind clouds of black smoke.

On its return to the host house, the oil was fired several more times, and individual participants in the procession, as well as members of the host family and anyone else who desired, passed their arms through the flames to purify their own bodies. Finally it was extinguished by blowing a larger amount of wine onto the oil than usual, so that the pan fairly exploded, filling the room first with blinding flame, then with smoky darkness. The attendant gods now revealed their satisfaction with the event: the *kiō-á* chairs pounded their message upon the lower family-altar table, one with such vigor as to put a dent into the hardwood surface, and the *tâng-ki* spoke words of pleasure. Then all three gods left. The *âng-thâu-á* chanted his closing words, and the rites were accomplished.[24]

In the evening the puppet show continued for the enjoyment of

24. I am told that in some years the rites are made even more elaborate by the performance of fire walking. For a description of fire walking, *see* Diamond 1966: 269 ff.

all who came to see it, and of the josses lined up on the family altar.

What are the themes rehearsed in this birthday drama? One is the integration of the Jang households within the larger village. This relation is echoed in the village-wide group that visits Nankuenshen with the palanquin filled with Bao-an's gods. But it is even clearer in the participation of extra families in the rites of worship conducted in the village. The extra worshippers are presumably motivated by reasons of piety and respect for His Highness Chyr, but they are also necessary if the event is to be appropriately *Rehnaw* 熱 鬧 and *Haokann* 好看. I recall that my first introduction to the word *Rehnaw/lāu-jiàt* was in a Chinese textbook, which glossed it "noisy confusion"; and so it certainly seems to the outside observer. To the Chinese participant, however, it is a sense of glorious festivity, characterized by noise and disorganization to be sure, but by levity and a disruption of routine as well. Cities are *Rehnaw*. Festivals are *Rehnaw*. Theatricals are *Rehnaw*. In general, crowds of people are *Rehnaw*. *Rehnaw,* in American terms, is "where the action is." Something *Rehnaw* is bound to be good, and in offering the god a *Rehnaw* birthday, an effort is being made to provide him with a kind of private carnival. This requires more people and more activity than usual.

At the same time the fête must be *Haokann/hó-khòn*$^{n}$. *Haokann* means literally "good-looking"; but it conveys not only an impression of beauty, but of propriety as well. Handsome is indeed as handsome does.

If the event is to be *Rehnaw,* a punch-and-judy show and a lot of people will suffice to make it so, but if it is to be *Haokann* as well, it requires the proper recognition of the god's position vis-à-vis his worshippers, and theirs to their god. This is where the baskets of food and the money fires come in. For although the number of baskets and the amount of spirit money is swelled to make the event *Rehnaw,* the relationships between worshippers and god, which are represented by them, are carefully distinguished to make the event *Haokann*. The god's obligations are laid out before him on the ground in sacrificial fires.

The second theme being rehearsed is the relationship that obtains between the god and his worshipping families: the celebration of their reciprocal obligations. When the worshippers have finished performing their portion of the drama, the god begins his part: he purifies the houses of the families of the god-worshipping group.

The ritual cleansing of the participant houses of His Highness Chyr's god-worshipping group is not done because there are known to be evil influences or malignant spirits in them; it is entirely prophylactic. People say this, too, is done in the interest of making the day *Rehnaw*. The rite, however, is an unambiguous dramatization of the god's interest in the welfare of the god-worshipping group, and of his power in cleansing its dwellings.

Two points are to be made. One concerns the divine presence, the other the houses which are purified by it. In connection with the first, we note that the purification is accomplished by the liturgy and oil burning of the *âng-thâu-á*. The power to create and use exorcist's oil resides in the formulae known to this cleric (which is one of the reasons they are secret). However the rite is performed only in the presence of the divine. It is a *tâng-ki* in trance who leads the procession for His Highness Chyr's birthday, and two supernaturally activated *kiō-á* accompany it. The activity is charged not only with magical power to purge baleful shades, but with the divine presence itself.[25]

The second point is that the protection accomplished by the oil in the central rooms of houses where participant families live is considered to extend both to the house, including such occupants as might not be in worshipping families, and to the families themselves, including such family members as might not in fact live in

25. In the nature of the case, a *tâng-ki* can present this presence in a greater variety of ways than can a bouncing divination chair, and accordingly the rite as described looks as though it is the Third Prince who bears the brunt of the godly responsibility. At that time there was no medium for His Highness Chyr in the village, and Chyr was therefore represented only by a *kiō-á* and could not be as active as the Third Prince. A *tâng-ki* has since been possessed by His Highness Chyr in Bao-an, and presumably this god is now able to take the lead role himself. Incorporating the Third Prince in a major role is not so odd as it might seem, however, for his *tâng-ki* has been well-established for more than twenty years, and with his success there has grown up a feeling that the village is under the immediate, beneficent, day-to-day protection of the Third Prince. That such an immediate and important god should participate in, or even lead, such rites is not strange. His participation, by the way, sneaks village interests and the village ritual group (as opposed to Jang interests and the Jang ritual group) in at the back door once more; His Highness Chyr is worshipped by the Jang. The Third Prince has no worship group and is at the disposal of the entire village.

the house but still have not divided formally from the family (as a child in boarding school in a city). The point is important when we remember that Chinese family splitting does not necessarily involve changing houses, and often several families live in one house, not all of whom are part of the god-worshipping group (though I believe in the case of His Highness Chyr's birthday celebration, this discrepancy did not arise). We are reminded faintly of the space/personnel association in village/surname definition that arose in connection with King Guo earlier. Just as the surname group does not fit exactly into its village, so the family does not fit perfectly into its building; and in both cases a divine being forms a species of integration by generously extending himself to cover anybody who can be included under either principle.

### EXORCISM: THE SHIEHTUU

When the rite of passing through oil is performed in connection with a god's birthday, it is a prophylactic rite, and its performance is primarily a drama of what the god *would* do if the houses of his devotees were threatened by disaster. This is not to say that such purification is not desirable or efficacious. Of course it is. But it is not necessary, save as it is a part of the festivity of the god's birthday.

The case is somewhat different when exorcism is performed for the relief of particular misfortunes of a specific family. During the period I lived in Bao-an, several families attempted to improve their financial fortunes and the health of their members by means of a rite called a *Shiehtuu* 謝土.[26]

This rite was typically performed when the family was suffering from generalized inharmony that could not be directly related to any specific misfortunes. Ill health, financial reversals, and domestic quarrels stalked in the family circle, and eventually it was decided

26. The term literally means "thanking the earth." According to Douglas (1899: 425) the expression (pronounced *siā-thó·* in Hokkien) means to give thanks to the earth god after a burial. Groot (1892–1910: 1.219 ff.) discusses these sacrifices at the grave, but makes no reference to this term. I have never come upon it used in connection with funeral rites. Although Douglas's interpretation makes sense in relation to the literal meaning of the characters, I can only insist that in my experience the rites denoted by the word have nothing to do with funerals, but with correcting family misfortunes through exorcism.

that something was wrong and an oracle was consulted which recommended a *Shiehtuu*.[27]

The *Shiehtuu* rites are complex and depend for their full exposition on an understanding of the chants themselves, which I do not have. In general, they are an exorcism and ritual cleansing of the house and the people living in it. The rite seems to be a composite of several different parts, which occur also in other contexts. I do not propose to analyze all of these here, but to mention certain ones that are directly relevant to our present purposes.

The priests perform chants in the afternoon which contain (as I understand it) magical formulae designed to bring the evil forces in the house under their power. Early in the evening one priest seats himself on the floor of the central room of the house and faces a crockery pot over which a piece of brown paper is tightly stretched and on which a few grains of rice have been placed. At one side of the paper there is a series of small holes, perhaps five to eight millimeters in diameter. As the priest chants and burns small yellow papers said to "open the eyes of spirits," an assistant bangs rhythmically on a small gong. The grains of rice make their way in short, irregular hops from their randomly scattered positions across the brown paper on the pot toward the holes, until they tumble into the pot through these small openings. When the last grain of rice has dropped into the pot, the evil forces of the house are considered to be concentrated in the pot, and it is carried as quickly as possible out of the village to a spot some distance into the fields, often the bed of a dry irrigation canal. Here it is staked to the ground with a charm stake of the same general type as we saw used in identifying the forts at the corners of the village. This expedition to the fields is overseen and led by a *kiō-á* borne by village people, although one of the *âng-thâu-á* bears the pot and stakes it to the ground.

27. The selection of this particular rite seems to have depended on the following facts. The oracle consulted was a *kiō-á,* which was read by Guo Maw-der. The oracle recommended that a *Shiehtuu* be performed, or so Maw-der interpreted it. Now Maw-der had a standing arrangement with a company of *âng-thâu-á* in Tainan city. They would perform a *Shiehtuu* for 2,000 *Kuay* ($50), and Maw-der, for recommending them, received a compensation. No one I asked about this devious arrangement thought fraud could possibly be involved. The *kiō-á* had recommended a *Shiehtuu,* and if Maw-der recommended priests, he was entitled to compensation if the priests chose to give it to him.

A godly presence, occupying the divination chair, overseas the burning of paper money on the site where a ceramic pot of evil influences, captured in a house, has been staked down outside the village.

The forces in the pot are dangerous. Were they driven from the house but allowed to remain in the village, they would endanger the houses of others, if not of their original host. Once they are taken outside the village, they can reenter it only by overpowering the soldiers who man the boundary lines and forts of the village itself. This is perhaps one of the most explicit points of tangency between the microcosm of the house and the macrocosm of the village, each seen as a sacred domain existing in space.

By the time this expedition has returned, a basin of oil has been heated for the rite of "passing through oil," which constitutes the heart of the rites. Under the direction of the *kiō-á* and usually a *tâng-ki* as well, the oil is fired in the central room of the house, where each object of the altar is passed through successive columns of flame. Then it is carried to the other rooms of the house and is fired once in each room. As it leaves the room, firecrackers are ignited in the room. Both the oil fire and the firecrackers are understood to frighten, purge, and destroy malign forces, and the house has already been emptied of those forces that were carried out magically captured in the pot. When all the rooms have been thus purified, the oil is carried to each corner of the house and fired once more, as a stake with a charm secured to the top of it is pounded into the floor of the central room, beneath the center of the red approach table, or higher of the two family altar tables.

When this has been completed, the *âng-thâu-á* performs a rite that by itself is known as "changing luck" 改 運. This is performed by some *âng-thâu-á* in public temples in Tainan, and occasionally occurs in Bao-an without an *âng-thâu-á* if someone else who knows the chants can perform it. Each member of the family is provided with a paper figure of himself, which he carries across a bench representing a bridge. Arriving at the end of the bench, he sits down and the officiant takes away the paper figure and recites charms causing malign forces affecting the body to rest instead in the paper body, which is subsequently burned outside the boundaries of the village.

The *Shiehtuu* rites usually last from early afternoon to just past midnight. Usually a punch-and-judy show is provided for the pleasure of household gods in the afternoon and early evening, and neighbors are invited to bring food for late-afternoon sacrifices to the Good Brethren, that is, to the hungry ghosts in the vicinity by way of propitiation. The punch-and-judy, whatever its supernatural effects, provides an added inducement to would-be sacrificers.

One of the features most striking about all this is that the core of the rites, the purification of the house, is a scaled-down version

An *âng-thâu-á* priest sets a stake, representing a fort, at the corner of a house so that supernatural soldiers will protect the house from malign forces.

of the rites of exorcism and purification described in connection with the protection of the village from generalized evil influences. The stakes at the four corners of the house represent the forts of the house, just as the stakes at the four trees around the village represent forts. The purification by oil is the same. The purification of individual sacred objects from the family altar is the same as the purification of objects on the altar of the village temple.

In other words, one part of this rite, and, so far as I understand it, the core part, makes the house a microcosm of the village. It is guided by the same logic (expelling malign forces), expressed in the same idiom (forts), performed by the same practitioners (*âng-thâu-á*) with the same equipment (oil, stakes) as the village exorcism described earlier. This general homology between the village macrocosm and the family microcosm has appeared more than once so far and is worth singling out for further examination.

# Chapter 7
## *The General Homology Between Village and Family*

We have seen that in Taiwan a widely shared ideology assimilates all supernaturals to the dead: the gods are the virtuous dead; the ancestors and ghosts, all the rest. The supernaturals—gods and ghosts—form the integration between social structure on the one hand and a generalized state of harmony or inharmony in the world on the other. The ghosts are used primarily as an explanation for disaster. Disaster is averted or (if it has already struck) expelled by the gods, and for this reason alliances are struck with the gods on the basis of mutual obligations.

We have also seen that this scheme works almost identically at the family and the village level. Both the family (taken as an internally undifferentiated unit) and the village (taken as an internally undifferentiated unit) involve themselves in cycles of mutual obligation to protecting divinities, and both deal with disaster through exorcism of ghosts using similar ritual dramas. The dangerous supernaturals, the ghosts to the north of the village, are dangerous for both. (The point is dramatized by the necessity, during the *Shiehtuu* rite, of carrying the pot of evil influences outside the limits of the village, not merely out of the house.)

In general, the relation between the village and its protecting gods and threatening ghosts is the same as the relation between the family and its patron gods and threatening ghosts. The discovery of such a detailed homology between different sets of religious data isolates a set of cultural constructs for religiously construing and manipulating the world which is independent of the particular units involved in any one instance or manifestation of the set (and that presumably is also available for use in the organization of additional contingencies not covered by the instances at hand). We are provided with a kind of least-common-denominator formulation of Chinese religious conceptions whereby contingencies in the human world are guarded against by organizations of people forming alliances with gods and exchanging worship for divine protection. The size and nature of the human unit involved seems to be related to the nature of the disaster guarded against (other villages, say, as opposed to individual bankruptcy), but the approach is consistent, even to the rites involved. And for this reason it is basic to our attempts to understand Chinese village religion.

The organizational elements common to the members of the homology are not the only features of note about them, of course. At least two extensions occur. One concerns the village. The village, unlike the family, makes use of its patron god as a symbol of itself, both internally, and in its participation in a complex pattern of relations with other villages. The patron god is used (as to some extent are other gods that have come to be seen as its special protectors, such as those with long established mediums in the village) as a symbolic point of cooperation and coordination in integrating groups of villages or groups within the village. We saw this in the instance of King Guo, whose worship by all people of Bao-an involves them in the Guo faction, including other Guo-dominated villages that also worship King Guo. Among other things, the handling of the god's statue forms the context for a dramatic enactment of both present and past tensions and alliances between villages throughout the Hsikang region. The same pattern of self-symbolization by means of one's patron god does not seem to occur at the family level. When a god is used for self-symbolization by his worshippers, his role is being extended beyond his more basic function as a protector. This extension at the village level does not find parallels in family action.

That is not to say that the self-symbolization function *could not* occur at a subvillage level, but only that in Bao-an it *does* not. In considering parallels between family and village, it is tempting to consider the loosely organized god-worshipping groups as parallel to groups of villages sharing a patron god. For the time being at least it is probably also wrong. In a god-worshipping group we do not actually find parallel patterns of self-symbolization by means of a god in contrast to and in competition with other god-worshipping groups. The worshippers of His Highness Chyr, for example, are not played off against (or allied with) the worshippers of Mhatzuu. Nor are members of such groups ordinarily recruited on principles standard and explicit enough for us to expect that that would happen.

This does not say that it does not or could not happen at other times or in other villages. The cult of His Highness Chyr is locally a Jang cult, after all, and one can imagine that in a more factionally inclined village than Bao-an, god-worshipping groups could easily be involved in factional groupings based on surname, kinship, or other principles. Perhaps if the historical battles of Hwang and Guo had not left such a clear mark in local memory, the symbolization aspect of the village-surname cult of King Guo might not be so clear as it is. Possibly the self-symbolization function of a worshipper's god is potentially as readily available to the family in its relations with other families through its god as to the village in its relations with other villages through its god. The former just does not happen to be the case in Bao-an.

The second extension concerns the family ghosts, whom we shall meet in the material yet to come. The family ghosts are spectres of particular family members who are structurally irregular in the context of normal family and descent-line expectations.* These shades haunt only their own families and are embodiments of the failure, mismanagement, or violation of various explicit principles of social organization, inevitably connected with the maintenance of a descent line. They are post-hoc explanations for perceived inharmonies, and typically they must be pacified by correcting the irregularities before the disaster they are reified to explain can be relieved. We shall return to them in a moment.

The homology between village and family is enlightening, but it cannot be pushed to extremes. It is perhaps more an overlap than an isomorphism.

It seems to me that the homology between village and family,

* The spectres that concern the village as a whole are not those anomalous in these ways, but rather those who died in "unnatural" ways. Hungry ghosts might endanger either village or family; what distinguishes them is their anonymity. Hungry ghosts are the ordinary ghosts of other people's families all across Taiwan (or perhaps all across China or all across the world). The frequent sacrifices for their pacification keep their sad condition constantly in mind and set the stage for the appearance of family and village ghosts, but they are seldom exercised or charged with responsibility for particular instances of inharmony.

TABLE 4
FAMILY-VILLAGE HOMOLOGY

| *Village* | *Family* | *Behavior* |
|---|---|---|
| Gods used as symbols of the village. | — | Interlocal festivals, war. |
| Gods worshipped as village protectors. | Gods worshipped as family protectors. | Sacrifices. |
| Outside ghosts that must be defended against. | Outside ghosts that must be defended against. | Forts, exorcism. |
| — | Ghosts of "unstructural" family members. | Social restructuring: deification, postmortal adoptions, spirit marriages, etc. |

even if it is not complete isomorphism, is still important. It means that within certain limits a single conceptual scheme is being applied to both realms, that within certain limits membership in one is seen as similar to membership in the other, and that problems in one might be solved as they are in the other. But more importantly it means that for the natives themselves this conceptual system, including the way in which it organizes experiences of success and failure and the way it meets potentially baleful contingencies by alliances (be it with a god, another village, or other members of a god-worshipping group), is separable from any specific context and is a more general set of principles which may be applied in other contexts. We should expect to meet the same phenomena again and again among diverse social groupings. In a religious idiom, we would expect to see the same scheme reproduced at, say, town or county levels. (Can we identify the cult of the "city god" 城隍 here?) But interactionally, we might wonder how much of a transformation is needed to relate this scheme to one describing Chinese social alliances in general.

# Chapter 8
## *The Family Ghosts*

So far we have been looking at the ritual aspects of the family as similar or identical with those of the village. The village has patron gods, and so does the family. The village offers them sacrifices, and so does the family. In this way the village indebts the god to it, and the same is true for the family. When disaster befalls, the village exorcises it. So does the family.

But let us not press the analogy too far. A family, after all, is not just a shrunken village, nor is a village merely an inflated family. There are, in the family, certain principles of social organization which are not normally an important focus of life at the village level, and prime among these is the ideology of the descent line.

We saw earlier that the descent line, and the idiom of caring for the elderly and deceased, was a vital part of the imagery of family life. We saw that in an attempt to approximate the ideal of a continuous descent line, Taiwanese resort to social fictions, such as adoption, when nature does not provide male offspring. When we turn our attention to ghosts and exorcism we find that the same principles arise, for persons who die without having descendants, that is, without becoming a link in a continuous descent line, are believed to be deprived of the offerings their descendants would normally provide, to be tragically impoverished in the land of shades, and to make all possible efforts to induce the living to take note of their condition and, if possible, to correct it.

Normally, little attention is paid to such spirits. In a sense they come into existence only when they are needed to explain a disaster. But should disaster occur, the medium need only find one of the family to have died without offspring, or for other reasons to be without a descent line, and a ghost is immediately reified as the cause of the current disaster. These structural anomalies are explanations *in posse,* which can be actualized when there is need for supernatural explanation.

How does one choose between a family ghost as an explanation for disaster and general ghosts of the kind we have just been discussing? Taiwanese answer that it depends on what kind of ghosts happen to be causing the trouble, which is revealed by gods through divination. Behaviorally, however, regularities emerge that do not require either ghosts or gods for their explanation.

The most common disaster interpreted as involving supernaturals is sickness. When somebody is sick, one gives him household remedies, or other medicines recommended by a traditional herbalist or a Western-style druggist. If recovery is not prompt, or if it is followed by relapse, a doctor is consulted, who administers Western-style medicine.[1] It is only when medical science has been tried and has failed, or when the patient is troubled by disease after disease in rapid succession, or when several members of the family become sick with different diseases that supernatural causes are considered, and a supernatural is consulted.

There is a tendency for some mediums to favor certain kinds of explanation. We have seen that if a man consults a *kiō-á* read by Guo Maw-der, he is apt to find he needs a *Shiehtuu.* If he consults a certain medium in nearby Chiali, it is likely to develop that he is troubled by a family ghost. However, to be troubled by a family

1. I insist on the term *Western-style* rather than simply *Western* because, although the commodities are themselves of Western invention and often Western manufacture, their application is somewhat different. Because many drugs are openly available in Taiwan which are sold only on prescription in the West, many Taiwanese readily use medicine more powerful than is usual in, say, the United States. Further, since instructions are normally not in Chinese or are not read (or both), there is a generally poor relation between drug and complaint. Doctors vary widely in licensing and quality, and rural people do not differentiate very precisely between a "doctor" trained for two months in the 1930s and one with a degree from an American or Japanese medical school trained in the 1960s. In general, doctors are perceived as people who give shots, and a session with a doctor which does not involve getting a shot is thought by many to be wasted money. Typically, the doctor's fee is based on his sale of medicine or a shot to the patient, and this may in certain cases also influence diagnosis and treatment. Impressive progress has been made and is being made in medical services in Taiwan, but it would be wrong to suppose that the presence or use of Western-style medical products implies either a standard of medical service or level and direction of popular knowledge comparable with that in the homelands of these products.

ghost he must first *have* a family ghost; that is, he must have a deceased family member who for some reason is outside a descent line. If he knows there is such a one among his family dead and he suspects it is the cause of his problems, he is likely to go to a medium whose god is known to be capable in handling family ghosts. If he does not have one, and suspects that he needs a *Shiehtuu* directed to more generalized forces of malice, he may consult Maw-der.[2] And often he consults several different oracles, trying to develop consensus among them or (seen another way) a solution he can live with.

SPIRIT BRIDES

Let us now turn our attention to some specific instances of families being haunted by ghosts of their deceased members and the ways in which these problems are solved. We might conveniently start by considering a phenomenon called by the Chinese "hell marriage" 冥婚, which we might more happily designate "spirit marriage" after the term most commonly used to designate the bride, "female spirit" 女鬼.[3]

Spirit marriage occurs when a girl who has died in childhood appears to her family in a dream some years later and asks to be married.[4] A groom is found by the family by laying "bait" in the middle of a road. This usually takes the form of a red envelope (used in China for gifts of money). A passer-by sooner or later picks up the envelope, and immediately the family of the spirit come out of hiding beside the road and announce to the young man that he is the chosen bridegroom. If he refuses, he is of course in danger of vengeance by the ghost, but his enthusiasm for the venture can be increased by an offer of a large dowry if necessary.[5] The ghost is

2. Maw-der, by the way, also gives penicillin shots for a moderate fee.
3. The more literary and more precise term is "lonely maiden" 孤娘, pronounced homonymously with the term for "young maiden" 姑娘, as Guniang/*ko·-niû$^n$*. The homonymy is dramatic, but can be confusing enough in spoken language to explain the preference for the term "female spirit" in Bao-an.
4. Some of the following material on spirit marriage is also examined in Jordan 1971b.
5. Wu Ying-tau (1970: 143) reports that in some cases the natal family of the ghost hires a go-between to find a poor country lad as husband, rewarding him with such a generous dowry that he can use it as brideprice when he takes a human bride later. I know of no such cases in Bao-an, but

married to him in a rite designed to resemble an ordinary wedding as closely as possible, although the bride is represented only by an ancestral tablet. No affinity is established between the groom and his spirit-wife's family in this way, and the only obligation he and his family have is to accommodate the ancestral tablet of the bride on their family altar and to provide it with sacrifices as though the spirit bride had married in life.

This at least seems to be the traditional form, and it is the form of spirit marriage described by Li (1968) on the basis of his fieldwork in Changhua. In Bao-an and the surrounding area spirit marriage occurs differently. The ghost seldom appears in a dream to her parents to demand a husband. In the cases with which I am familiar she strikes misfortune upon her natal family or the families of her married sisters. This usually takes the form of sickness of one or more family members. When the sickness is not cured by ordinary means, the family turns to divination and learns of the plight of the ghost through a séance. Usually several sessions are held with different gods before a marriage is finally agreed to by the living. The most common oracle to which problems of spirit marriage are put is the female medium of a so-called Little God [6] in Chiali. This particular god's *tâng-ki* specializes in spirit marriages and has a stock of equipment for their performance which can be rented by the day. Therefore, in deciding to consult the Little God, an individual or a family is fairly clearly anticipating a spirit marriage, and it will be one of my assumptions in what follows that a spirit marriage is initiated by the family involved.

Another point in which spirit marriage in Bao-an differs from the spirit marriage Li describes is that in recent years virtually all bridegrooms have been the husbands of married sisters of the ghost brides. This is a point we shall consider in detail below.

Finally, the ritual itself has been elaborated somewhat in Bao-an

---

the variant seems credible. Eberhard (1968: 153) notes at least one case in antiquity of a ritually dangerous parcel being passed on by leaving it on the ground for an ill-starred finder. Apparently the custom is not confined to postmortal matchmaking.

6. The term "little god" 小神 is used to refer to the divinized spirits of local people, whose oracles are consulted primarily by women for information on the rearing of children and other of the family's affairs that are entirely or largely under the government of women. We shall have more to say of them later on.

(and other villages that have access to the Little God), for the bride is no longer represented only by her ancestral tablet, but by a paper, wood, and cloth dummy, who represent her in a more graphic way and, to me at least, increases her dramatic value considerably.

In his book on Taiwanese customs, Lin Tsair-yuan (1968) has described "hell marriage" as dying out (p. 110). During the time I lived in Bao-an, however, such marriages were enjoying great popularity throughout the region. And although informants often could not recollect similar marriages from their childhood, everyone seemed aware of their frequency at the present time.

But spirit marriage, for all its "popularity" in southwestern Taiwan today, is not something local people take pride in as they are proud, say, of lunar New Year or of the triennial festival at Hsikang. On the contrary it is rather a shameful thing. Lou Tzyy-kuang (1968: 24) writes: "In Taiwanese custom having a deceased, maiden daughter is a shameful business. When one's daughter dies, she is buried in a simple grave, and her ancestral tablet is then put in a secluded place in the house, such as the room where people slept before she was born or behind some door, to guard against other people finding it." [7] Arthur Wolf (personal communication) reports similar attitudes in northern Taiwan: "In the Sanhsia area [of Taipei county] most families place the tablet of an unmarried girl in a back room because 'it looks so bad to have an unmarried girl's tablet on the altar.' The motive for a ghost marriage is to remove the unsightly tablet from the house."

Accordingly, and to my frustration, I would often learn of a spirit marriage only some days after the event. The two recorded here were examples I stumbled onto after about a year and a half of residence in the village. When I left the village, a third potential groom was negotiating with the ghost to avoid marriage with her. All three follow very nearly exactly the same form, which I understand is typical for this region at this time.

In both spirit marriages described below the bride's family lived in Bao-an, and, as it happened, both grooms lived in the same nearby village, and both confirmed the oracle of the Little God

7. 在台灣民俗中，有孤娘的是很可耻的事，他們自己的女兒死了，極簡單地埋葬之後，就将其神位另外擺在屋裏的僻處，例如她生前睡的屋子裏；或者某個門後；以防别人的發現。

through the same god, Yang Fuu Tayshy 楊府太師,[8] who is the patron of their village. These particular points of similarity can probably be taken to be coincidence.

The bride, in the first instance, was the spirit of a woman who would have been in her middle forties had she not died in her first year of life. After her death her mother bore another girl, who grew up and was married to a man in a village some ten kilometers from Bao-an. This same husband of the spirit's younger sister was the groom selected by the spirit for her "hell marriage." Here is a summary of his account of the experience:

Three or four years ago I had a dream of a woman. At the same time things were not going very well with my family. I told my mother about the dream, and she went to the Little God in Chiali. The Little God revealed that there was a ghost from a certain place haunting me. The Little God simply gave me some incense ash to eat and told me to offer some cups of tea and worship in such and such a direction, asking for peace. At that time I was incredulous, and unwilling to believe in what I couldn't see. Later on my mother asked the Little God several more times. One time the Little God said that a female spirit wanted to marry me. Of course no one wants to marry a spirit! You only marry a spirit when there is nothing else you can do. When I heard that a spirit wanted to marry me, I was very skeptical. Could such a thing really happen? I wanted to get to the bottom of the business, so I invited the god Yang Fuu Tayshy [to activate a divining instrument in a séance] so I could ask.

The first time he came, Yang Fuu Tayshy said it was correct that the spirit was from a certain place, and he promised to help me and make her leave. After the séance I went to my wife's mother's house in Bao-an to ask her opinion about it; things were not going very well there either, because of the spirit.

From then on for almost three years I did not visit my wife's mother, not because I didn't like my mother-in-law, but because I thought perhaps if I avoided going there the ghost would leave by herself and would stop coming to haunt me. Later the people in my family began getting sick. Whenever this happened I would go to the Buddhist temple and get some incense ash and they would get well. We paid no attention to the spirit. But although we would take medicine or eat incense ash and then get well, still sickness and other problems kept coming back.

8. The form *Tayshy* appears to be a localism, the more general form of the god's title being Yang Fuu Dahshy 楊府大師, "Great Master Yang."

About eight or nine months before I got married to the spirit I had a dream about her in which she let me see her body. I had another séance with Yang Fuu Tayshy and asked him to help in inducing the spirit to leave. This time Yang Fuu Tayshy said I should have to marry her, so I went to Bao-an and told my wife's mother, and with Chyuan-shoei [全水] [the younger brother of the ghost] I went to Chiali to ask the Little God about it. The Little God said the ghost did not demand an elaborate wedding; just a simple affair would do. The day was selected by Yang Fuu Tayshy because he is the patron god of our village, and I wanted him to be sort of host in the whole business. After all, a spirit is something we cannot see. If you are going to marry a spirit, how do you know it is the right spirit? If it is the wrong one, then later on things become even more troublesome, so the reason for inviting the host god of my village on the wedding day was to make sure it was the right spirit; and the divination instrument of Yang Fuu Tayshy led the bride's taxi. Since the wedding with the spirit, the family has been very peaceful, and nothing unfortunate has happened. . . .

Yang Fuu Tayshy says the spirit was haunting me as much as twenty-four years ago. At that time she was about nineteen. Even then I used to get sick, but was cured with Western medicine or, if that didn't work, I got a bit of incense ash from the Buddhist temple and ate it, and then I would recover. I never thought I was being haunted until I had the first dream.

The second case is similar to the first. The groom was named Dah-tour大頭. This time, however, there were two brides, both of them deceased younger sisters of the groom's wife. Dah-tour's wife, named Shiow-yueh 秀月, was from Bao-an. Shiow-yueh was thirty-six years old, had been married to Dah-tour for nearly fourteen years, and had several healthy children. About a year before the ghost wedding she became subject to periods of illness characterized by weariness and aches. Western medicine, the family maintained, did not seem to help her, and although she never considered herself to be especially religious, she was persuaded by friends and neighbors to consult an oracle. She selected the Little God of Chiali. The Little God, not unpredictably, announced that she was sick because a spirit in her home wanted to marry her husband, Dah-tour. Dah-tour relates that he did not believe this, so he went to Chiali to consult the Little God once more, who repeated the information. At length a divination session was held with Yang Fuu Tayshy. The results were about the same as in the first case.

Two spirit brides, made of paper and cloth and wearing jewelry, represent girls who died in childhood. They await the arrival of their living groom before their father's family altar.

Yang Fuu Tayshy was implored to drive the ghost away, but finally declared that the only thing to do was marry the spirit and have done with it. Dah-tour accordingly agreed to marry the ghost. It is not clear just when he learned that there were two ghosts involved, but presumably it made no particular difference to him. As soon as he agreed to marry the ghost Shiow-yueh recovered. Things went well for a couple of months, and he decided that perhaps the marriage would be unnecessary. At this Shiow-yueh fell ill again, and another interview with Yang Fuu Tayshy convinced them that the marriage was indeed a business to be taken seriously.

Meanwhile, Shiow-yueh's family in Bao-an was holding divinations of its own, although I do not know the details of these. They learned from them that Shiow-yueh's two deceased younger sisters both wanted to be married. One wanted to marry Dah-tour, and the other wanted to place an envelope in the road in the usual way. This was done, but the groom so selected did not please the ghost, who backed out of the agreement, and decided to marry Dah-tour too. According to Dah-tour, the family later learned that the groom selected by placing an envelope on the road was "a hoodlum who never does any work and just goofs around all the time." Perhaps more to the point, he was from a village with which Bao-an has long had rather chilly relations.

The reader is best equipped to understand the unique features of a spirit marriage rite if he is familiar with such rites among the living. These have been described in detail elsewhere.[9] For present purposes it is enough to know the following. At an appointed hour on the day selected for the wedding the groom and members of his family appear in a fleet of taxis to meet the bride at her house and take her to the groom's house.[10] Before she leaves the house, she and the groom bow before the bride's ancestral tablets. She is escorted to the taxi with a rice-winnowing basket held over her head to screen her from the view of heaven, so that her absence from her traditional home will not be noticed until after she is integrated into her new home. With her come her parents and other family members, who will be the guests for the day at the house of the young husband.

On arrival at the groom's house, the bride and her party are welcomed very formally, even stiffly, and served a banquet to which the groom's friends and relatives are invited. At the groom's house the bride and groom bow before the groom's ancestral tablets to symbolize her new position as a member of his line.

When the bride is a spirit, the rites are somewhat different and include repeated symbolization of the status of the marriage as appeasement to a deceased spirit. Here is a description of part of the rites for the first spirit marriage described above.

For the ceremony itself the bride was represented by means of a

9. Gallin 1966: 204–213, Nĝ 1955: 41–67 (English edition: 62–96), Lin Tsair-yuan 1968: 62–111.

10. The use of a palanquin to carry a bride to her husband's house is extinct in Taiwan in all but a very few mountainous areas at the time of this writing. Apparently this ancient method of nuptial transport has been successfully replaced by taxis in the short space of ten to twenty years, for even middle-aged women report they were carried to their husband's house in sedan chairs. The hour of the groom's arrival is important to the success of his married life and is ordinarily selected by a professional almanac interpreter.

dummy of paper and cloth. She had a head made from a picture of a smiling young girl clipped from a wall calendar. This was pasted to a narrow strip of wood, which formed the backbone. Arms were made from padded newspaper and were jointed at the shoulders to allow them to be lifted in dressing her. She wore a pair of trousers and a skirt of white, then a red dress, covered over with a white lace outer dress that was considered part of the red dress.[11] This counted as three layers of clothing. On her feet were red children's shoes. Her hands were made of white gloves, stuffed with newspaper, and then decorated with numerous gold-colored bracelets and rings of the same kind that a real bride would wear, except that real brides use real gold. Round her neck dangled a gold pendant, also imitating the costume of living brides. The figure was seated, and measured perhaps seventy or eighty centimeters from her shoes to the top of her veiled head. Her head, and her hands even more, were out of proportion with the rest of her, and her face smiled in a way most unseemly for a Chinese bride.

Early in the morning of the day she was to be taken to her new home, the dummy of the bride was moved into the central room of the house and seated facing the door with her back to the family altar. The ancestral tablet, which had been kept in the shrine box with the other family tablets, was carefully removed and inserted into the figure of the bride, so that it rested inside her, invisible from outside. In this way the bride's dummy was animated with the ghost that was to be married.

In the central room of nearly every rural Taiwanese house stands an altar. At the center of it is an incense pot in which joss sticks can be placed to honor the gods. At the left end of the altar are the family's ancestral tablets, usually enclosed in an outer shrine box, behind a separate incense pot. Incense can also be burned in a censer hanging just inside and above the front door. Normal sacrifices of incense in these places are one or three joss sticks. Throughout the time the bride sat in the central room of the house, rows of seven sticks were kept burning in all three places, and in addition powdered incense smouldered in a pot placed on a tray bearing money and other of the smaller items from her dowry.

The dowry consisted of 14,000 *Kuay* ($350) in cash, three suit-

11. Most spirit brides, like most modern living brides, wear white. Red is a traditional wedding color, however, and the use of red together with white made a perfectly credible and recognizable wedding dress.

cases full of clothing and cloth, several bound parcels containing, I was told, "similar items" and sundry foods used in worship. In addition there were symbolic bits of charcoal, leeks, cigarettes, and other items conventionally exchanged between marrying families and symbolizing long life, fertility, etc.[12]

The groom arrived at the appointed hour of the forenoon by taxi. He wore black rather than white gloves, but was in every other way indistinguishable from any other groom. The bride was escorted to a waiting taxi, her head being shielded from the heavens with a rice-winnowing basket, in every way like those used for ordinary brides, save somewhat smaller and bearing a yellow paper charm, said to be written by the divining stylus of Yang Fuu Tayshy, with the words "Rice-Sieve of Peace" 安米台.[13]

In a separate taxi rode the divining stylus of Yang Fuu Tayshy and his statue. It was he, of course, who had overseen the engagement, had finally given in to the ghost, and had fixed the day for the marriage, a day, I might add, satisfactory by the Chinese almanac.

The marriage included a feast at the house of the groom, as do all weddings. On the second day, there was also a feast at the house of the bride's family, again following the pattern of all weddings. With this the marriage was accomplished. The ancestral tablet was removed from the dummy bride and placed among those of the groom's family on his altar. The three layers of clothing were removed and returned to the establishment that leased them. And the remainder of the dummy, including the artificial gold rings and bracelets, was burned.[14]

12. For a discussion of ritual exchanges related to dowry and bride-wealth, *see* Nĝ 1955: 52 f. (English edition: 73–75), Lin Tsair-yuan 1968: 85–90.
13. This is the usual name for a sieve used in a wedding, the object of its use being, as noted above, to screen the bride from heavenly sight. The paper charm is novel to ghost marriages, to the best of my knowledge, although it seemed intended more as a label than as a charm. The Taiwanese term for such a sieve is *an-bí-thai,* and it is properly written 安米篩. The simplified writing used on the charm can be read homonymously in Taiwanese, although not in Mandarin.
14. Burning is the usual method of sending items to the supernatural world. Messages are sent to the gods this way. Temple money is sent aloft by burning, and clothes, houses, and other possessions for the dead are communicated to them by burning. It is not clear that the body of the dummy bride was being sent anywhere, except perhaps as one might reason that her presence was no longer required and her ghost was being sent back to the misty regions it came from. Burning in any case does not imply disrespect. The dummy was being treated as a sacred object, not as trash.

Although the rites associated with a ghost marriage are very similar to those of an ordinary marriage among the living, they are not exactly the same, for at every turn one is reminded that the bride is dead, and that she is aggressive and potentially dangerous. The following points are noteworthy.

It was emphasized that the bride wore three suits of clothing, although it would have been possible to count them as four. To the best of my knowledge the number of layers of clothing one wears as a bride is unimportant, but the number of layers of clothing that swathe a corpse can be crucial. If this is so, then it becomes important that the ladies of the household who had charge of preparing the dummy felt obliged to point out to me that she wore three layers of clothing, for what in effect was being said was not (or not only) that she was a proper bride, but that she was a proper corpse!

The quantity of incense in the central hall of the house would be unnecessary for an ordinary wedding, although some incense would be offered. The sticks of incense used in the various braziers were in groups of seven. I know of no rule that governs the number of sticks of incense offered in a censer, except that it be an odd number. However when offering wine, three or five cups are used for gods, seven, nine, or eleven for ancestors. By a transfer of this reasoning to incense, it is possible that the use of seven sticks of incense in each brazier emphasized the position of the bride as a deceased family member. There was also a pot of powdered incense on the dowry tray. Powdered incense is used in the worship of gods and ancestors during sacrifices, but it is most generally associated with purification by smoke. Incense offerings by guests at funerals, however, are always made with powdered rather than stick incense.

The groom wore black gloves. The normal color would be white, and although white would ordinarily be the color of mourning, apparently it symbolizes nothing at all in the case of a bridegroom because he is dressed in Western clothing, and white gloves are a part of the Western costume being imitated. In switching to black gloves, however, something seems to be symbolized, for black in Chinese, as in most languages, has associations with darkness, evil, and secrecy. In Mandarin one speaks of "black and white" 黑白, meaning wrong and right, or of a "black curtain" 黑幕, referring to devious practices performed in secrecy. In Taiwanese one can speak of something as "white white white" 白白白, very white or immaculate, whereas something "black black black" 黑黑黑 is not only very black, but very dirty. Fierce gods, such as plague gods, are often represented with black faces; [15] corpses are thought of as black, particularly if they have died by drowning (a most horrible death in Chinese eyes as we have seen, and one productive of equally impressive ghosts). Indians are imagined to be black, and I have been told they are the ugliest people in the world. One Chinese scholar passing through Chicago confessed to being so nauseated on seeing Negroes in O'Hare Airport that he was unable to eat his dinner when it was served by a Negro waitress. In wearing black gloves the groom is prepared for black business: a wedding with the dead.

Perhaps the culminating point of this *grotesquerie,* however—for the Taiwanese do indeed consider ghost weddings to be rather a morbid business—was the smile on the face of the bride. On the original Japanese wall calendar such a smile against a background of pagodas or spring blossoms may have been very attractive. Transferred to a ghost bride, it became a sneer of triumph, for Chinese brides never smile. Smiling, it is maintained, would be immodest, and the correct attitude for a bride is one of great embarrassment at the proceedings. A Taiwanese bride is said to feel *pháiⁿ-sè* 歹勢: embarrassed, awkward, intrusive, in a word, *gauche,* and her eyes are kept downcast and her head lowered. Yet the face selected for the ghost bride does exactly what no bride would do or be allowed to do: it peers into the eyes of the beholder, and grins.

In these ways a consistent difference is maintained between a spirit marriage and an ordinary wedding. The stain of death is kept constantly before the eye, and the reminder that the wedding is a dirty but necessary business, rather than a truly joyful occasion, is expressed over and over again. It is merely a way of appeasing an aggressive and triumphant ghost.

What is happening in these cases? The family is first faced with a problem: illness. They also have a deceased, unwed girl in the family, or, as is the case in the present examples, in the wife's natal family. The medium puts these two facts together and decides that the ghost is causing the illness, and adds that her motivation in causing the illness is that she wishes to be married. The cure is to marry her so she will stop making a nuisance of herself and retreat back into ghostly oblivion where she belongs.

15. Curiously, the goddess Mhatzuu is also represented with a black face in some instances.

The credibility of such an explanation and such a proposed course of action in the eyes of the participants hangs on a number of things. There is first, of course, the belief in ghosts and the belief that ghosts can make one sick. The remainder of the diagnosis and the prescribed cure follow from this, if we first note certain facts about the treatment of women in Taiwanese society.

I mentioned the simplicity in which a child is buried. I overstated the case somewhat by concentrating upon infants and young children. With a young man, who is older but unmarried, another solution becomes more frequent and socially more graceful: he is allowed to adopt a son postmortally, who then adopts the necessary ritual obligations toward his deceased "father," including serving as chief mourner at his funeral. This was done for Guo Tong-ming 郭通明, who died orphaned and unwed at the age of thirty after several years of illness. He was the fourth of five sons and lived in a little hut near the house of his eldest brother. After Tong-ming died, his brother "gave" Tong-ming two of his own sons, and they will have the duty of making sacrifices to their adopted father for the rest of their lives, although the adoption will have no effect upon their legal status as sons of their biological father, nor on their claim to his inheritance, nor on their residence or emotional attachments.[16] It is a matter of form only, a convenient fiction to provide Tong-ming's spirit with descendants able to worship him and to maintain the history of the family in accord with the proper blueprint for families.

If the deceased is younger, a son might be adopted for him later if the family feels a need to do so; that is, if there is evidence his ghost is dissatisfied.

But this cannot be done with girls who die early, for a woman takes her descent-line membership from her husband. No husband, no descendants, and no participation in the ritual of ancestor worship, either as an ancestor or, during ancient times, even as a worshipper. The Later-Han Confucian commentator Jenq Shyuan 鄭玄 (A.D. 127–200) writes: "Those who die early, who die before eighteen so they have not yet taken husbands, do not take part in the rites while they are alive, and to do so after death would also

16. The relationship of elder brother is irrelevant in the present case. The problem was to find a son for Tong-ming, and any relative with an abundance of male offspring could equally well have contributed one of them to the cause.

be a breach of proper behavior." (quoted by Lou Tzyy-kuang 1968:23).[17] If her spirit is to be worshipped by an unending line of descendants, she simply has to have a husband. This, informants say, is why a deceased spirit wants to be married.[18] In short, the reason female children should become ghosts may well lie in the possibility of adopting fictive offspring for male children, a process impossible for females because a woman can have children only in the line of her husband, and if there is no husband, she has no line.[19]

There are subordinate problems. (There are always subordinate problems.) There is little point in examining them in detail here because most of them are not really relevant to the main point and because the data in hand simply are not enough for us to make decisions about the validity of one hypothesis as opposed to another. I cannot resist a short excursion into one of the most important of these issues, however: why should a ghost want to marry her sister's husband? It is not a necessary match, and informants insist it is a recent development. It is possible that sisters' husbands were occasionally chosen in the past, but now it has become a preferred form. Why the sister's husband? Why a change?

We might begin by noticing that there has been a change in who

17. 殤，十九以下未嫁而死者，生不禮相接，死而合之，是亦亂人倫者也。

18. Li (1958: 98) writes: ". . . there has never been a ghost bridegroom, but always a ghost bride. . . . I found that if a boy died before he married, and comes back to his parents in a dream, he would not ask them to find a bride, rather he would ask them to find an offspring for him, possibly from one of his brother's sons or any classified nephew. In this way he would be entitled to have a place in the family shrine with many of his forebears. . . . In such a patrilineal society as China, a girl who died young is not allowed to have a place in her own parents' family shrine, thus she has to find a husband in order to have a proper position in this world. Conversely, a boy can occupy a place in the shrine of his natal family only when he has an adopted heir."

19. This hypothesis predicts that adoptions of children should occur for unwed males regardless of age at death, whereas unwed females should be available to serve as explanatory ghosts regardless of their age at death. I do not know of any actual instances of male children who died in childhood demanding adopted progeny later on, although Li, cited above, says that they exist. Similarly, I know of no actual instances of girls who died in late childhood or early adulthood demanding mates after death. On the contrary the ghost brides I am familiar with died as infants. Yet both of these other instances should occur theoretically, and one could feel more comfortable about the proposed sex difference in ghosts if such examples could be found.

is suffering from the attacks of the ghosts. Presumably under the system as Li describes it, a family, under pressure from the ghost of an unmarried daughter, seeks a husband for her. A man would never go to a medium and be told he was sick because of an anonymous ghost and that he had best pick up a red envelope on a road somewhere. The initiative in the traditional practice comes from the ghost's family.

In the Bao-an region, by contrast, it is often the married sister or her husband who falls sick. In the Bao-an cases it is the groom-to-be who initiates the wedding on the basis of his own illness or an illness of his wife or children. We can distinguish two types of spirit marriage. In the first type the offending ghost is from the victim's family circle and must be found a husband. The way to find a husband (any husband will do) is to leave a red envelope on the road. In the second type the offending ghost is from outside the family group in which the victim is living, and the problem is not to find a husband for the ghost but to find a ghost for the husband! The question in this latter case is not really (or not primarily) why the ghost picks her sister's husband as a groom, but why the groom feels (or can be made by the oracle to feel) that his wife's sister wants to marry him. If a family can randomly seek a husband for a daughter's ghost, why can one not randomly seek a ghost for one's own illness? And, indeed, if type-two marriages are new, or even merely on the rise, how do we explain the change?

One attractive hypothesis arises if we take the view of the medium. A client arrives suffering from illness, and we know that each deceased unwed sister or daughter is a potential cause. These are of course limited in number. If we are free to use his wife's sisters as well, we have increased the chances of being able to find a deceased, unwed girl who has not already been postmortally married, and thereby we have increased our chances of delivering our client from his misery, and incidentally of being able to lease equipment for a spirit marriage to the client.

If we take this view, then it becomes the more interesting that informants report the custom to be more prominent in recent years. Remembering that villages tend to have heavy surname clusterings and that surnames are exogamous groups, most marriages take place between villages. It may be that the supply of deceased, unwed girls of a village gets used up in a period of popular enthusiasm for this kind of explanation. They must then be replaced as more babies die over a period of years, or they must be supplemented by changing the explanation so as to allow the introduction of other dead babies from villages where the fashion has not come at the same time; hence the admission of deceased sisters of wives whose natal families live in other villages where the supply of deceased, unwed girls has not been used up.

If this is possible, a clever medium or two in one or two villages near Bao-an might simply have discovered a principle that allows the use of deceased unwed girls from other villages after the local supply is gone. It would, of course, take far more examples to begin to entertain such a notion seriously rather than speculatively.

Another argument, whether or not we choose to take seriously the somewhat conspiratorial reasoning just outlined,[20] is that in recent years the greater say of young people in marriage arrangements has resulted in closer ties between affines, so that a husband's family ties now include his wife's family to the extent that it has become more credible for imperfections in her family to make him ill.

We might also investigate intermediate types of Taiwanese spirit marriage. One of the ghosts that ultimately married Dah-tour, after all, began as a type-one ghost and ended up as a type-two ghost; how separate, therefore, can the two types be except analytically? Is the distinction possible, given the amount of communication in Taiwan today? How similar can the types become? Is it really accurate to associate marriage between the ghost and her sister's husband only with type-two marriage, or is it in fact becoming common in type-one marriages as well?

I mention these problems more because they suggest interesting questions for further consideration and research than because of their pressing relevance to our main interest here. In all instances of spirit marriage the theology (or more exactly the eschatology) is the same. There are shades who suffer if they have no descendants; women have descendants only through their husbands; spirits cause illness to draw attention to themselves; and the like. The point

20. Note that nothing in the argument implies conscious decision on the part of a medium to defraud anyone. It is convenient to speak of a medium making a selection of possible explanations and the like, but I do not imply that any bad faith is involved. On the contrary, I have the impression that the vast majority of rural *tâng-ki* believe very firmly in the divine origin of their revelations.

is that those ghosts used to explain family disaster are the shades of persons who are social-structurally anomalous, and the way the disaster is alleviated is by changing their status so they and the living may rest in peace.

### REIFIED GHOSTS

In the previous section we saw that spirit attack was used as an explanation of illness when the family contained some structural irregularity that could reasonably be thought to be dissatisfying to the ghost. And we turned this around and suggested that the ghost (who exists potentially for every deceased human being in Chinese cosmology) was reified as a representation of the family irregularity to which illness was attributed, and that the illness was cured by symbolically correcting the irregularity.

The ghosts we examined were those of deceased, unwed girls seeking husbands. Let us now pursue this same theme with some other kinds of ghosts. The first example came to public attention when a child was stricken gravely ill. His family first took him to medical doctors and complained of having spent over 3000 *Kuay* ($75) to no avail. They also used a *kiō-á* and a *tâng-ki* to consult at various times with King Guo, Marshal Shieh, and the Third Prince. These three gods all agreed on a supernatural explanation of the child's illness. The boy's father was in Japan at the time of the illness, but it was he who was held responsible for the problem. The father's father (the boy's grandfather) had died before the boy's grandmother, and this lady had married again into another family. She had apparently lived happily with her new husband and eventually died in the bosom of her second family. Some time after the old lady's death, the sick boy's father built a new house and equipped it handsomely. He decided it was rather awkward not to have his mother's ancestral tablet beside his father's on the new family altar, however, so he negotiated with the old lady's second family and ultimately received permission to take the tablet home to worship at least temporarily.

The arrangement was apparently satisfactory to the living parties involved, but not to the old lady herself, for it was revealed by the three gods consulted that she was in a quandary about which house was properly hers, and she dared enter neither to take advantage of the offerings provided her. This left her in a state of painful deprivation, so as a sign of her displeasure she brought illness upon this small child, her grandson, and also upon an adult in the other family (although I was unable to procure details of the other illness). To cure the boy, the gods explained, it would be necessary to go to a certain temple in Tainan and ask the enshrined deity to make the decision about which family the ghost should consider her proper descendants.

Once again we are faced with the problem of explaining illness. And once again the explanation centers on irregularities in the family. In this case what is called into question is the family affiliation of the stricken boy's paternal grandmother. And the question on which the ghost demands decision is whether she is affiliated ritually with the line of her first husband or with that of her second. Whereas the spirit bride was anomalous in lacking any descent line until she married into one, the grandmother is anomalous in being retained in two simultaneously. Naturally enough, the grandmother demands a decision. And apparently the medium doing the interpreting preferred to put the burden on an anonymous competitor by recommending that the problem be taken to a temple in the city.

Before we try to see just what it is about the double descent line that is bothering the grandmother, let us turn briefly to Chinese ideas about second marriages. A woman ideally lives to a ripe old age. So does her husband, and her life is one of service to him. The wedding rite not only separates her from her natal family but joins her *in perpetuity* to her husband's family.[21] In fact, of course, not everyone lives to his desired longevity. However, in dynastic times Chinese custom and morality, and in certain ways law as well, tried very hard to maintain the polite fiction of longevity for all by enjoining the woman to remain with her husband's family and not to remarry (even should her husband die between their engagement and the actual marriage).

The ethnographic literature suggests that throughout the Chinese population, remarriage of a widow has at least until very recently been considered a most dishonorable thing. At the same time it appears to be done often enough. Kulp (1925: 158) writes of the

21. Divorce was possible, under traditional law, if initiated by the husband on charges of disobedience, failure to bear a son, jealousy, etc., the so-called "seven ousts" 七 出. *See* Chiu 1966: 61–74.

town of Chao-chow near Swatow: "Re-marriage of widows in respectable families is a negative value throughout the region." The same seems to have been true of Yunnan, where Hsu (1967: 255) suggests that "although socially it is more honorable for [childless] widows to adopt sons and remain faithful to their departed husbands than for them to remarry, a large number of widows do prefer the latter way out, in spite of the fact that the remarriage of widows is treated with much social and ritual censure." The same values seem to hold for north China as well. M. Yang (1945: 113) reports for Taitou in Shantung that "a second marriage is a matter of shame." Further, "Public opinion is that a decent woman should be the wife of only one man" (p. 117). Gamble (1954: 37) reports for Ting Hsien in Hopei that "Widows can and do marry in Ting Hsien." It is not the most common thing, however. Twenty women of one hundred and sixty-one who had been widowed remarried. However, C. K. Yang (1959a: 48) reports for an adjacent province that "The Preparatory Committee of the Honan Provincial Women's Association under the Communist regime reported in 1949 that in the northern part of Honan, the current rule of the clans was that a widow could not remarry. Should she remarry against the objection of the family, the whole clan had the right to interfere, even the right to kill her." By way of evidence that the rule was indeed followed, Yang cites a grisly example or two in which remarrying widows actually were murdered. Doolittle (1865: 1.100) tells us that in Foochow "It is considered a disgrace to a family for one of its sons to marry a widow, no matter how intelligent, interesting, and handsome she may be, as well as a disgraceful and shameful step on the part of the widow to consent to marry again. No rich and fashionable family ever marries a son to a widow."

In modern times the law has been on the widow's side if she wanted to remarry, but even the lawmakers seem not really to have approved of such behavior. Su, writing in 1922 of the Provisional Civil Code and its relation to traditional Chinese marriage law writes:

> A widow might remarry if she so desired, but the ancient traditions and customs exerted upon her a strong pressure to remain unmarried. If she did remarry, she forfeited all claim to her first husband's estate and the property she had added to it by marriage. If she remained unmarried and in her husband's family, she inherited his titles and emolu-

ments and succeeded to his position in the family organization.[22] It is well known that the Chinese people have always delighted in honoring and respecting the widow. In the old days, the good widow who had properly brought up her children to maturity and faithfully fulfilled her other duties received an imperial reward in the form of a gateway or arch erected in her honor in the community where she lived. These gateways and arches are to be seen in almost every village in China (p. 67).

Vannicelli (1943: 386) shows us an even clearer picture.

The widow who remains faithful to her deceased husband till her death, living in chastity and serving her in-laws, is held in great honour in China. Chinese law, as we have seen, erects a triumphal arch to such widows. *The same law permits the widow a second marriage, and noone can oppose her in it.* The widow is free to remarry, and in the second marriage she acts *sui juris*. . . . Further, to contract a second marriage, it is necessary to have a go-between. If there is a written contract, it is written not on red paper, but on white (the colour of mourning) and composed in different language from those we have already reported, and it comes signed by the widow herself and by one of her kinsmen. (Emphasis added.) [23]

It seems clear that the widow who remarried suffered numerous social disadvantages (*see* Vannicelli 1943: 387 f.). Vannicelli quotes Escarra (1931) in listing various folk expressions referring to the dowry of the second marriage, all of them derogatory. Supernatural disasters awaited her too: "It is feared that the spirit of the deceased husband may follow his wife and do her harm in her new home, therefore when the widow moves to her second husband's house she leaves from a neighbour's house, or from an abandoned one, or else leaves during the night, as in Shensi" (Vannicelli 1943: 387).[24]

22. "Ta-Tsing Leu Lee, sec. 47."

23. La vedova, che resta fedele al suo defunto marito fino alla morte, vivendo in castità e servendo i suoceri, è tenuta in grande onore in Cina. La legge cinese, comme si è già veduto, eriga a tali vedove un arco di trionfo. *La stressa legge permette alla vedova le seconde nozze e nessuno può opporvisi.* La vedova è libera di rimaritarsi e nelle seconde nozze si comporta come persona *sui juris*. . . . Anche per concludere le seconde nozze è necessaria l'azione del mediatore; se vi è un contratto scritto, non si scrive in carta rossa, ma in carta bianca (il colore del lutto) e redatto in termini differenti da quelli, che abbiamo già riferiti, e viene firmato dalla vedova stessa e da uno dei suoi parenti. (Emphasis added.)

24. Si teme che lo spirito del marito defunto segua la sposa e le dia molestia nella nuova dimora, perciò la vedova si recherà alla casa del secondo

One solution to the problem was to marry the second husband in life, with the proviso that at death the woman would revert to her first husband's line. Von Möllendorff (1895: 49) writes: "A curious practice exists in some parts of China, as in Ningpo [Nationalist Ninghsien, in Chechiang Province]: a widower and a widow, both of advanced years, join in second matrimony, with the stipulation that the widow will continue spiritually with her earlier husband, that is that after her death her body will be reclaimed by his family and be buried with him." [25]

The point of all this is fairly simple: the grandmother should never have remarried in the first place. Marriage is supposed to be permanent. It makes a woman not only her husband's wife, but a member of his descent line, a membership by no means dissolved by his death. In a sense, his death has no effect on the status of his wife. Social relationships, as ritually defined, continue *as though* the man were yet alive.[26] When a woman breaks this bond by remarrying, she threatens the entire nature of the bond itself. What is immoral about widow remarriage is that it is subversive of the ideology of the marriage tie, which binds a woman not only to her husband but to his line as well.

The fact that widow remarriage is so widespread in China (as

---

marito, partendo dalla casa di un vicino o da una casa abbandonata, oppure durante la notte, come nello Scen-si.

25. Eine seltsame Sitte besteht in einigen Theilen Chinas, z. B. in Ningpo. Ein Witwer und eine Witwe, Beide in vorgerücktem Alter, gehen eine zweite Ehe mit einander ein, mit der Bedingung, dass die Witwe spirituell ihrem früheren Manne verbleibt, d.h. dass nach ihrem Tode ihr Leichnam von seiner Familie reklamirt und mit ihm begraben wird.

26. The strain to maintain the fiction of a natural life for all family members reaches fascinating extremes. Marjorie Topley (1955, 1956) reports spirit marriages in Singapore in which both bride and groom are deceased. She writes that spirit marriages are contracted *inter alia* "when a younger son wishes to marry and his elder brother has died before taking a wife." According to Chinese custom, a younger son should not marry before his elder brothers; a ghost marriage is, therefore, sometimes arranged for an elder brother so that the younger may then proceed with his own nuptials without fear of incurring the disfavor of his brother's ghost. The same principle appears in the Taiwanese wedding rite at the point when the bride and groom must ceremonially bow before the groom's parents. At one wedding I attended the parents were both deceased, but the ceremony was accomplished around two empty chairs, where the parental presence was symbolized by a square of red paper laid on each. (Red cloth or paper placed over a chair is widely used to symbolize occupation by a supernatural being.)

well as perfectly legal) suggests that other factors are also involved, which somehow run at cross-purposes with the sanctity of the marriage bond. Perhaps in some cases economic considerations are paramount. In others, no doubt personal antipathies between the widow and her husband's family become unbearable after the husband is no longer there to mediate them. Probably in certain instances love affairs between the widow and outside men may lead to her remarriage.

But let us return to our ghostly grandmother. Her son (by her first husband) was building a new house and providing it with a new family altar. On this altar belonged his family tablets, and normally (or normatively) he would include among them the tablet of his dead mother. The new house and the new family altar represented a tidying-up of things. A new house is *hó-sè*好势: clean, orderly, proper, deserving of pride; and to complete this the tablet of his mother was missed as presumably it previously had not been, for in a family that is *hó-sè,* that is where a mother's tablet belongs. The notion of *hó-sè,* applied to families, makes no provision for remarried widows.

But the grandmother *had* remarried. She had separated herself from her first nonnatal line and attached herself to a second. And the remarriage produced a conflict between two lines of reasoning. One was that the grandmother belonged to the line she had most recently married into. The rights of the first line to her were gone. The other reasoned that her tablets belonged on her son's altar. Filial subservience dictates that a son worship his mother's shade. That is the duty of a son to his mother, and there is no clear provision for mothers that opt out of their son's family altars. The matter might have been overlooked, had it not been a *new* altar, and had it not been therefore a point of pride that it be a proper one.

The solution was a compromise. The grandmother's ghost could be shared, providing the benefits of respectability and completeness to both households, if not exactly at once, then at least serially. Unfortunately, neither the lineage principles nor the ideals of the family were to be that easily overlooked, and they reasserted themselves when explanation for sickness provided an opportunity for the community, in the person of a medium for a god, to inspect the family for structural irregularities.

In summary, the ghost was thought to be haunting her grandson because she was improperly located in the social structure. As a mother, she belonged in her son's ancestral shrine, while as a wife she belonged in that of her most recent husband. The families involved decided that she could be in both. The ghost disagreed. Or the community disagreed. Or the *tâng-ki* disagreed. The social rule that is important is that a woman can belong to only one lineage. Double lineage membership is not an acceptable compromise, for it begs the point. One can get away with widow remarriage; one cannot get away with flaunting it. Which family she is to belong to is unimportant, but that she can belong to only one is crucial. Hence it provides an acceptable reason for her to be held responsible for the illness of her grandson.

So far we have two patterns of ghostly explanation of family disaster, and two ways of dealing with the ghosts. The ghost might be a family member who is social-structurally anomalous, in which case one ordinarily acts to correct the anomaly. Or the ghost might be a set of vaguely defined malign forces, associated in some way with ghosts, but not identified as a particular person. And in this case one exorcizes it.

But not all ghosts fall into one or another of these two types. In the following examples we have an instance of a particular ghost, representing structural principles once again, and she is a more dramatic and exciting presence than we have met thus far. The reaction, however, is exorcism, an exorcism, I would add, not that different from the exorcism we considered above when a child drowned in the fishpond. The haunting in question occurred some months after I left Bao-an and was reported to me in a letter. Here is a slightly abbreviated translation of the report I received:

Last night something happened at Guo Ching's family, so I am writing you a special letter to tell you. I hope you will find the matter of interest. The story goes this way: Guo Ching has a son who lives in Taitung and who is already married. I have heard that this boy had struck up with a girl in Taitung who already had a husband, so her husband divorced her. Although the girl's husband had already divorced her, her husband's mother became very angry, and as a result fell sick and died. Before this old mother died, she was particularly angry with Guo Ching's boy because the latter had damaged their family. For this reason she used some superstitious method (the kind of [Taiwanese aboriginal] wizardry you photographed when you were in Taitung) to wound Guo Ching's son's wife. The objective was to cause his wife to become sick and die so that Guo Ching's son wouldn't have a wife. Not long afterward Guo Ching's son's wife took sick (a neurosis like the one Guo Tong-ming died of). Guo Ching's boy saw that his wife had already developed a neurosis and was terrified, so two weeks ago he sent his wife back to our village. After this woman got to our village, she upset [鬧] the family every day, and struck people. So Guo Ching's family had three gods come down. Two [*tâng-ki*] were from our village: Guo Tian-huah [Third Prince] and Guo Ching-shoei [the Great Saint], and one *tâng-ki* from another village. I hear that these three gods used very peaceful means in taking care of this matter to implore the ghost who was bothering the woman's body to leave. Finally the three gods used impolite words and told the ghost who was bothering the woman's body that if she didn't leave, the three of them would be impolite to her. At length the ghost left, and the three gods [left and their *tâng-ki*] sat down to rest. After the three *tâng-ki* had stopped, they had some refreshments, and when they had finished their refreshments the three left together to go home. But . . . they had only just arrived at the pond behind Guo Ching's house (for it was the road beside the village pond) when the ghost, who had been standing there waiting for them, struck the Third Prince's *tâng-ki,* Guo Tian-huah. Tian-huah was knocked to the ground by her, but just as the ghost was about to strike the other two *tâng-ki* their two gods possessed them, so they began to fight vigorously with the ghost. The two *tâng-ki* fought very boisterously [*Rehnaw*], sometimes chasing into the trees, sometimes onto a roof, sometimes chasing her through the fishpond. Finally that invisible ghost lost the fight and ran away.

So the two *tâng-ki* said, all right, she has run away; we'll leave it at that. And the gods left them again. The row was very true to life. More than fifty of the village people stood around and watched the hooplah. Especially in the night we have been attacked [害] to the point that a lot of village people don't dare to go home alone.

Immediately I responded, inquiring exactly what sort of possessing force it was they were dealing with, and speculating, as politely as possible, that it might be the old mother. Here is the reply:

The ghost at Guo Ching's family was indeed the mother of the first husband of that woman from Taitung. But that evening I hear that that mother who had died did not have enough strength, so she ran back to

Taitung and invited their ancestral spirits, a whole lot of them, to come [請了他們祖先的靈魂很多鬼來的]. So only then did she dare fight with the *tâng-ki* of the gods. But that business still hasn't come to anything much. If there is good news later on, I shall tell you.

In our discussion of ghost marriage, we were concerned largely with the role of family and kinship and with the role of the ghost incident in the context of family and kinship. In the present instance, too, standards of family behavior are involved, for the Bao-an man has played the ghost's son for a cuckold. In China adultery is a very serious crime. Not only is it grounds for divorce under Republican law, but under the Ching marriage code adultery by the wife was the one offence for which she could be divorced regardless of any of the usual protections the law maintained to protect her from arbitrary divorce.[27] But I raise the example not because of the outrageousness of the boy's act nor even because of the vitriolic response of the ghost. A different point is illustrated by the present ghost and a rather more subtle one: the response to the ghost was an exorcism, performed by *tâng-ki* in trance and overseen by a large number of neighbors. Just as the voice of the medium can be that of the moral community when it detects structural irregularities and declares that their associated ghosts must be pacified, so in the present case this same voice (and presumably again that of the community) undertook instead to resist the principles that had been violated. It is easy enough to speculate as to why this should be done. Perhaps it was because the ghost was from outside, representing an unknown woman unrelated to the village; perhaps it was because the ghost was considered to be using aboriginal magic belonging to an exotic and therefore threatening system whose validity must not be acknowledged.

Whatever the reasoning, the point is that the community is a partner in the crime. The people and the gods of Bao-an took a collective stand in support of "their man" in opposition to some-

27. Just as there were "seven ousts" 七出, or seven grounds for divorce, so there were "three non-ousts" 三不出, or three protections from divorce. In the presence of a non-oust (such as the family having become rich after she married into it), a woman was exempted from divorce on the basis of an "oust" (such as loquaciousness). The sole exception was adultery. (*See* Chiu 1966: 61–70, 94 f.)

one else's ghosts. The instruments of the exorcism were the *tâng-ki*, the tools of the gods. And the guiding power that drove the vile presence from the hamlet before the very eyes of the fascinated and affrighted populace was the community's gods. Durkheim would be pleased.

## DEIFIED GHOSTS

By this time we ought to have had our fill of ghosts. There have been general malevolent forces, at the village and at the family level, whom the people of Bao-an have had to build forts against and to expel through exorcism with fire. Then there were ghosts of family members wanting to marry human husbands to put themselves in a descent line, and the family members had to give in to them and see them married. There was next the ghostly grandmother, who would not compromise her descent-line scruples (even though the historical grandmother had created all the problems by remarrying), and her family had to find her a single line. Finally there was the cuckold's mother, who threatened the adulterer and his wife and then the village mediums because her line had lost a potential mother of offspring.

But there are more.

We have seen that the supposed malice of ghosts is directly related to their own discomfort. The usual idiom for this is the availability of offerings to provide for their sustenance. A ghost must have descendants charged with providing offerings to him; otherwise he comes to share the tragic fate of the "hungry ghosts" who wander the world pitiously picking up such crumbs of offerings as best they can.

There is another way, however, for the deceased to be worshipped: he can be deified. A deity builds his following on a nonkinship basis (at least after the first few years of his cult, during which time recruitment may be based on kin ties). In theory gods have positions in the celestial hierarchy, to which they are duly appointed on the basis of merit. However, certain ghosts claim the benefits of such positions with apparently little attention to orthodoxy or legitimacy. They can perhaps be thought of as celestial bullies who force people to worship them as though they were really important gods. This turns out to be a solution often chosen by the same sort of female spirit who wants to be married to have offspring, for it is a solution to the same kind of problem: securing sacrifices. But this time she demands to be worshipped as though she were a deity.

Let us look at some examples. To begin, let us consider another god-worshipping group, similar in general outline to the eight we discussed earlier. We can call it Group 9. The worshippers are the sons of two deceased brothers and a concubine of one of the brothers (and of course the households these people head). The membership of the worship group exactly corresponds with the households living in one building. I can think of no very likely reason why this should be so. Possibly it is fortuitous. The normal worshipping unit, as we have seen, is the household or family, and expansion to a worshipping group does not seem to have any necessary relation to physical buildings. Possibly this was the group charged (more or less at the whim of a medium) with worshipping the ghost; for a ghost is indeed the object of their worship, a deceased daughter of one of the two dead brothers.[28] She was born in 1907 and died in 1908. According to her worshippers, her cult began "about thirty years ago," which would be 1938 or so, or when the spirit was about thirty years old. We will recall that this is about the age at which less ambitious female spirits decide to get married and settle down. She is worshipped under the name of the Little Maid 小女娘. The worshipping families are quite reluctant to discuss the matter. Apparently they undertook her worship because she insisted upon it, and an attempt to rid themselves of the "goddess" was unsuccessful. One informant told the story of the Little Maid this way:

The Little Maid was from our own family and died and became a goddess, so we had a joss carved to worship. . . . Later on the father of the Little Maid and another man from this village were very good friends, and this gentleman suggested to her father that he stop worshipping the Little Maid. Her father agreed, the two of them being on very good terms, so at the time of the great rites of Hsikang, her father brought the joss of the Little Maid [to the Hsikang temple] and put it into the Kings' Boat to be burned at the end of the ceremonies to send her back to heaven.[29] But the Little Maid herself didn't go, it

28. A third brother still lives in a nearby house and does not participate in Group 9.
29. *See* Liou Jy-wann 1963, sec. 2 for a description of these rites.

was said; she came back to haunt people here, and the family became very inharmonious. The family of the man who had proposed burning the joss (now moved to Tainan) was the same: the family was inharmonious. . . . Because nothing else could be done, they had another joss carved to worship: the present joss. This was about ten years ago.

Scanty as the available information is, and inconspicuous as the cult attempts to be (easy enough when it is confined to a single building), it persists: the Little Maid insists upon it! As a goddess, even a bogus goddess (for anyone will readily concede she is, in fact, a ghost that has got the upper hand), she can be worshipped by nonoffspring and enjoy sacrifices even without being married.

Her cult, furthermore, might even grow. One way it can grow is for her to select a *tâng-ki.* I do not have enough cases to be able to generalize safely, but my impression is that many or most of the female *tâng-ki* in Taiwan are mediums of such "little maids," and some at least bear a kinship relationship to their possessing goddesses. Let us consider the case of a Bao-an woman *tâng-ki,* Jang Shiow-yeh.

Like virtually all *tâng-ki,* Jang Shiow-yeh tells of her long efforts to avoid being possessed. However, one theme that rises over and over from her tale is that what really bothers her is possession by such a divinized *Goei* rather than by a bona fide *Shern.* Shiow-yeh began by having odd physiological symptoms. A few months later, after unsuccessful medical treatment, she began to be possessed, but she did not speak intelligibly while possessed.

After a time my husband's older brother said: "You've been to a doctor, and he couldn't find anything wrong, and the medicine he gave you had no effect. It would be best to ask the gods and see. Otherwise you may never be able to be rid of this." I took his advice and went to a "little god", 小神 in XYZ, and the little god told me: "There is a little god descending upon your body. When you go home you ought to consult with one of the important gods in your village. You are not sick."

Shiow-yeh went home and held a session with a *kiō-á* to inquire of King Guo, but King Guo failed to possess the *kiō-á.*

So I went back to XYZ. . . . The little god possessing me was [supposed to be] my husband's younger sister, and I wanted to ask her if this was really true. . . . [The little god of XYZ possessed the medium, and I asked her why my husband's sister] was making me so sick. I was told she wasn't making me very sick at all, and that she had become a little god too and wanted me to be her *tâng-ki.* I was too stunned to react. A little god has no power and can't satisfy people. If one is thinking about being a *tâng-ki,* everyone would agree it is better to be the *tâng-ki* of an important god. Basically nobody pays much attention to the words of a little god's *tâng-ki.* . . . I thought perhaps the words of the little god's *tâng-ki* in XYZ might be inaccurate, so I went to four or five more little gods in [five other villages]. Each time I asked the little gods myself, and what they told me was the same as what the little god in XYZ had told me: a little god wanted me for her *tâng-ki.* Even then I didn't believe it, for I had no respect for the little gods. If there was no way to avoid becoming a *tâng-ki,* I could at least be the *tâng-ki* of an important god; I would feel better about that.

Before I left Bao-an, Shiow-yeh was initiated as a proper *tâng-ki* for her husband's deceased younger sister, her little god. It was a simple enough event, conducted by an *âng-thâu-á,* who equipped her with weapons and introduced her to mortification of the flesh, the sign of her trade.[30] Throngs of village people looked on as she flailed her back, shouting, sputtering, drooling, and muttering. When it was over, she was, willy-nilly, a *tâng-ki,* and could begin counselling people on behalf of her little god.

As mentioned, a deified ghost with a *tâng-ki* can develop a body of devotees. Shiow-yeh, after all, consulted with several such little gods about her symptoms. One little god in another village, known locally as Little God Hwang, has expanded her cult far enough that there is one family in Bao-an which considers itself to be under her special patronage, even though, unlike the two little gods we just considered, there is no kinship relation. The story of Little God Hwang is sketchy, but her relationship to the family of Guo Tong-kwei 郭通奎 of Bao-an seems clear

30. There was no exorcism, because the possessing presence had never pretended to be a high god. For the same reason the rites took place before her father's house, not before the temple. Details of the initiation are not relevant here, although I hope to go into the matter in another paper devoted entirely to *tâng-ki.*

enough. It is said that Little God Hwang lived in a certain village about three kilometers from Bao-an, which we may designate ABC. After her death (we know not how many years before) she "chose" her younger sister as her *tâng-ki* and began curing the sick with charms. It is said she gave her sister an extra ten years of life in order to make use of her as a *tâng-ki*. That was about ten years ago, and when I was in Bao-an some of Little God Hwang's devotees speculated she must have granted the *tâng-ki* an additional ten years. So successful was the Little God Hwang that when one of her protégé families moved to Kaohsiung they apparently set up a small temple for her in their own central room and, using a *kiō-á*, formed a kind of branch temple. Guo Tong-kwei and his family began worshipping Little God Hwang in 1960.

His family was very inharmonious, and it seemed as though harmful forces had come upon the family. He asked several gods about it, but they didn't clear up the problem. Later his wife's mother [who lived in ABC village] introduced him to Little God Hwang of ABC. . . . Little God Hwang told him, "Take home my incense and worship me and your problems will be solved." [31] It seems strange, but from the time he began to worship Little God Hwang, his family became very harmonious. At night there was no sign of ghosts coming to disturb them. In the same year when he brought home the incense of Little God Hwang, his second boy child was born, and so he gave this child to Little God Hwang as an adopted child.[32]

31. The implication is that the worship should be permanent. We recall that the transfer of the incense pot is the key act in establishing a new temple from an old one.

32. The Hokkien term is *khòe-kiá*$^{n}$ 契 囝 . The word designates a child who is taken under protection by a "foster father," as by adoption, but not so close. In Taiwan this is ordinarily done when real parents have lost several children. The foster father who is selected is one with many living sons. The child addresses his foster father as he would his father, and it is believed the child will thus have a better chance of survival. Cf. Douglas 1899: 282. By extension, the same term refers to a male child put under the protection of a god. (This is the only usage mentioned by Elliott 1955 for this word in Singapore.) In this latter arrangement, kinship terms are not used, and the arrangement would seem to be closer to a child's relationship with his patron saint, say, in the West. In the present context the child was ceded to Little God Hwang, not because its elder siblings had died—for they had not—nor because the little god had to be paid in some way for bringing harmony to the house, but because the family was confident that a tiny child's chances of survival could be materially improved with the

Infrequency, secrecy, and former legal suppression all conspire to make the matter difficult to see clearly, for the number of cases one can study is small, and the amount of information about each, unhappily little. But it seems *as though* the same kinds of structurally anomalous dead who require husbands can be handled in two other ways. One is to exorcise them. The other is to divinize them. In the former case one is dismissing them and refusing to deal with them as credible problems, giving community sanction to the family over and against the skeletons in its closet. In divinizing them one is adding them to a corpus of gods, however minor and inferior a role therein the divinized ghosts must play.[33] We have gone in a circle: the exorcised become the exorcisers; the tormentors become the protectors against torment; and the system closes in upon itself.[34]

Such a state of affairs is a bit disconcerting, because it does no little violence to the analytic scheme I put forth at the beginning of this essay when I said that supernaturals were of three types: gods, ghosts, and ancestors. The gods, I said, were the spirits of those who had been outstandingly virtuous on earth. Ancestors were such other mortals as had descendants to provide sacrifices

---

aid of a goddess they had just discovered to be generally efficacious in dealing with other of their family affairs.

33. Liou Jy-wann (1963, 1966) has argued that many far nobler southwestern Taiwanese deities are also divinized ghosts, including the five kings of Nankuenshen and the Twelve Plague Kings invited temporarily at the time of the triennial festival of Hsikang. I have never heard confirmation of this from a Taiwanese concerning the Nankuenshen gods, but when I mentioned them to religious Chinese in Manila, they laughingly informed me of their "mere ghosts" status. Similarly, only the most directly involved, well informed, and religiously active laymen in Hsikang gave any hint whatever of recognizing anything amiss with the Plague Kings, despite the presence of the word "plague" 瘟 in their title. A successful cult apparently obscures the ominous origins of the deity and converts him in time to a mighty and important god whose help is sought to drive out *Goei* and who is no longer thought to be a *Goei* himself. It is an interesting question whether this same process happens in the case of little gods, little maids, and the like. Dare we suspect that the Queen of Heaven herself might have begun her career as a little god?

34. We *may* have gone in a circle in another way too. Shiow-yeh was selected as the *tâng-ki* of her husband's sister. Could it be that ghosts with marriageable sisters' husbands wed them, whereas those with only brothers' wives to possess possess them? If I may be forgiven for suggesting work I have not in fact done (yet), this is an inviting hypothesis it would be well to keep in mind when working in rural Taiwan.

to them. Ghosts were the rest: spirits that were not gods, yet had no descendants to provide for them or were otherwise specially distinguished from the normal dead. In all of this I quoted informants' statements as evidence. Now we discover somewhat abruptly that, behaviorally, certain ghosts can be treated as gods, to the point that they become indistinguishable. How can this be?

The answer probably depends on a related question: how different are ghosts and gods when we define them by human responses to them? In the course of the discussion it developed that the distinguishing characteristic of most village gods was that one can come to an agreement with them which will bring one protection against disaster in exchange for sacrifices.[35] And the distinguishing characteristic of a ghost is that he is the cause of the disaster one must be protected against. Unlike Western ghosts, the familial ghosts of Bao-an do not attack man out of pure devilishness and malice, but out of necessity. Morally they are neutral beings. The operation that stops the disaster in the case of familial ghosts is the correction of the unsatisfactory and anomalous position of the ghost. This renders it a nonghost, usually an ancestor.[36] If a ghost can be converted from causing disaster to preventing it, and if the prevention is accomplished because of alliances between humans and ghosts on the same basis as those made between humans and gods, then the ghost, seen in terms of human behavior, has been changed from a ghost to a god.

We have two sets of definitions in this. One is intellectual, moralistic, and related to the genesis of these beings in human virtue. The other is behavioral and relates to the supposed motivations and behavior of supernaturals and to the use human beings actually make of gods and ghosts as elements in a system of explanation and interaction. Both, at their respective levels, are native definitions; however, there is not a perfect correspondence between them, but rather a kind of slippage when one tries to line the models up.

The identification of this area of slippage, or noncorrespondence, between the two models enables us to understand certain

35. We exclude in this the Jade Emperor, who is conceived to administer the system, and a few other specialized gods.

36. The same operation is impossible for generalized anonymous ghosts, because their kinship status is unknown. It is not clear why they cannot be deified, although sacrifices to the Good Brethren are perhaps a step in that direction.

points that were previously obscure. For one, the deified ghosts are only "little gods" rather than gods properly so called. So long as their unsavory origins are remembered, they can be gods only with respect to the treatment accorded them, but not gods in the sense of the virtuous dead. It is important to the integrity of the belief model that only the virtuous can become gods. On the other hand, the possibility of flattering ghosts to alleviate human suffering is an important means of coping at the behavioral level. The term "little god" preserves both models when the deed must be done. Should a little god prove powerful, only human memory, easily obliterated with passing generations, prevents its attainment of full divine status.

TABLE 5
THEOLOGICAL (BELIEF) MODEL

| Ancestors (ancestral dead) | Gods (virtuous dead) | Ghosts (desperate dead) | |
|---|---|---|---|
| | | SLIPPAGE | |
| Ancestors (irrelevant dead) | Gods (tractable dead) | Little Gods | Ghosts (intractable dead) |

BEHAVIORAL (ACTION) MODEL

The difference between the two models, and the odd ambiguity in the behavioral one also suggests why the words *Shern* and *Goei* historically do not correspond to the modern stated conceptions,[37] and even today one finds such seemingly contradictory terms as *Goeishern* 鬼神, a ghostly god or ghost, and *Shyeshern* 邪神, a false god, a ghost in a malicious manifestation.

The slippage also suggests a partial explanation of one other problem not directly met in the text, namely the reluctance of *tâng-ki* to accept their calling. For to be a *tâng-ki* implies contact with the supernatural, which it is no longer possible for us to see as inevitably benevolent.

37. The problem particularly troubles Groot (1892–1910), who devotes all of Book II (vols. 4–6) to manifestations of the *Linghwen*. The same problem can be seen in dictionaries that try to take account both of popular and of classical usage.

# Chapter 9
## *Structure and Change*

In closing, something should be said about the extraordinary model we have been slowly assembling of perceptions of disaster and religious ways of coping with it. It seems to me that this model is logically independent of the social practices to which it is attached and is therefore able to accommodate social change without suffering displacement. When one deals with a culture as longevous as the Chinese, such systems are doubly suggestive. It is truly striking that the structural principles involved in membership in a descent line should be so well internalized and so important as to result in ghosts when violated. In a sense, it is amazing that an infant girl who died after a year of life should thirty years later be so alive in the memories of the living that her ghost is thought to have come back for a husband or to demand a cult.

But how closely is this system of explanation actually tied to *these* principles and *these* explanations? We recall that the real "professors of the system" (Groot's happy phrase) are the *tâng-ki* and the readers and wielders of the *kiō-á*. These men are free to reify a ghost and attribute particular motivations to it within the range that their clients believe credible and that other oracles are apt to confirm. These two important provisions are highly limiting within any one time, place, and family context. Such limits make the system intensely conservative, for at intervals it lays open the family history to community critique, and the medium solemnly decrees that this or that irregularity, this or that failure to follow out descent-line obligations in a particular way, has brought about disaster and will continue to do so until the family takes steps to undo the mischief it has brought upon itself. We have seen how an innovation such as sharing the descendantship from a remarried widow brought censure upon the house, in theory from the widow herself, in fact from a community that thought this a violation of its principles.

Nevertheless, such a system is also able to accommodate change, if slowly. We must not overlook the fact that exactly the same personnel *could* manipulate exactly the same supernaturals to explain exactly the same disasters with a very different set of reasons, and they *could* propose a different set of solutions. Decisions about ghosts as the cause of disaster, about whether the ghosts should be exorcized (formally dismissed) or accommodated (caused by ritual manipulations to conform to the structural norm), provide opportunity for a variety of ways of manipulating and operating the system so that it remains in concord with contemporary expectations, norms, morality, and, in general, the world as it actually is.

The only restriction is that the principles on which the ghosts are asserted to function be principles within the Taiwanese system of practices. Should these practices change, there is no reason at all why the ghosts should not change their demands as well.

To the Taiwanese (whose focus is on the ghosts), the pattern is clear: ghosts not properly following certain explicit principles are malicious, and the Taiwanese are obliged to do something about them (and probably should avoid producing them). To the outside observer (whose focus is on behavior), the pattern is also clear: the framework of gods, ghosts, *tâng-ki*, and what-not allows plenty of room for these principles to be applied differently or to change utterly from time to time, place to place, application to application with comparatively little adjustment needed in anything more than the proportions of different kinds of decisions made by the *tâng-ki* (read: community).

One way change is accommodated is for certain social principles to be openly contravened and set aside. Thus, not only is exorcism used to drive out the ghosts that nothing can be done about (as those who die by drowning), but to drive out ghosts with a good case (the cuckold's mother), who are inconvenient on other grounds (local solidarity and support of "their man" against an anonymous outsider). Without trying to judge whether this particular case represents a new practice in Taiwan (which I doubt), we can see that room is made for the accommodation of new social practices when there is a shift in the understanding about which ghosts can be exorcised and which must be humored: in Taiwanese terms, a shift in the power 力量 of a certain kind of ghost. Seen the other way about, there is a shift in the estimates of the power of particular categories of ghosts as social practices change. We can easily imagine that over time social practice and power of certain kinds of ghosts change together in a kind of mutual accommodation.[1]

There is another way, too, in which such a system is able to accommodate change, and that is in the kinds of cases that may be dredged from the family history and made into ghosts, and the kinds of reasons that may be given for their being ghosts. Returning to our earlier vocabulary, there are changes in what is socially irregular enough to excite local interest, curiosity, or censure. This can work to shift the corpus of available ghosts. Some evidence in this direction is provided by the examples in the text.

We saw that in recent ghost marriages the groom's illness was explained by reference to his wife's deceased sister. Although deceased girls have turned into ghosts for years, informants maintained that their special passion for sisters' husbands was a relatively recent development. We cannot predict this development by reference to the groom's closer emotional relationship to his wife's family than in previous times (if indeed that can be firmly established!), however we do know that this has its effects in making it credible to him that a ghost should be found in his wife's family to explain his illness, whereas informants say this would (probably) not have been the case half a century ago. A change in social pattern seems to have cleared the way for a change in available supernatural explanations, resulting in explanations from a body of ghosts previously unavailable for this use.

Can changing social patterns also *restrict* the body of credible ghosts? We noted that in many Bao-an families the family-head's father is worshipped as an ancestor but his grandfather is not, whereas in other families the grandfather continues to be worshipped. Presumably in earlier times in Taiwan worship extended back further. It seems certain it did on the continent, even among classes unable to support lineage halls for the worship of truly

1. We cannot see this happening because of the lack of historical material on ghosts in Taiwan. The point is the flexibility of the system, not whether it has in fact changed or not. My prediction is that it has and it will.

remote ancestors. If that is so (and for Taiwan we do not know), then might there have been a period in which unworshipped grandfathers stalked about serving as explanations for the illness of their unfilial descendants? [2]

There has been a great deal of interest, discussion, and criticism in anthropological circles of equilibrium models, models of social systems and belief systems that are so well integrated that they are self-correcting. Each part of the system reinforces each other part in a tight web of relations that move to maintain the stability of the entire system in the face of various kinds of external disruption. Such models have the advantage of manifesting clear pattern (which is inspiring), but the disadvantage of failing to accommodate our experience of social change (which is disconcerting). It seems to me that in the case of Taiwan the question is perhaps beside the point. The scheme of ghostly explanations of disaster and divine correctives behaves as a good equilibrium model should in adjusting things to a tightly defined, socially sanctioned norm, and it is clearly a major force in the maintenance of descent-line and other traditional principles. But it can also easily accommodate changes in the norms (or differences in the acceptable deviation from them: another kind of norm), in response to any number of impinging social realities (including those associated with modernization). And that is the essence of a dynamic model.

The same general picture seems to emerge if we turn back to the gods we discussed earlier. In the case of relationships between families and particular gods, there are at least two ways in which the role of the divine can be altered without damage to the conceptual system of alliances and reciprocity as a whole. First of all, men are free to change their allegiances from one god to another, to bring problems to any of a host of deities. A man's, or a family's, alliances may change as it is discovered or decided that a different set of gods would provide a more effective defence against current difficulties and frustrations. Gods vary in popularity over time and space in response to a variety of forces, as we have seen,

2. The closest we come to this today is word-of-mouth tales of appearances of dead parents to their children "in a certain village—I am not just sure where" to complain of inadequate food or shelter in the land of the dead and to ask for more offerings. Grandfathers seem to be quite out of focus today.

ranging from the effectiveness of a god's local *tâng-ki* to a neighbor's success in curing headaches with prayers to another. To the extent that gods are functionally undifferentiated, or nearly so, these changes can be discounted as trivial: mere replacement of identical elements. To the extent that they come to have local associations (with medicine, say, or with crops), the changes may represent differences over time and across space in the anxieties uppermost in people's minds.

When the human unit in the alliance is a village, additional variants on this same theme are also available, all of which are built on the principle of changing the gods without switching man's alliances: one axis of movement in the system is the possibility of changing the alliances obtaining among the gods themselves (as we saw in Bao-an's union with the Jang village). Another is the fact that, although gods are conceived of as participating in a hierarchy, local gods generally do not have known and fixed positions in it, and different views may prevail at different times. A third axis of movement is the possibility of assigning different local gods to different temporary positions to receive visiting divinities at occasions like the triennial Hsikang festival, thereby ordering their protégé villages anew each three years (and ordering them also according to the pervasive idiom of bureaucracy).

In brief, the possibilities for rearrangement of the gods and of human relationships with them are endless, and each arrangement is susceptible to a variety of locally determined and understood meanings. However the gods are used by families or deployed by villages, their existence and superhuman power, and the efficacy of calling upon them for assistance are not threatened.[3]

Changes in the exact role of the divine can occur in a second, more subtle way as well, requiring no changes in alliances or other reorderings of the family or village religious loyalties. Much human contact with the divine is through divination of one kind or another, and (as with ghosts) there is no reason to suppose there

3. For the Chinese, as for polytheistic peoples in general, there is no problem explaining how the efforts of a single, omnipotent god could have failed to produce the desired results. The polytheistic god is easily overcome by alliances against him, whether of other gods or of darker forces, and the worshipper copes with the situation by reordering his alliances. In this way intervillage relations and individual fortunes, gains and defeats alike, can be represented, explained, and to some degree manipulated.

are not changes over time in what subjects are appropriate for divination—I recall a quite heated debate over whether a political faction might choose its candidate by use of *poe*—or in what construction the divine, in the person of a spirit medium or a *kiō-á* reader, might wish to put upon a given event. The existence of on-going dialogue with the supernatural raises the possibility of constant review and updating of revelation. The gods have the ability to say something as relevant about the expenditure of village funds to install a public telephone as they did to suggest military strategies or alliances during the Ching. Continuous revelation allows the gods to be the constant voice of public approval or disapproval and a usual peacemaker in village or family disputes and decisions. Because their ultimate source is human (the *tâng-ki*, the reader, the farmer interpreting his home oracles), divine morals are free to change with human morals, divine strategies with human strategies. Even very substantial changes in these spheres need have no effect upon the belief in the gods themselves, or upon the practices involved in worshipping and in communicating with them. Once again we face beliefs and practices that can accommodate change in response to evolving social reality, without themselves suffering displacement.

Ultimately this belief system will probably be undermined. It will be undermined by essentially external forces—westernization, science, political paranoia—which maintain that there are no ghosts, that there are no gods (or that God is a Christian), and that divination is a rather perverse kind of induced autosuggestion. But it will not be undermined by its own inconsistencies or by its inability to cope with problems intrinsic to Chinese social life. And this is true because the system is flexible and geared tightly enough to the changing realities of Chinese life that it cannot be subverted by gradual social change.

# Selected Chinese Words
# Glossary of

The following list includes Chinese words that appear romanized in the text, English words that have been used more than once as glosses for specific Chinese terms, and place and dynasty names. Each entry begins with the form found in the text (following conventions established earlier for capitalization) with an *aide-mémoire* where necessary. This is followed by the Mandarin characters and the Hokkien characters if they are different. The final portion of each entry contains the romanized Mandarin and Hokkein pronunciation. The lack of any one of these is represented by a dash. For example:

Taiwan (province of China) 台灣 Tair-uan / tâi-ôan

The form found in the text is *Taiwan*. The Mandarin writing is 台灣. The Hokkien writing is the same as the Mandarin. The Mandarin pronunciation is *Tair-uan*. The Hokkien pronunciation is *tâi-ôan*.

ancestor 祖先 Tzuushian / chó·-sian
âng-thâu-á ("redhead" Taoist priest) 紅頭仔 Horngtour / âng-thâu-á
bad thing — /歹物— /phía$^{n}$-míh
Bao-an (pseudonym for a village in Taiwan) 保安 Bao-an / pó-an
buddha 佛 For / hu̍t
censer master 爐主 Lujuu / lô·-chú
Changhua (city and county in Taiwan) 彰化 Janguah / chiong-hòa
Chern (surname) 陳 Chern / tân
Chernghwang (city god) 城隍 Chernghwang / sêng-hông
chhiam (fortune verse) 籤 Chian / chhiam
Chiayi (city and county in Taiwan) 嘉義 Jiayih / ka-gī
Ching (dynasty) 清 Ching / chheng
Chingming ("clear and bright," a festival) 清明 Chingming / chheng-bêng
city 市 Shyh / chhī
county 縣 Shiann / kōan
devil 魔神/魔神仔 Moshern / mô·-sîn-á
divine rascal 神棍 Shernguenn / sîn-kùn

dog tub 狗桶 Gooutoong / káu-tháng
Education and Recreation Center 育樂中心 Yuhleh jongshin / iȯk-lȯk-tiong-sim
eight immortals table (part of family altar) 八仙桌 Ba sian juo / pat-sian-toh
evil fairy, *see* Iauguay, Iaujing
evil god, *see* Shyeshern
family 家 Jia / ke *or* ka
female spirit 女魂 Neuhwen / lú-hûn
Fukien (Chinese province) 福建 Fwujiann / hok-kiàn
ghost 鬼 Goei / kúi
god 神 Shern / sîn
Goei (ghost) 鬼 Goei / kúi
Goeishern (ghost-god, alternate term for ghost) 鬼神 Goeishern / kúi-sîn
Good Brethren (euphemism for hungry ghosts) 好兄弟 Hao Shiongdih / hó-hia$^{n}$-tī
Great Saint Equal to Heaven (god) 齊天大聖 Chyitian Dahshenq / chê-thian-tāi-sèng
Guangong (god) 關公 Guangong / koan-kong
Guan-in (goddess) 觀音 Guan-in / koan-im
Guardian (title used for manifestations of King Guo) 太保 Tay-bao / thài-pó
Guo (surname) 郭 Guo / koeh
hangings (paintings of gods over a family altar) 佛祖漆仔 Fortzuu chitz / pu̇t-chó·-chhat-á
harmony / harmonious 平安 Pyng-an / pêng-an
headman —/頭家仔—/ thâu-ke-á
Heitour Dawshyh ("black-head" Taoist priest) 黑頭道士 Heitour dawshyh / o·-thâu-tō-sū
hell marriage 冥婚 Minghuen / bêng-hun
His Highness Chyr (god) 池府二千歲 Chyr fuu ell chian suey / tî-hú-jī-chhian-sòe
His Highness Lii (god) 李府大千歲 Lii fuu dah chian suey / lí-hú-tāi-chhian-sòe
His Highness Wu (god) 吳府三千歲 Wu fuu san chian suey / gô·-hú-sam-chhian-sòe
Hopei (Chinese province) 河北 Herbeei / hô-pak
hó-sè (proper) —/好勢— / hó-sè
hó-khòa$^{n}$ (pretty) —/好看— / hó-khòa$^{n}$
household 户 Huh / hō·
household head 户長 Huhjaang / hō·tiú$^{n}$

Hsikang (town near Bao-an, in Tainan county) 西港 Shigaang / sai-káng
hungry ghosts 餓鬼 Ehgoei / gō-kúi
Hwang (surname) 黃 Hwang / n̂g
Hwen (soul) 魂 Hwen / hûn
Iauguay (evil fairy) 妖怪 Iauguay / iau-kòai
Iaujing (evil fairy) 妖精 Iaujing / iau-cheng
immortal 仙 Shian / sian
In (negative principle) 陰 In /im
inharmony / inharmonious 不平安 Bu pyng-an / put pêng-an
initiation 開光 Kaiguang / khai-kong
Jang (surname) 張 Jang /tiu$^n$
Jiaw, *see* poe
Kaohsiung (city and county in Taiwan) 高雄 Gaushyong / ko-hiông
King Guo (god) 郭聖王 Guo shenq wang / koeh-sèng-ông
郭姓王 Guo shinq wang / koeh-sèng-ông
kiō-á (divination chair) — / 轎 — / kiō-á
kong-chhò· (village temple) — / 公厝 — / kong-chhò·
Kuay (New Taiwan Dollar = US $.025 in 1971) 塊 Kuay / kho·
Kwangtung (Chinese province) 廣東 Goangdong / kńg-tang
large family 大家 Dah jia / tōa-ke
Lin (village subdivision) 臨 Lin / lîn
Lin (surname) 林 Lin / lîm
Ling (higher soul) 靈 Ling / lêng
Linghwen (soul) 靈魂 Linghwen / lêng-hûn
little god 小神 Sheaushern / sió-sîn
Little Maid (ghost) 小娘 Sheauniang / sió-niû
lonely spirit 孤魂 Guhwen / ko·-hûn
Lunghsi (city in Fukien) 龍溪 Longshi / liông-khe
漳州 Jangjou / chiang-chiu
Marshal Shieh (god) 謝府元帥 Shieh fuu yuan shuay / chiā-hú-gôan-sòe
Matou (town in Tainan county) 麻豆 Madow / mâ-tāu
Mhatzuu (goddess) 媽祖 Mhatzuu / má-chó·
Miinnan (frequent term for southern Fukien or its people or dialects) 閩南 Miinnan / bân-lâm
Ming (dynasty) 明 Ming / bêng
Nankuenshen (temple in Tainan county) 南鯤鯓 Nankuenshen / lâm-khun-sin
palanquin 轎子 / 轎 Jiawtz / kiō
passing through the oil 過油 Guohyou / kòe-iû

Peikang (town in Taiwan, near Chiayi) 北港 Beeigaang / pak-káng
Peiman (town in Tainan county) 北門 Beeimen / pak-mn̂g
phái$^{n}$-khòa$^{n}$ (ugly) — / 歹看— / phái$^{n}$-khòa$^{n}$
phái$^{n}$-sè (embarrassing) — / 歹勢— / phái$^{n}$-sè
Phoenix Mountain Monastery (temple in Fukien, home of King Guo) Fenq shan syh / hōng-soa$^{n}$-sī 鳳山寺
poe (divination blocks) 筊 / 筶 Jiaw *or* Jiao / poe
Poh (lower soul) 魄 Poh / phek
portion (administrative section of a village) 股 Guu / kó·
portion representative 股首 Guushoou / kó·-siú
power (of gods) 力量 Lihlianq / la̍t-liōng
Queen of Heaven (=Mhatzuu) 天后 Tianhow / thian-hō· 天上聖母 Tian shanq shenq muu / thian-siōng-sèng-bó
red approach table (part of family altar) 紅格桌 Horng ger juo / âng-keh-toh
Rehnaw (festive) 熱鬧 Rehnaw / lāu-jia̍t
River Bank Hamlet (part of Bao-an) 溪埔寮 Shibuuliau / khe-po·-liâu
seven ousts (grounds for divorce) 七出 Chichu / chhit-chhut
Shaangbing (rite of appreciating soldiers) 賞兵 Shaangbing / siú$^{n}$-peng
Shanghai (city in China) 上海 Shanqhae / siōng-hái
Shensi (province of China) 陝西 Shaanshi / siám-sai
Shern (god) 神 Shern / sîn
Shieh (surname) 謝 Shieh / chiā
Shi Luo Diann (temple in Tainan City) 西羅殿 Shiluo diann / sai-lô-tiān
Shiehtuu (ceremony) 謝土 Shiehtuu / siā-thó·
Shyeshern (false god) 邪神 Shyeshern / siâ-sîn
Shyu (surname) 徐 Shyu / chhî
soul, *see* Linghwen
South-of-the-River (part of Bao-an) 溪南 Shinan / khe-lâm
spirit marriage, *see* hell marriage
splitting the family 分家 Fenjia / hun-ka
súi (pretty) — / 美 — / súi
Sung (dynasty) 宋 Sonq / sòng
Swatow (city in Kwangtung) 汕頭 Shantour / sòa$^{n}$-thâu
Tainan (city and county in Taiwan) 台南 Tairnan / tâi-lâm
Taipei (city and county in Taiwan) 台北 Tairbeei / tâi-pak
Taiwan (province of China) 台灣 Tair-uan / tâi-ôan
Tamsui (town in Taipei county) 淡水 Dannshoei / tām-chúi
Tang (dynasty) 唐 Tarng / tông

tâng-ki (spirit medium) 乩童/童乩 Jitorng / tâng-ki
Third Prince (god) 三太子爺 San taytzyy ye / sam-thài-chú-iâ
three non-ousts (guarantees against divorce) 三不出 San bu chu / sam-put-chhut
township 鄉 Shiang / hiong
Tsengwen Chi (river) 曾文溪 Tzengwen shi / chêng-bûn-khe
Tsinkiang (city in Fukien) 晉江 Jinnjiang / chìn-kang
Tuucherng (town in Tainan city) 土城 Tuucherng / tó·-siâ-á
Twelve Plague Kings (gods / ghosts) 十二瘟王 Shyr-ell uen-wang / cha̍p-jī un-ông
泉州 Chyuanjou / choân-chiu
Tzwu (lineage) 族 Tzwu / cho̍k
Venerable King of the Broad Marshes (god = King Guo) 廣澤尊王 Goangtzer tzuenwang / kóng-te̍h-chun-ông
Wangjiaw (ceremony) 王醮 Wangjiaw / ông-chiò
water ghost 水鬼 Shoeigoei / chúi-kúi
Wugongshern (god) 蜈蚣神 Wugongshern / gô·-kang-sîn
Wulin (pseudonym for village near Bao-an) 梧林 Wulin / gô·-lîm
Yang (positive principle) 陽 Yang / iông
Yang Fuu Tayshy (god) 楊府太師 Yangfuu tayshy / iûⁿ-hú-thài-su
Yunnan (province of China) 雲南 Yunnan / hûn-lâm

# Bibliography

WESTERN WORKS

Álvarez, José María

1930 Formosa geográfica e históricamente considerada. Barcelona: Libería Católica Internacional. 2 vols.

Barclay, George W.

1954 Colonial development and population in Taiwan. Princeton: Princeton University Press.

Bredon, Juliet and Igor Mitraphanow

1927 The moon year: a record of Chinese customs and festivals. Shanghai: Kelly & Walsh, Ltd.

Bynner, Witter

1929 The jade mountain. Reprint. New York: Anchor Books, Doubleday & Co., 1964.

Campbell, William

1903 Formosa under the Dutch, described from contemporary records with explanatory notes and a bibliography of the island. Reprint. Taipei: Ch'eng-Wen Publishing Co., 1967.

Chen Cheng

1961 Land reform in Taiwan. Taipei: China Publishing Co.

Ch'en Ch'i-lu

1967 A brief history of Taiwan. Journal of the China Society 5: 77–91.

Chen Shao-hsing

1956 Social change in Taiwan. Studia Taiwanica 1: 1–19.

Chen Ta

1923 Chinese migrations, with special reference to labor conditions. Bulletin of the United States Bureau of Labor Statistics, no. 340. Reprint. Taipei: Ch'eng-Wen Publishing Co., 1967.

China Yearbook

1969–1970 China yearbook. Taipei: China Publishing Co.

Chiu, Vermier Y.

1966 Marriage laws and customs of China. Hong Kong: Institute of Advanced Chinese Studies and Research, New Asia College, Chinese University of Hong Kong.

Christie, Anthony

1968 Chinese mythology. Feltham, Middlesex: Hamlyn Publishing Group.

Cohen, Myron L.

1967 Variations in complexity among Chinese family groups: the impact of modernization. Transactions of the New York Academy of Science, 2d ser. 29, 5: 638–644.

1968 A case study of Chinese family economy and development. Journal of Asian and African Studies 3: 161–180.

1969 Agnatic kinship in south Taiwan. Ethnology 8: 167–182.

Comber, Leon

1958 Chinese temples in Singapore. Singapore: Eastern Universities Press.

Davidson, James W.

1903 The island of Formosa: historical view from 1430 to 1900. Reprint. Taipei: Book World Co., 1963.

Diamond, Norma Joyce

1966 K'un Shen: a Taiwanese fishing village. Ph.D. dissertation, Department of Anthropology, Cornell University.

1969 K'un Shen: a Taiwan village. New York: Holt, Rinehart & Winston.

Doolittle, Justus

1865 Social life of the Chinese with some account of their religious, governmental, educational, and business customs and opinions with special but not exclusive reference to Fuhchau. Reprint. Taipei: Ch'eng-Wen Publishing Co., 1966.

Doré, Henry

1917 Researches into Chinese superstitions. Vol. 4. Translated with notes by M. Kennelly. Reprint. Taipei: Ch'eng-Wen Publishing Co., 1966.

1931 Researches into Chinese superstitions. Vol. 9. Translated by D. J. Finn. Reprint. Taipei: Ch'eng-Wen Publishing Co., 1967.

Douglas, Carstairs

1899 Chinese-English dictionary of the vernacular or spoken language of Amoy, with the principal variations of the Chang-chew and Chin-chew dialects. New edition. Reprint (n.p.).

Du Bose, Hampden C.

1886 The dragon, image, and demon: the three religions of China, Confucianism, Buddhism, and Taoism, giving an account of the mythology, idolatry, and demonolatry of the Chinese. London: S. W. Partridge & Co.

Eberhard, Wolfram
1967 Guilt and sin in traditional China. Berkeley and Los Angeles: University of California Press.
1968 The local cultures of south and east China. Translated by Alide Eberhard. Leiden: E. J. Brill.

Elliott, Alan J. A.
1955 Chinese spirit-medium cults in Singapore. London: University of London.

Escarra, J.
1931 Codification du droit de famille et du droit de succession (livres IV et V du code civil de la republique chinoise), rapport presenté au conseil legislatif du gouvernement national. Shanghai: Zikawei.

Freedman, Maurice
1958 Lineage organization in southeastern China. London: University of London.
1966 Chinese lineage and society: Fukien and Kwangtung. London: University of London.

Fung Yu-lan
1948 A short history of Chinese philosophy. Edited by Derk Bodde. New York: Macmillan Co.

Gallin, Bernard
1960 Matrilineal and affinal relationships of a Taiwanese village. American Anthropologist 62: 632–642.
1963 Cousin marriage in China. Ethnology 2: 104–108.
1966 Hsin Hsing, Taiwan: a Chinese village in change. Berkeley and Los Angeles: University of California Press.

Gamble, Sidney D.
1954 Ting Hsien: a north China rural community. Reprint. Stanford: Stanford University Press, 1968.

Goddard, W. G.
1963 The makers of Taiwan: lectures to student groups in Britain. Taipei: China Publishing Co.
1966 Formosa: a study in Chinese history. East Lansing: Michigan State University Press.

Granet, Marcel
1934 La pensée chinoise. Reprint. Paris: Éditions Albin Michel, 1968.

Groot, Jan Jacob Maria de
1886 Les fêtes annuellement célébrées à Emoui. 2 vols. Paris. Ernest Leroux, Éditeur.
1892–1910 The religious system of China. 6 vols. Reprint. Taipei: Literature House, 1964.

1903 Sectarianism and religious persecution in China. 2 vols. Reprint. Taipei: Literature House, 1963.
1910 The religion of the Chinese. New York: Macmillan Co.

Hoogers, P. J.
1910 La téorie et la pratique de la piété filiale chez les Chinois. Anthropos 5: 1–15, 688–702.

Hsieh Chiao-min
1964 Taiwan—ilha formosa: a geography in perspective. London: Butterworths.

Hsu, Francis L. K.
1967 Under the ancestors' shadow: kinship, personality, and social mobility in village China. 2d ed., rev. and enl. Garden City, New York: Doubleday & Co.

Imbault-Huart, C.
1893 L'île Formose: histoire et description. Reprint. Taipei: Ch'eng-Wen Publishing Co., 1968.

Jordan, David K.
1969a The languages of Taiwan. La Monda Lingvo-Problemo 1: 65–76.
1969b Supernatural aspects of family and village in rural southwestern Taiwan. Ph.D. dissertation, Department of Anthropology, University of Chicago.
1971a A guide to the romanization of Chinese. Taipei: Mei-Ya.
1971b Two forms of spirit marriage in rural Taiwan. Bijdragen tot de Taal-, Land- en Volkenkunde 127: 181–189.

Kulp, Daniel Harrison, II
1925 Country life in South China: the sociology of familism. Volume I: Phenix Village, Kwangtung, China. Reprint. Taipei: Ch'eng-Wen Publishing Co., 1966.

Laufer, Berthold
1923 Oriental theatricals. Field Museum of Natural History, Department of Anthropology, Guide Part 1. Chicago: Field Museum of Natural History.

Li Yih-yuan
1968 Ghost marriage, shamanism and kinship behavior in rural Taiwan. *In* Folk religion and the worldview in the southwestern Pacific: papers submitted to a symposium, the Eleventh Pacific Science Congress held in August–September 1966, edited by N. Matsumoto and T. Mabuchi, pp. 97–99. Tokyo: Keio Institute of Cultural and Linguistic Studies, Keio University.

Liao, J. W. K.
1949 L'épopée chinoise à Formose: les premières guerres de libération. Bulletin de l'Université l'Aurore 3rd ser. 10: 1–20.

Marsh, Robert M. and Albert R. O'Hara
1961 Attitudes toward marriage and the family in Taiwan. American Journal of Sociology 67: 1–8.

Maspero, Henri
1950 Mélanges posthumes sur les religions et l'histoire de la Chine. Volume 1: les religions chinoises. Paris: Presses Universitaires de France.

Möllendorff, P. G. von
1895 Das Chinesiche Familienrecht. Shanghai.

Nĝ Bú-tong, ed.
1955 Ki-tok-tô kap tâi-ôan kòan-síok. Tainan: Presbyterian Church of Taiwan. English translation by Ardon Albrecht and Gô· Sīn-gī. 1965. A guidebook for Christians on Chinese customs and superstitions. Taipei.

Pasternak, Burton
1968 Agnatic atrophy in a Formosan village. American Anthropologist 70: 93–96.
1969 The role of the frontier in Chinese lineage development. Journal of Asian Studies 28: 551–561.

Pletcher, Charles Hutchinson
1949 The Formosan uprisings of 1868. Master's thesis, Committee on International Relations, University of Chicago.

Praag, H. van
1966 Sagesse de la Chine: les grandes valeurs d'une culture millénaire. Paris: Editions Gérard & Co.

Reichelt, Karl L.
1951 Religion in Chinese garment. London: Butterworth Press.

Saso, Michael R.
1966 Taiwan feasts and customs: a handbook of the principal feasts and customs of the lunar calendar on Taiwan. 2d ed. Hsinchu: Chabanel Language Institute.

Schipper, Kristofer M.
1966 The divine jester: some remarks on the gods of the Chinese marionette theater. Bulletin of the Institute of Ethnology. Academia Sinica 21: 81–96.

Smith, Robert J.
1966 *Ihai:* mortuary tablets, the household and kin in Japanese ancestor worship. Transactions of the Asiatic Society of Japan, 3rd ser. 9: 83–102.

Soothill, William Edward and Lewis Hodous
1937 A dictionary of Chinese Buddhist terms with Sanskrit and English equivalents, a Chinese index, and a Sanskrit-Pali index. Reprint. Taipei: Buddhist Culture Service, 1962.
Su Sing-ging
1922 The Chinese family system. New York: Columbia University.
Topley, Marjorie
1955 Ghost marriages among the Singapore Chinese. Man 55: 29f. (sec. 35).
1956 Ghost marriages among the Singapore Chinese: a further note. Man 56: 71f. (sec. 63).
Tun li-ch'en
1965 Annual customs and festivals in Peking. 2d ed. Translated and annotated by Derk Bodde. Hong Kong: Hong Kong University Press.
Vannicelli, Luigi
1943 La famiglia cinese: studio etnologico. Milan: Società Editrice «Vita e Pensiero».
Walls, Jim
1960 Chinatown, San Francisco. Berkeley: Howell-North.
Welch, Holmes
1957 Taoism, the parting of the way. Boston: Beacon Press.
Werner, E. T. C.
1922 Myths and legends of China. London: George Harrap & Co.
1932 A dictionary of Chinese mythology. Reprint. Taipei: Book World Co., 1963.
Wolf, Arthur Paul
1964 Marriage and adoption in a Hokkien village. Ph.D. dissertation, Department of Anthropology, Cornell University.
1966 Childhood association, sexual attraction, and the incest taboo: a Chinese case. American Anthropologist 68: 883–898.
1968 Adopt a daughter-in-law, marry a sister: a Chinese solution to the problems of the incest taboo. American Anthropologist 70: 864–874.
Wolf, Margery
1968 The house of Lim: a study of a Chinese farm family. New York: Appleton-Century-Crofts.
1970 Child training and the Chinese family. *In* Family and kinship in Chinese society, edited by Maurice Freedman, pp. 37–62. Stanford: Stanford University Press.
Wu Ch'eng-en
1943 Monkey. Translated by Arthur Waley. Reprint. New York: Grove Press, 1958.

Yang, C. K.
1959 The Chinese family in the communist revolution. Cambridge: Massachusetts Institute of Technology.
Yang, Martin M. C.
1945 A Chinese village: Taitou, Shantung province. New York: Columbia University Press.
1962 Changes in family life in rural Taiwan. Journal of the China Society 2: 68–79.

CHINESE WORKS

Anonymous
1964 台灣史話 [The history of Taiwan]. Taipei: 台灣省文獻委員會.
Chern Ching-gaw and Shieh Shyr-cherng 陳清誥與謝石城
1963 台南縣市寺廟大觀 [A guide to temples in Tainan City and County]. Kaohsiung: 光台文化出版社.
Chyau Yann-nong 喬硯農
1965 中文字典 [Chinese dictionary]. Hong Kong: 華僑語文出版社.
Duh Erl-wey 杜而未
1966 鳳麟龜龍考釋 [An inquiry into the phoenix, unicorn, tortoise, and dragon]. Taipei: 台灣商務印書館.
Ferng Tzuoh-min 馮作民
1966 台灣歷史百講 [One hundred talks on Taiwan history]. Taipei: 青文出版社
Fuh Chyn-jia 傅勤家
1937 中國道教史 [History of Taoism in China]. Shanghai: 商務印書館.
Her Lian-kwei 何聯奎
1955 台灣省通志稿卷二人民志禮俗篇 [Draft for a Taiwan provincial gazeteer]. Taipei: 台灣省文獻委員會.
Hwang, Der-shyr 黃得時
1967 鬼神的人格化.
[Anthropomorphism: a characteristic of Taiwan folk belief: Proceedings of the Third meeting of the Seminar on Taiwan Studies]. In 台灣研究研討會紀錄 [Proceedings of the Seminar on Taiwan Studies], pp. 56–58. Taipei: 國立台灣大學文學院考古人類學系印行.

Jenq Sheng-chang 鄭昇昌
1967 神明來曆及年節由來 [Histories of gods and origins of annual festivals] Changhua: 陽光出版社.

Jiang Jia-jiin 江家錦
1957 台南縣志稿卷二人民志宗教篇 [Draft for a Tainan county gazeteer]. (n.p.)
1959 台南市志稿卷二人民志宗教篇 [Draft for a Tainan city gazeteer]. (n.p.)

Kokubu Naoichi 國分直一
1962 童乩的研究 [Researches on spirit mediums]. Translated by 周全德 [Jou Chyuan-der]. 南瀛文献 8: 46–53.

Liaw Hann-chern 廖漢臣 ed.
1960 台灣通志稿卷二人民志民族篇 [Draft for a Taiwan provincial gazeteer]. Taipei: 台灣省文献委員會

Liaw Yuh-wen 廖毓文
1967 台灣神話 [Taiwanese mythology]. Taipei: 生生出版社.

Lii Tian-chuen 李痜春
1956 台灣省通志稿卷二人民志宗教篇 [Draft for a Taiwan provincial gazeteer]. Taipei: 台灣省文献委員會.

Lin Tsair-yuan 林財源
1968 台灣採風錄卷一 [Selected Taiwanese customs, vol. 1]. Pingtung: 普天出版社.

Liou Jy-wann 劉枝萬
1960 台灣省寺廟堂名稱，主神，地址調查表 [Tables of names, patron gods, and addresses of temples in Taiwan Province]. 台灣文献 11 (2): 37–236.
1963 台灣之瘟神信仰 [Belief in cholera gods in Taiwan]. 台灣省立博物館科學年刊 6: 109–113.
1967 台北市松山祈安建醮祭典:台灣祈安醮祭習俗研究之一 [Great propitiatory rites of petition for beneficence at Songshan, Taipei. Volume I: Studies on Taiwanese propitiatory rites]. Nankang: 中央研究院民族學研究所.

Lou Tzyy-kuang 婁子匡
1968 婚俗志 [Marriage customs]. Taipei: 台灣商務印書館.

Shieh Jin-sheuan 謝金選
1954 神祕的關渡媽祖 [Mysterious Mhatzuu of the passage]. 台灣風物 4 (2): 15f.

Tsay Wen-huei 蔡文輝
1967 有關中國家庭研究参考書目 [Bibliography of studies on the Chinese family]. 國立台灣大學社會學刊 3: 179–189.

Wu Ying-tau 吳瀛濤
1970 台灣民俗 [Taiwan folklore]. Taipei: 古亭書屋.

# Index

TALLAHASSEE
LIBRARY
COMMUNITY COLLEGE